Students and External Research

THE BRITISH
IRON & STEEL SHEET INDUSTRY
SINCE 1840

BELL'S ADVANCED ECONOMIC GEOGRAPHIES

General Editor
PROFESSOR R. O. BUCHANAN
M.A.(N.Z.), B.Sc.(Econ.), Ph.D.(London)
Professor Emeritus, University of London

A. Systematic Studies

AN ECONOMIC GEOGRAPHY OF OIL
Peter R. Odell, B.A., Ph.D.

PLANTATION AGRICULTURE
P. P. Courtenay, B.A., Ph.D.

NEW ENGLAND: A STUDY IN INDUSTRIAL ADJUSTMENT
R. C. Estall, B.Sc.(Econ.), Ph.D.

GREATER LONDON: AN INDUSTRIAL GEOGRAPHY
J. E. Martin, B.Sc.(Econ.), Ph.D.

GEOGRAPHY AND ECONOMICS
Michael Chisholm, M.A.

AGRICULTURAL GEOGRAPHY
Leslie Symons, B.Sc.(Econ.), Ph.D.

REGIONAL ANALYSIS AND ECONOMIC GEOGRAPHY
John N. H. Britton, M.A., Ph.D.

B. Regional Studies

AN ECONOMIC GEOGRAPHY OF EAST AFRICA
A. M. O'Connor, B.A., Ph.D.

YUGOSLAVIA: PATTERNS OF ECONOMIC ACTIVITY
F. E. Ian Hamilton, B.Sc.(Econ.), Ph.D.

AN HISTORICAL INTRODUCTION TO THE ECONOMIC GEOGRAPHY
OF GREAT BRITAIN
Professor Wilfred Smith, M.A.

In Preparation

AN ECONOMIC GEOGRAPHY OF CARIBBEAN AMERICA
Peter R. Odell. B.A.. Ph.D.

AN AGRICULTURAL GEOGRAPHY OF GREAT BRITAIN
Professor J. T. Coppock, M.A., Ph.D.

AN ECONOMIC GEOGRAPHY OF BRAZIL
J. D. Henshall, M.A., M.Sc. & R. P. Momsen, A.B., M.A., Ph.D.

The British
Iron & Steel Sheet Industry
since 1840

An Economic Geography

KENNETH WARREN
M.A. Ph.D.

*Department of Geography
University of Newcastle upon Tyne*

LONDON
G. BELL & SONS, LTD
1970

SBN 7135 1548 1

Printed in Great Britain by
NEILL & CO. LTD., EDINBURGH

Preface

This is an analysis of the stages and causes of the transfer of sheet metal manufacture from numerous small West Midland works to only five plants on or near the coast and mainly in Wales over a period of 130 years. It is accordingly a case study in the transformation of the location pattern of the first industrial revolution into that of the new industrial age, and of the associated constraints on radical redevelopment. It touches on one of the chief causes of depressed areas and of our difficulties, partly material, partly conceptual, in meeting the competition of newly industrialised nations.

Until 1837 iron sheets were widely used under the name blackplate as the chief material in tinplate manufacture and, on a smaller scale, in the production of numerous other finished products, including nails, japanned ware and the 'toys' of Birmingham. After that date galvanised 'iron' gradually emerged as an important new outlet, darkening heavy industrial districts with quickly erected, impermanent-looking structures, providing a cheap building material for the farmer which was later to become a good index of rural poverty wherever its reddened corrugations were left rotting away, and scattering 'tin' roofs throughout the underdeveloped areas of the world. In the process the galvanised iron trade also built up new localised centres of manufacture. The need for iron of good quality concentrated the early firms, so that even when each year more and more of the sales of the finished product were being made overseas, localisation of the trade was largely within a ten mile radius of Dudley in the centre of the Black Country of South Staffordshire and Worcestershire. Galvanising works beyond, even as far away as Scotland, depended very largely on iron sheets from this area. For at least two decades in the second half of the

v

nineteenth century buoyancy and expansion in sheet was the largest single check to the downward trend in the Black Country iron trade. From the mid-1890s overseas business grew more important, steel replaced iron and then imported steel sheet bars displaced a large proportion of home supplies. The West Midlands area declined while new sheet making districts developed in the coastlands, especially in South Wales and near the estuaries of the Mersey and the Dee. In this period techniques were improved but there was no change of principle and the number of producers remained large.

In the late twenties galvanised iron exports collapsed and new markets, requiring steel sheet of much higher quality, grew in importance. Among these outlets were the manufacture of steel furniture, steel drums but especially steel motor car bodies and domestic appliances. The old techniques of sheet manufacture were modified to meet these changes but in both quality and costs of production proved unable to match the achievements of the new continuous wide hot strip mills serving the new markets in the United States. Twelve years after the Americans, and very gingerly, British firms first ventured into strip mill construction. Inevitably such giant units revolutionised the trade so that in less than thirty years the manufacture of sheet steel was concentrated in only five locations. A century earlier economic growth had been almost free of external restraints, but now, in a mature, relatively slow-growing national economy, and after a painful realisation of the social implications of company policies, governments were concerning themselves with industrial location. As a result, even though the strip mills had completely different locational requirements from the old hand mills, they were located in the existing sheetmaking areas. The growth of the Black Country sheet iron trade, the emergence of the coastal steel sheet making centres, and their replacement by the strip mills provide three main subdivisions for the analysis which follows.

Over the last few years geography has undergone a shaking of the foundations, so that I owe some explanation of my perspective to my academic colleagues. Throughout this study I have been sifting material which others have also used in part in a number of excellent volumes on the steel industry.

My sieve has had a very different mesh, in accordance with my aim to write an economic geography, and emphatically not another, and rather different, economic analysis or economic history.   Concern throughout is with location and the factors shaping it, and therefore I have avoided considera- tion of technical details for their own sake, have penetrated only so far into the industry's economic structure as seemed essential to understand its geographical changes and have excluded aspects of company growth, changes in management and developments in labour unless they were directly related to locational change.   In the process of selection I have drawn confidence from H. J. Mackinder's dictum of over 70 years ago '. . . no theoretical consideration can hold the investigator within set bounds, though he is none-the-less practically limited by the nature of the arts of investigation to which he has served his apprenticeship'.

The reader of part of an earlier draft of this work criticised an absence of analysis and of generalisation and so isolated two aspects of my approach which, not unnaturally, I see in a rather different light.   Many of the new analytical techniques seem likely to take the industrial geographer only a short way towards insight into the reasons behind the patterns of development.   In much of modern manufacturing the popu- lation of plants and still more of firms is too small for successful application of many of the tools of the locational analyst, and where perhaps no more than three or four groups dominate a particular industry, the actions of one of them, actions probably not wholly rational, may precipitate a revolution in technology, a change in the organisation of the trade and in its location.   Even in an earlier period, when many firms were involved, the situation was amazingly complicated.

Locational theory provides the economic geographer with his generalisations, gives an essential conceptual framework and a standard against which to measure the suitability of locational choices.   It is clear that efficiency would have been greater if its principles had been followed in the develop- ment of the sheet industry, but they were not.   Neither the Black Country publicans or grocers who spent their savings to buy bankrupts' rolling mills which they carried on until they too went down, nor the stubborn, short-sighted directors of Welsh sheet and tinplate concerns who would not cooperate with Sir William Firth in strip mill development had much idea about locational theory, but their actions shaped the context for future development decisions. I have worked with a concept of the ideal for each stage of evolution in the industry, but my analysis is of the actual, for I cannot be happy with August Losch's often quoted opinion that '. . . the question of the best location is far more dignified than determination of the actual one'.

Many must have shared the author's experience when visiting industrial firms. There seem to be so many escape routes through a variety of technical devices from the consequences of an apparently bad location. In the end one leaves amazed at or still suspicious of claims of low costs in what seem the most unlikely places. From this I conclude that analysis in economic geography requires a resolution to probe as far as possible into the reasons for locational decisions, to master the rudiments of technology and to look into the contingencies of industry and company development. In the end one will obviously wish to refurbish theoretical concepts and to sharpen one's analytical tools, but acceptance of some of the current pleas for the ending of ideographic studies would prove ruinous for geography. This book has been written in the conviction that, while by no means ignoring the value of the general or the theoretical, the geographer is still primarily concerned with unique areal associations of phenomena, the outcome of decisions taken at particular times and in a particular setting. To ignore that nowhere else are there very satisfactory analogues of the Black Country, the industrial valleys of South Wales, the Mersey and Dee estuary industrial areas or the manufacturing complex of mid-Scotland leads both to academic half truths and wholesale disappointment in planning.

In an old established country substantial analysis of the past is essential in order to understand locational patterns which are inevitably anomalous from the point of view of modern technology or the present economic setting. Sixty years ago, in his *Principles of Economics*, Alfred Marshall painted a picture of a progressive and rational society—'In backward countries there are still habits and customs similar to those which lead a beaver in confinement to build himself a dam: they are full of suggestiveness to the historian and must be reckoned with by the legislator. But in business matters in the modern world such habits quickly die away'. No one who studies the Ebbw Vale controversy, or that surrounding the fourth strip mill, or who grapples with the material and psychological aspects of development area problems could endorse such an opinion when applied to industrial location. Yet the fullness of the following analysis increases from the earlier to the later periods and it is not a historial geography of the evolutionary persuasion but a 'realistic' economic geography.

Naturally one must recognise that no such analysis can ever be more than partial and that much which is still hidden will always remain so. The writer has on occasion been intrigued and frustrated when visiting the homes of those who have occupied responsible or even key posts in the sheet steel industry. A chance query sends a most helpful host up-stairs to fetch a file from a cache of documents and, returning, he consults this and comments from a position tantalisingly located at the other end of the sofa or from the armchair across a wide hearth rug! At that point one recognises any belief that one has uncovered the full story of locational development as delusion.

In preparing this study I have had the good fortune to meet or correspond with many men who have been concerned in very various ways with the iron and steel sheet industry over a period which in exceptional cases extends back as far as the 1890s. As a result I began to appreciate something of the wonderful spirit of adventure and comradeship that characterised those who worked in the old-type sheet mills and to realise how, in a dimension completely other than that of locational change, the strip mill may appear a monster destroying old values. Throughout I have taken and evaluated recollections, evidence and advice and in no case are my helpers responsible for any mistakes I may have made. To all of them I wish to say how much I enjoyed the work, how greatly I valued their conversation, their letters or in some cases their considerable commentaries on my drafts, and their hospitality. I have listed those to whom I am so much indebted together with the most relevant of their industry affiliations. I dedicate this book to them and to their industrial forebears as well as to an academic purpose.

F. C. Braby, *Frederick Braby*: G. H. Brook, *Briton Ferry Steel*: J. Bryden, *Smith and McLean*: W. F. Cartwright, *Guest, Keen, Baldwins, Steel Company of Wales*: E. Cross, *Ebbw Vale Steel, Iron and Coal Company, Richard Thomas, and Richard Thomas and Baldwins*: G. F. Gillott, *Pressed Steel*: A. R. Gray, *John Summers*: A. Jackson, *United Steel Companies*: G. H. Latham and Sir Ernest Lever, *Richard Thomas, Richard Thomas and Baldwins*: W. S. Lewis, *Gilbertsons and Richard Thomas and Baldwins*: E. C. Lysaght, *John Lysaght*: J. Malborn, *John Lysaght, United Engineering and Foundry*: J. M. Parkes, *Birmingham Corrugated Iron Company*: T. W. Roberts, *Ellesmere Port*: G. A. V. Russell, *United Steel Companies*: H. H. Stanley, *John Lysaght, Steel Company of Wales*: Sir Geoffrey Summers, P. J. Summers and Sir Richard Summers, *John Summers*: C. T. Thomas and F. H. T. Thomas, *Richard Thomas, Richard Thomas and Baldwins*: D. J. Young, *Guest, Keen, Baldwins, Steel Company of Wales*.

Finally, but by no means as a mere formality, I would like to record my appreciation of the kindly editorship of Professor R. O. Buchanan.

Contents

PART IV: WORLD WAR II & POST-WAR DEVELOPMENT

Maps

Tables

INTRODUCTION

Sheet Steel: Past and Future

In 1967 British steelworks turned out 19·2 million long tons of finished products. Well over one third of this, 7·3 million tons, was sheet, strip and tinplate. Although other plants made small contributions, most of this output came from five works, each having a continuous wide hot strip mill. These products have been the outstanding growth sector of the industry over the last twenty years, output increasing from a level of 22 per cent. below that of the main heavy rolled products in 1951 to 26 per cent. above in 1967. Yet even a superficial examination shows how unsatisfactory is the location pattern of British strip mills. The Ebbw Vale works stretches magnificently in its narrow bed at the head of a coalfield valley 900 feet above and 19 miles inland by rail from Newport docks, into which its iron ore is brought. The imposing black silhouette that shocks the traveller coming over the hilltop from the leafy quiet of Hawarden, Flintshire, is the highly successful mill of John Summers and Sons, but the embanked River Dee alongside is unusable either for ore carriers or for shipments of finished products. Iron ore is railed across the Wirral from Birkenhead, coal comes from Staffordshire and Lancashire and the biggest markets are in the Midlands. Port Talbot, by far the biggest strip mill, has operated since its start in 1951 beside an ore dock which even then was realised by many to be far too small, and despite the substantial economies of full integration its finishing operations spread to three major outlying plants, one of them as far away as Newport, Monmouthshire. Ravenscraig, the only strip mill in the whole of northern Britain, and the most recently built of all, is landlocked in mid-Lanarkshire, and much of the product of the hot mill is cold rolled some distance away at Gartcosh. Finally, Llanwern, Newport, the most highly automated and best located of all, is none-the-less at an inadequate port and a considerable distance from its markets. Why, one might enquire, was such a magnificent plant not put down at deep water in closer proximity to big sheet markets not so well served by the other mills—perhaps even on the Thames Estuary?

To these enquiries or criticisms there is a simple, if not wholly satisfying, answer—the locational commitment of history. Iron was first made in the Ebbw Vale area in the 1780s, and thirty years earlier there were ironworks at Taibach near Port Talbot. In the late nineteenth and early twentieth centuries Ebbw Vale was one of the biggest steel works in South Wales. Along Swansea Bay openhearth steel plants were built in the 1870s and 1880s, in 1898 Port Talbot Docks were rebuilt and within four years Gilbertsons from Pontardawe were building steelworks and mills there. An integrated works at Margam on an adjoining site was erected by Baldwins after 1915. The Summers' Hawarden Bridge works occupies the extension of a site purchased in 1895 and developed for export of galvanised sheet steel, and the Ravenscraig mill is the last stage in the metallurgical evolution of an area whose development began 130 years ago when blackband iron ore and splint coal made Scotch iron the terror of the metallurgical world. The development of Llanwern, on a marshland site grazed by cattle until 1959, was least trammelled with the past in the material sense. Locational choice here was shaped by the availability of specialised mill labour and the conviction that tinplate and sheet were Welsh trades, a persuasion of great significance in a time of socially biased decision taking. Traces of an earlier era, one in which Welsh claims to sheet rolling expertise were much less secure, can still be discerned. In the West Midland conurbation small and increasingly specialised sheet production survived until the 1960s. Almost extinct now, this is the legacy of a time when Staffordshire, not Wales, was the centre of the sheet trade, when Black Country methods and men built up the industry in other districts and countries. Alongside sheet production there grew up a metal fabricating industry which was probably as dominant in national sheet consumption in the nineteenth century as it is today. Elsewhere the traces of former sheet production are less noticeable. Until recently the discerning traveller could find such fascinating puzzles as the existence of the Wolverhampton Corrugated Iron Company in Ellesmere Port or the Birmingham Corrugated Iron Company operating amidst the piles of Leblanc alkali waste on the edge of Widnes. Along the railway route from Buchanan Street, Glasgow, in the Iron-masters District, Middlesbrough or along the Avon Feeder Canal in Bristol were other reminders of a past pattern of the industry. These, however, are relics, the flotsam of locational history, not the major inheritances that the strip mills represent. The latter are more than an anomaly for academic study: they constitute a serious planning problem. They operate in locations moulded in the past but they must compete with foreign plants built with few or no ties of this nature, with the strip mills of countries which, in their heavy metallurgy, are fortunate in having no economic history.

SHEET STEEL: the International Arena

Five British strip mills were involved in the 1966 production of 7·4 million metric tons of sheet, coiled strip and tinplate. Early in the year Japan had 5 fully continuous and 8 semi-continuous hot strip mills and rolled, of sheet and strip alone, 13·5 million tons. The 3 hot strip mills operated by Fuji and Tokai Steel had a capacity of 6·0 million metric tons.[1] Built up in the fifties and sixties, these plants have not surprisingly proved more productive than the older British strip mills, but the difference is striking, at any rate for the hot mills (Table 1). There is a notable contrast in assembly and

TABLE 1

Hot and cold mills at Tokai and Hawarden Bridge, 1964/1967
(annual capacities thousands metric tons)

	Hot mill	56″ cold reduction mill
Hawarden Bridge*	1426/1528	702
Tokai†	2400	660

*1967   †1964

Sources: John Summers. Works Information October, 1967
Fuji Steel, 1966, p. 18

marketing costs, for the Japanese strip mills have all had deep water access from the first. Process costs, too, are lower, largely because of the newness of equipment and more particularly the installation of oxygen steelmaking plant in new works. Overhead costs are less for various reasons. The relatively high cost of capital in Japan encouraged economy, the lower cost of oxygen as against openhearth capacity helped. Lack of room forced the plant engineers to design a layout which economised space and therefore heat and movement costs, while the designing of the various units of plant for capacity operations from the start reduced the burden of standing charges per unit of output (Table 2).

TABLE 2

Approximate interest and depreciation charges on steel developments at Newport, Taranto and in Japan (£ per ingot ton)

	£	s.
Newport (1962)	15	14
Taranto (1965)	9	15
Japan (1967)	8	8*

*possibly less
Note: Annual charges of 12½ per cent. on capital are assumed
Sources: Various

Not surprisingly Japanese exports of strip mill products have grown much more rapidly than those from Britain (Table 3). In the four years 1963-1966 British sheet and strip exports ranged between 1·02 million and 1·26 million tons, while Japanese exports of hot and cold rolled sheets increased from 0·99 to 2·11 million tons.

TABLE 3

United Kingdom and Japanese exports of strip mill products, 1957, 1960, 1966 (thousand metric tons)

	1957	1960	1966
TINPLATE			
United Kingdom	442	515	385
Japan	39	100	397
SHEET AND STRIP			
United Kingdom	623	497	1257
Japan	278	716	2787

Sources: British Iron and Steel Institute
Japanese Iron and Steel Federation

Japan provides one measure, admittedly harsh, wherewith to estimate the international competitiveness of the British sheet and tinplate industries. By this assessment their performance is clearly indifferent. Overextension of world strip mill capacity caused over-production and a tumble in prices. From a high of 175 dollars cold reduced sheet had fallen to a mean annual price of 109 dollars a ton by 1966.[2] Competing in this field, British companies with home trade prices of £59 13s. 3d. per metric ton were selling in a market whose price averaged only £38 10s.

The evidence from the British companies themselves is proof that all is not well. In the year 1964-1965 the 25 per cent. of their output which Richard Thomas and Baldwin exported provided only 21 per cent. turnover value. As the Chairman's statement put it, if all exports had been sold at home trade prices results would have been £7 million better— in a year when the group's operating profit before depreciation was £13·9 million. In 1965–1966 exports were 28 per cent. of total deliveries in tonnage but only 22 per cent. by value.[3] The experience of the Steel Company of Wales when contrasted with that of Fuji steel illustrates decreasing British competitiveness.

TABLE 4

Net income as percentage of net sales for the Steel Company of Wales and Fuji Iron & Steel, Company, 1954–1964

	Steel Company of Wales	Fuji Steel
1954	5·5	1·3
1956	4·6	3·0
1960	7·0	3·6
1962	2·6	2·1
1963	2·4	4·0
1964	0·4	3·9

Based on company reports

Clearly these considerations are not decisive. For instance, could home trade prices not be too high? Certainly the companies themselves were not willing to concede that. The Chairman of Colvilles in his review of 1964 business reported that the returns for the Strip Division were insufficient to cover the interest on the Government loan. In 1966 a new chairman was complaining that the Iron and Steel Board prices did not permit sufficient trading margin to ensure the continued efficiency of the industry. The price increase of April, 1966, was inadequate in his opinion. At the time of this increase John Summers and Sons of Hawarden Bridge initiated a zonal pricing system which gave substantial concessions in the North West. The Chairman of the Steel Company of Wales, commenting on this, observed 'It seems to me to be extremely unfortunate that the health of the industry should be undermined by ill-considered price reductions at a time when money is required for capital expenditure to keep the iron and steel plant abreast of modern developments'.[4] In short, prices are uncomfortably high for foreign trade but not high enough to justify all the extension or rebuilding that is desirable at home. This is a basic problem of an old industry in an old industrial country, a problem perhaps best known to the general public in cotton textiles. When looked at more closely other deficiencies of the British strip mill industry become apparent and these are more directly the result of its evolution.

REORGANISATION AND THE BRITISH SHEET STEEL INDUSTRY

It is now universally agreed that plants should be much bigger than the present average size. In 1966 the four British plants concerned mainly with strip mill products—excluding Ravenscraig, whose output is closely involved with other products as well—made an average of 1·67 million tons ingots. This is small considering the economy of L.D. converters as compared with other plant, and the need, for obvious reasons, to have at least a 2 vessel L.D. shop. For low phosphorous iron, steel conversion costs were in 1966 reckoned 38–40 per cent. less than with fixed openhearth furnaces. With 2 vessels of 275 tons advanced current practice by 1966 gave a possible output of 3·1 million tons[5]. Such a steel capacity could be adequately supported by 2 large new blast furnaces, and 3 such works could meet the needs for strip mill products envisaged for 1975.[6] Two years before the Benson Committee discussed these output targets, W. F. Cartwright, Managing Director of the Steel Company of Wales, had examined the costs of thoroughly overhauling the equipment of the British flat rolled products industry. He envisaged the number of plants reduced from 5 to 2. For their 8 million tons ingot capacity the historic cost of the present five plants was £77 per ingot ton. These could be replaced by two plants with fully modern equipment for an investment of £70 per ton—and, with improved finishing plant, the additional advantage of at least a 4 per cent. increase in the sale of finished products and a greater proportion of output at the prime quality level. Further, the savings of such a reconstruction and concentration in operating costs were reckoned spectacular.[7] (Table 5).

TABLE 5

Resource utilisation in British strip mills to produce 5·9 million tons finished products per year
(consumption per ton of finished product (tons))

	Five existing works	Hypothetical 2 new works
Coking coal	0·965	0·712
Injected oil in ironworks	—	0·171
Iron ore	1·62	1·69
Scrap	0·585	0·426
Fuel oil in steel plant	0·20	—
Electricity	47 KWh	36 KWh
Man hours	24·2	7·6

Other economies, from centralised material assembly and dispatch were not considered by Cartwright. Capital investment would be lessened overall and the installation of equipment of the highest efficiency could better be justified if the utilisation rate of the new ore docks were higher than the present scatter of British works allows. And yet there are, in addition to the new £15 million tidal harbour of Port Talbot, plans for at least three other deepwater ore docks whose main customer will be a strip mill—at Newport, on the Mersey and on the Clyde.

A reduction in the number of plants is desirable, but clearly also those which exist are in poor or indifferent locations.

Ebbw Vale, Hawarden Bridge and Ravenscraig are land-locked plants and all are distant from the chief consumption centres for steel sheet or indeed for tinplate. In 1965 three of the 12 Ministry of Labour Regions, the Midlands, London and the South East and Eastern, consumed over half the sheet steel marketed at home. They produced none. Projections of overall steel consumption to 1975 suggest that there may be a decline in their share of the nation's total but that they will still remain pre-eminent. Why not plan for steel capacity where the Medway could provide deep anchorage and the Isle of Sheppey ample sites to accommodate the immensity of continuous strip mill operations?

Consideration of the ideal, in size and type of plant or in location, must continually cause dissatisfaction among those concerned with the actual, but in a mature industrial economy such as that of Britain those who plan to realise the contemporary ideal must take account also of legacies and liabilities from the past. In terms of works this is obvious, but there are added to the immobilities of plant in being, those of management and labour and all round rigidity of attitude. In a democratic society, deeply committed to the philosophy of a welfare state, these in turn exercise very great pressures to make the future conform to the past in order to avoid the dislocations inevitable in a wholesale change in industrial structure. The past shaped not only present industrial problems but also the framework of thinking within which British society has so far tried to solve these problems. So the study of the development of a basic industry in Britain becomes an analysis also of the emergence of welfare economics as a dominating principle in reconstruction and, since society is so firmly rooted in space, in relocation. An historical perspective in economic geography becomes a prelude to realistic planning.

REFERENCES

1 Fuji Iron and Steel Co. Ltd. *Engineering and Consulting Services of Fuji Steel*. 1966, p. 27.
2 E.C.S.C. *La Situation sur les marches siderurgiques dans les pays tiers* 1967, p. 10.

3 R.T.B. Chairman's *Statement* 1964/65, 1965/66.
4 *Annual Reports and Statements* 1964–1966. John Summers, Colvilles and Steel Company of Wales.
5 The Steel Industry. *The Stage 1 Report of the Development Co-ordinating Committee of the British Iron and Steel Federation* (Benson Committee) 1966 pp. 39–41.
6 *ibid* p. 30.
7 W. F. Cartwright. 'The Future of Automation in the Iron and Steel Industry'. *Iron and Steel* 17 December 1964.

PART I

THE BLACK COUNTRY PHASE

CHAPTER 1

The Growth and Geography of Sheet Iron Manufacture in the Mid-Nineteenth Century

SHEET & SHEET ROLLING

The first iron sheets made in Britain were rolled at the end of the eighteenth century, either in south Staffordshire or in Pontypool, for the recently introduced tinplate trade. Whether as blackplate for the tinning pots or as the wider, thicker sheets for other markets this product of the iron industry had a slower growth in the second quarter of the nineteenth century than for instance the rail business. It had also special production conditions which substantially affected its location.

Sheets were rolled from puddled iron bars in rolling mills, known as two-high mills, for which a simple analogy is found in the old-fashioned kitchen mangle. As with the mangle the distance between the two rolls could be adjusted according to the thickness of the material to be rolled. With each 'pass' the gauge of the sheet was reduced. Necessarily its surface area was increased so that, when thinner sheet was needed, it was necessary to fold over or 'double' the sheet and for very thin sheets to fold again, so producing 'triples' or 'lattens'. Until the 1880s individual works had their own individual gauges, so that only an intimate connection between the mill and the consumer enabled the trade to function. When gauges were standardised, singles ranged down to 20 gauge, doubles from 21 to 24 G and lattens from 25 to 27 G with extras for even thinner sheets. Other extras were charged for exceptional sizes or for particular qualities.[1]

Sheets have a large surface area for their weight and therefore lose more heat in rolling than larger masses of iron such as rails or plates. Much more than with these also the form of the product was completely different from that of the puddled bar iron from which they all were rolled.   Several reheatings, many passes through the mill and consequently much handling was involved.   Each of these requirements had important implications for the location of the industry.   In the early 1870s manufacture of each ton of iron sheets required 25 to 26 hundredweights of rough bar, and 4 hundredweights was cropped from the sides of the finished sheet.   Similarly about 25 hundredweights of coal was consumed or 10 to 11 hundredweights more than in manufacturing boiler plate.[2] On both the bar and the sheet mill account proximity to low cost coal supplies was highly desirable.   The iron had to be of high quality to undergo the extreme reduction necessary in rolling thin sheet and still more the forming operations to which the purchaser was likely to subject such a product. Use of furnace or puddling forge cinder in the production of pig iron, which was common in the mid-nineteenth century, was quite unsuitable,   Precision in rolling, in measuring gauge and superficial dimensions and in the annealing processes that imparted the essential physical properties necessitated a large labour force of high quality in relation to tonnage produced.   These considerations made sheet production a costly trade and ruled certain iron producing areas out of sheet manufacture.

New iron producing districts only gradually built up a skilled labour force, and in their early stages, helped by virgin mineral resources, they usually made their main impact in lower grade lines.   The Scots in the 1830s were an outstanding example of this.   As pits for ore and coal dotted the Monkland parishes, and furnaces sprang up around Coatbridge, they became the ogres of the world of pig iron production.   Their success there contrasted sharply with their problems in finishing. Over 100 years later there still survived brick-built cottages in a style alien to Lanarkshire which had been put up to accommodate mill men enticed from South Wales or the English Midlands to make good the early Scottish inadequacy. Even in the 1850s Scotch iron could be converted into bars in South Wales and yet undersell local malleable iron in the Glasgow market.[3]   Cleveland, the pacemaking district in pig iron production by the late 1850s, had similar difficulties, and, when these were overcome concentrated heavily on iron rails. In this trade its chief rivals were to be found on the northern outcrop of the South Wales coalfield, a line of works which debased their iron to meet competition yet still went down one by one. In the valleys leading to Newport, Cardiff, but especially in those running into Swansea Bay the tinplate mills did roll iron comparable with that from sheet mills, but expanding demand for tinplate led them to concentrate on a narrow quality range and on the limited sizes required by the tinning houses, so that, although they retained some foothold in the sheet trade, they were never significant in it. Low quality iron, prosperous alternative finishing trades, lack of labour skills or a function tributary to older established iron districts ruled out Derbyshire, Northamptonshire or Lincolnshire.

North Staffordshire produced good iron but developed late, its first forge and mills dating from 1840. Rapid expansion in the next twenty years concentrated its finishing capacity on angles, plates, and a highly successful bar iron trade. The substantial Lancashire finished iron industry served the wide ranging needs of the country's chief manufacturing district, with special emphasis on wire and wire products. West Yorkshire on first consideration seemed an ideal sheet district. The quality of Best Yorkshire iron made from Better Bed coal near Leeds and Bradford was higher than that of iron made in any other district of Britain. The labour of Low Moor, Bowling, Monkbridge and others was of high quality, and ample fuel was available. The district iron trade, however, specialised instead on materials for the local textile and engineering works, and most notably on railway material and boiler plate. Sheet remained a minor line. In a sense indeed the iron of West Yorkshire was too good for the ordinary sheet trade.

In the mid-nineteenth century each of the chief ironworking districts of Britain already had some representation of each product, but every district had its distinctive emphasis. Sheet manufacture was conducted in most of them and was often to form a basis for much more important future growth. The centre of the sheet business was, however, in the Black Country, where gradually, between 1840 and 1880, production of sheet iron emerged to play a dominant role. Its location there reflected a complex of factors reflecting both the strength and the weaknesses of the Midlands as an ironmaking district. The main factors in its localisation fall under three headings, the structure of the sheet industry, material supply conditions and marketing.

THE ECONOMIC STRUCTURE OF SHEET MANU-FACTURE, AND OF SOUTH STAFFORDSHIRE IN THE MID-NINETEENTH CENTURY

A sheet mill and its ancillary plant had a small output compared with a plate or rail mill. The capital investment was also much smaller. Bigger concerns could be built up by a duplication of units, but throughout most of the nineteenth century the trade was characterised by numerous smallish concerns. Capital charges were small compared with running costs, and especially with labour costs. Such a trade attracted the small entrepreneur, the ironmaster for whom organising material supplies and marketing in inland locations like the North Crop or away from fuel supplies, as with Cleveland, would have been too much. Its nineteenth century characteristics made the sheet trade most suitable for small scale operation near skilled labour, materials and markets. In all respects the Black Country was a favoured location.

The typical Black Country ironmaking enterprise was small. There were some notable exceptions: at Gospel Oak, and in their mines, Walker and Yates are said to have employed 2000 men as early as 1824,[4] and later the Earl of Dudley's enterprises were on a very large scale, but in general the outsider was impressed by the number of individual enterprises. Joseph Butler, the West Yorkshire ironmaster, wrote of his tour in 1815, 'there is hardly an ironmaster in this district worth a groat'. In the 1830s, in competing with Welsh firms for rail contracts, Staffordshire ironworks sometimes had to join together to command the necessary capacity, and in 1845-1846 when the Chillington Iron Company contracted to supply the Oxford, Worcester and Wolverhampton Railway Company with 17,500 tons of rails it had to buy the Leabrook Works near Wednesbury to complete the order.[5]   At that time many Staffordshire ironmasters were dependent on loan capital from local banks. The small enterprise probably also reflected favourable raw material supply conditions, especially in the flat country north of the central ridge, where the Thick coal—or Ten Yard Seam— lay near the surface, iron ore supplies were plentiful, at least at an early period, and the whole district was knit together by the Birmingham Canal Navigation network. Such conditions permitted success with small capital outlay. In turn the trades to which the early iron firms turned accentuated the emphasis on smallness.

Writing in 1838 William Hawkes Smith summarised the genesis of the Black Country iron district with a neat locational theory. 'It is obviously fitting that the preparation and manufacture of a heavy article should, if possible, be carried on in the neighbourhood where the raw material is produced. It was therefore natural that, all obstacles being removed by the operation of . . . three great agents . . ., viz the steam engine, navigable canals, and the use of coke for smelting, the iron trade would congregate into the immediate mining district'.[6]   Already the area had been stamped with that distinctive character within which the developing sheet trade took its form '. . . the traveller appears never to get out of an interminable village, composed of cottages and very ordinary houses . . .   These houses for the most part are not arranged in continuous streets, but interspersed with blazing furnaces, heaps of burning coal in process of coking, piles of ironstone, calcining forges, pit banks and engine chimneys, the country being besides intersected with canals crossing each other at various levels, and the small remaining patches of surface soil are occupied with irregular fields of grass or corn intermingled with heaps of refuse of mines or from the slag of blast furnaces. Sometimes the road passes between mounds of refuse from the pits, like a causeway raised some feet above the fields on either side, which have subsided by the excavation of the minerals beneath.   These circumstances in the state of the surface and the substrata, united to the clouds of smoke from the furnaces, coke hearths, and heaps of calcined ironstone, which drift across the country according to the direction of the wind, have effectually excluded from it all classes except those whose daily bread depends upon their residence within these districts'.[7] Within this uncongenial environment the mineral supplies on which its whole evolution had depended were beginning to fail before the middle of the century.

By the mid-1840s the pig iron production of the Black Country was estimated to require from 3.3 to 4.2 million tons of minerals.[8] Many furnaces were at half work through inability to obtain supplies.[9] Within the Black Country itself there was a serious imbalance in mineral supply, iron-stone being relatively abundant on the north east of the central ridge where coal was in short supply, while south of the ridge, linked by the congested Dudley tunnel, the reverse situation prevailed.[10] By 1852 S. H. Blackwell of Dudley was remarking that clay band ores cost from 4s. to 9s. a ton to raise, whereas Cleveland ore could be delivered to the works for 3s. to 3s. 6d. and Cumberland hematite could be raised for under 2s. 6d. a ton.[11] By the mid-1850s most of the 50 to 100,000 tons of limestone raised annually around Ruabon and Wrexham was delivered to Black Country works, and in 1854 213,500 tons of calcined North Staffordshire ore and 120,000 tons of ore from Northamptonshire, as well as Cumberland ore, were delivered in the district by rail or canal. A few years later Welsh and Durham coke ovens were contributing to Staffordshire furnace fuel supplies, and the forges were using pig iron from North Staffordshire, South Wales and Cleveland.[12] By 1870 the coal resources of the Black Country coalfield were already being described as very largely exhausted. The iron ore resources in the centre of the field were by then said to be almost wholly worked out, although there was hope of ore from the north east between Bloxwich, Wyrley and Essington and in Cannock Chase or, very hypothetically, to the west between the Staffordshire and Shropshire coalfields. Inefficiency and lack of co-operation, which contributed to the drowning out of millions of tons of ore and coal, and rising labour costs from at least the 1840s hastened the district's relative decline.[13]

The bankruptcy of a once great mineral endowment caused outsiders to anticipate the decline of the Black Country. As Henry Scrivenor put it in 1854 when discussing the use of Northamptonshire ore and Llangollen limestone '. . . is not this, as regards South Staffordshire, the beginning of an end?'[14]   The more enlightened local ironmasters realised that adjustment was necessary.   Once, as Samuel Bailey told the North of England Mining Engineers in 1861, South Staffordshire could afford to pay 12 shillings a ton for its coal and 20 to 24 shillings a ton for ironstone.   'But now, in consequence of railway communication, when we have all the world to compete with, and when coal is delivered in this district from north, east, south and west, and at nearly the same prices as we are paying for getting, it is indeed time for us to bestir ourselves if we are to exist and compete with other districts'.[15]   In general the coal owners and ironmasters of the Black Country were individualist and stubborn and reacted only slowly to the conditions Bailey spelled out in 1861, so that decline continued.   In the depression of the mid-1870s even Cleveland suffered severely, but the furnace plants of South Staffordshire were much more acutely afflicted. By March 1875, when 125 of the 157 blast furnaces in the North East were still working, only 79 of the 149 in the Black Country were in blast.[16]

With a similarly shrinking local mineral resource base, and keen outside competition in the thirties and forties, Welsh works had lowered the quality of their iron: Staffordshire firms generally avoided this policy.   True, John Gibbons of Corbyns Hall introduced cinder into the blast furnace charge, so producing that class of iron known as 'part mine', but overall the emphasis on quality was reinforced rather than diminished.   As a result Scrivenor found that as early as 1854 many South Staffordshire ironmasters had stopped using Northamptonshire ore.[17]

For similar reasons it was impracticable to reverse the whole trend of development in the district by lowering Staffordshire wages 'to place the several districts on an equality', as Mackelcon recommended as early as 1843.[18]   William Truran of Merthyr found that high wages were linked with a lower tonnage but also with much better finished iron.   Welsh puddling furnaces, worked for about 140 hours a week, turned out about 18 tons each;   in Staffordshire a 100 hour week and a turn out of 10 tons was usual.[19]   Four years later Edward Williams of Dowlais visited the ironworks of the Midlands and the North to survey their competitive position. In the Black Country he inspected only three works, Old Park, Round Oak and Smethwick Ironworks, but he too was impressed by the quality of the iron that was used and the care taken in puddling.[20] Pig and finished iron prices reflected the emphasis on quality (Table 6).

TABLE 6

Welsh and Staffordshire iron prices summer, 1856 (shillings per ton)

	Forge pig iron	Rails	Bars
South Wales	70	160	160
Staffordshire	90	170	180

Source: G. Wilkie. *The Manufacture of Iron in Great Britain*, 1857, p. 11.

In June 1861 in a period of deep depression, Blackwell made a balanced assessment of the problems and prospects of the district's iron trade.[21] Many works were not only idle then but would probably never work again, raw materials were difficult to obtain, mineral royalties extortionate, wages too high and men were leaving for other districts where regular work could be obtained even though for lower wages. It was necessary to take note of the advantages of other districts, and iron masters '. . . certainly must not blind themselves to the progress which the manufacture of iron has made during the last 25 years'. Blackwell, however, stressed that South Staffordshire was not finished, and listed its advantages —the ability to bring in ore and iron from elsewhere, its central position, high quality products and great local market. Both its difficulties and these advantages made it a congenial home for the sheet trade.

While rising material costs priced the Black Country out of the rail trade, so that, whereas in 1850 twelve works or combinations of works were said to be making rails, Edward Williams nine years later found that few or no rails were being rolled,[22] the wider margins in quality products increasingly attracted the ironmasters' attention to them (Table 7). The basis for an emphasis on sheet iron was found partly in this, partly in its requirements of high grade iron and partly in the advantages of a local market. In the last few decades of the

TABLE 7

Margins between puddled bar and finished product prices, 1860

Rails	5s. to 5s. 6d.
Heavy angles	20s.
Light angles	30s. to 40s.
Sheet and hoops	30s. to 40s.

Source: W. Fordyce, *Coal and Iron*, 1860, p. 164

nineteenth century the Staffordshire sheet mills became largely concerned with overseas markets, but this trade was built on proximity to the largest home market for the product in Britain. The traditional sheet-using trades of the West Midlands were nailmaking, the 'toy' trade of Birmingham, japanning and holloware manufacture, and tinplate production. To these was added in the 1840s a trade which eventually dominated all the others, the manufacture of galvanised iron sheets.

MIDLAND MARKETS FOR SHEET IRON

The domestic manufacture of hand-wrought nails had once been the biggest Black Country finishing trade, employing upwards of 50,000 persons, but by 1830 nails cut from strip had made the hand nailers the most depressed class in the district. The growing cut nail trade provided a substantial market for sheet iron. By 1866 Birmingham's cut nail trade, estimated to be equal to the combined output of Wolverhampton, Leeds, Newcastle and Lancashire, used 15,000 to 16,000 tons of iron a year, largely sheet. This outlet for the sheet mills remained important until wire nail replaced cut nails at the end of the century.[23] The important Black Country sheet firm of Morewood and Company installed some 200 nail machines to use the 'strong iron' which was produced before the mill rolls reached the temperature required for sheet for galvanising.[24] Outside the Black Country in at least one significant case the reverse happened, and an important nail maker gained a first small footing in the sheet business, from which was built up the great firm of John Summers and Sons.

In the eighteenth century the button and even the buckle trade of Birmingham provided a small market for the early Midland sheet mills, and in 1794 Pitt described the tobacco and snuff box makers of Darlaston and Willenhall, and the plated, lacquered, enamelled and japanned goods of Bilston.[25] Japanning became much more important during the nineteenth century, when its products became essential requisites of Victorian household respectability. Japanning involves the covering of materials, mainly papier mâché or iron, with varnishes to produce a resemblance to the lacquered wares of the Far East. The trade came to the West Midlands about 1740, and Birmingham, Wolverhampton and Bilston became the chief centres of manufacture. The needs of countless country stores at home, the exertions of travellers and the amazing catalogues of the bigger firms kept the japanned ware works, the fertile imaginations of their resident artists, and the iron sheet mills which supplied them busy. Trays, waiters, coal vases, scoops and scuttles of bewildering variety left the district, and in the 1870s, with the growth of holiday-making, japanned trunks became another important line, requiring a much larger tonnage of sheet iron. By then the japanned ware trade of Wolverhampton and Bilston had doubled since 1849 and employed 2000 people. Even though the trade remained important until after the end of the century, other trades had already become more important to the sheet mills.[26]

Holloware, largely for domestic use, was made either of cast or of wrought iron and, if of the latter, from iron sheets. Originally the goods were hammered into shape, but in 1841 stamping, introduced by T. Griffiths, greatly speeded the process, which increasingly was localised in the Midlands. Here iron holloware manufacture grew at the expense of holloware in copper or brass. Tinning, enamelling and later galvanising became important finishing operations of the holloware firms. The sheet iron used in this trade had to be capable of standing the forming operations of either hammer or press work and therefore of good quality. Throughout the century such specialised activities as those of the frying pan makers of Ettingshall and Bilston were to remain of vital interest to some of the sheet makers.

In the mid-1820s Staffordshire and Worcestershire each had one tinplate works and by 1850 together they had nine, or one more than Glamorgan. There was a substantial local market for tinplate in trades similar to those which used uncoated sheet, although the scanty evidence suggests that quite early much Midland tinplate was sent to the ports or other industrial areas.[27] The maximum number of tinplate works in the West Midlands was reached in the 1870s but relative importance of the area in the trade was already declining. Wages were from one third to one half as high again as in South Wales, two days' output in a Welsh mill was said to be equal to one week's in a Staffordshire mill and the area had to concentrate on higher grades, largely for the home and German markets. Soon after the change to steel as a raw material in the tinplate trade and the con- centration on exports brought a rapid withering in South Staffordshire.[28] That this was a warning also for the sheet makers perhaps only a contemporary of exceptional discern- ment could be expected to recognise.

With such local outlets, trades which had grown up beside it from the mid-eighteenth century, the iron sheet business of South Staffordshire was already important in the 1830s, but then and for long after was never singled out as a pre-eminent trade either in tonnage produced, in activity rates of the mills or in expansion of capacity. The district's chief glory was in the quality of its bar iron and nothing suggested that within fifty years many famous marked bar houses would have failed while others turned over to the only notable growth line in the whole finished iron range of the district, the manu- facture of iron sheets. This growth depended partly on expansion in the outlets discussed above, but was essentially and increasingly connected with a completely new trade, the manufacture of galvanised iron sheets. This trade was initiated elsewhere, but manufacture was soon strongly localised in the West Midland metallurgical complex.

The progress of the industrial revolution and especially the growth of commerce and of new transport facilities, involved a large expansion of the constructional industries. While brick and stonework, and soon iron beams, provided essential materials for walls, suitable material for the very extensive roofs of factories, warehouses, railway stations was less easy to provide. There was a great extension in the use of Welsh slates but also attempts to use iron. In the late 1820s Walker of Rotherhithe introduced corrugation, which gave sheet iron greatly increased strength and made it much more suitable for use in structures. 'It is called *corrugated* iron' wrote the *Mechanics Magazine* in 1833, 'which in plainer English means *furrowed* or *fluted* and derives its very valuable properties simply from being passed through fluted rollers when in a red hot state'. At that time little had been done with the material, although there were several corrugated iron roofs in the London docks. Sheet iron, plain or corrugated, was already being used in new buildings as far afield as St. Petersburg and Moscow.[29] A basic problem checked more rapid progress, the difficulty of providing resistance to weathering. Oil or tar paints were recommended by the *Encyclopaedia of Cottage, Farm and Villa Architecture*, the Russians first painted their roofing sheet on both sides and after fixing on the roof a second coat was given—'The common colour is red, but green paint, it is said, will stand twice the time'. A few years later paints, varnish, wax, oxide and zinc were tried on the sheet iron of steamers in India. The zinc was, however, adulterated with lead and failed to give protection, and eventually coal tar was used.[30] It was then that a practical galvanising process was introduced, with the result of large increase in demand and consequently a major new outlet for good quality iron sheet.

Experiments in immersion of iron in molten zinc to provide good weathering properties date back at least to the experiments of the Frenchman Melouin in 1741, but industrial development began only with the work of his fellow countryman, Sorel, in Paris in 1836. In 1837 Henry Crawford took out British patents on the lines of Sorel's work for the galvanising of copper or iron with powdered or molten zinc. In 1841, and frequently over the next few years, E. Morewood took out further patents covering improvements in galvanising processes. There remained considerable obscurity about processes, helped no doubt by the word 'galvanising', which quite wrongly suggested an electrolytic process, and by business policy, which made the practical processes '. . . a

sealed book, save to the few who make it their business pro-
fession, and they in accordance with their own motives of
personal interest, appear disposed to preserve it a trade
secret'.[31]   Nevertheless technical advance was rapid, there
were both many patents and many infringements of patents,
vituperative correspondence in the trade journals, hard words
at company meetings and litigation.

Galvanising required good quality sheet which, though not
of the standard used in stamping, retained its malleability
when dipped into molten zinc and then directly quenched
in cold water, and also, later, when shaped in the corrugating
machine.   In October 1866 the journal *Engineer* described
the standard good practice of the time.   Piles of sheet iron—
now known as black sheet to distinguish it from the grey or
whitish colour of the galvanised product—were first pickled
in tanks of sulphuric acid to clean them, then washed, scraped,
dipped in hydrochloric acid, washed again and dried.   After
this, by the use of tongs, they were slipped edgeways into
molten spelter in a bath made from best Low Moor iron
plates and surrounded in turn by a coke fire and outer wall
of bricks.   The sheets were pulled out on the other side by
men who checked that the zinc had taken.[32]   Although
there was some dispute about the quality of the new product,
so that, as late as 1857 the Vieille Montagne Zinc Mining
Company of Moresnet, Belgium, was claiming boldly that
its zinc roofing was cheaper, more durable and lighter,
galvanised iron quickly established a reputation as an ideal,
easily erected roofing material.   By 1845 it had been used
in the naval dockyards at Woolwich, Deptford and Portsmouth
and for the sheds and warehouses at Liverpool docks, and
Morewood, now a manufacturer, was offering it as 'peculiarly
adapted for railway stations, as forming a light, strong and
incorrodible covering'.[33]   It also helped to change the appearance and the crafts of rural England and Seebohm later gave
it scant and grudging recognition when discussing improved
materials—'. . . the useful but deplorably unsightly corrugated
iron for all sorts of purposes'.   Contemporary farm sceptics
noted that the material was seldom covered with a zinc coat
so pure as to prevent rust in a few years and hence, unless
the material was painted, the annoyances of a leaking roof.[34]

Nevertheless it was employed in parts of the roofing of Barry and Pugin's new Houses of Parliament, though later Sir Charles Barry expressed doubts about the material.[35]

The materials, processes and skills involved in galvanising were completely different from those in the black sheet trade and there seemed no reason for combining their production either in company structure or in location. Indeed lack of integration, organisationally and geographically, was not uncommon up to the end of the nineteenth century. On the other hand desire of the galvanisers to control the source of material and later, though more hesitantly, that of the sheet mill to ensure an increasingly important outlet, brought about many instances of backward and forward integration. The manufacture of black sheet had grown out of and was frequently conducted alongside other lines of iron production, fuel consumption was still high and good iron was needed. The coalfields and especially the Black Country remained its centre. Galvanising used little coal, was consumer oriented and quickly also developed large exports. It was soon more widely spread and frequently coastal. Yet the tendencies discussed above meant that the Black Country had a substantial share of the new trade, attracted other outlying, small-scale enterprises to relocate there, and, for those established elsewhere, ensured that Staffordshire black sheet was long their chief raw material.

REFERENCES

1 G. K. V. Gale, *The Black Country Iron Industry* 1966, pp. 96–98.
2 H. Bauerman, *Metallurgy* 1874, pp. 362, 364.
3 W. Truran, *The Iron Manufacture of Great Britain* 1855, p. 169.
4 Sir J. Clapham, *An Economic History of Modern Britain*, 1. *The Railway Age* pp. 188–189.
5 *Mining Journal* 23, 1853, p. 467.
6 W. Hawkes Smith, *Birmingham and South Staffordshire* 1838, p. 11.
7 *Midland Mining Commission* 1843. *Report* 1.
8 Estimates of Benjamin Guest and Richard Smith (Lord Ward's mining agent) *Select Committee on the Oxford, Worcester and Wolverhampton Railway Bill* 1845, Vol. 10, pp. 6, 19.
9 G. R. Porter, 'On the progress, present amount and probable future condition of the iron manufacture in Great Britain'. *Reports of British Association, Southampton meeting* 1846, p. 107.

10   B. Guest, *op. cit.*, p. 6.
11   S. H. Blackwell, 'The Ironmaking Resources of the United Kingdom'. *Lecture 5 of 2nd Series Great Exhibition Lectures* 7 April 1852.
12   *Mineral Statistics of the United Kingdom. Transactions of the North of England Institute of Mining Engineers* 2, 1854, pp. 242–255. *Colliery Guardian*, 31 January 1863, p. 212. 6 June 1863, p. 454. 13 April 1868, p. 355.
13   Report of Commission on the Distribution of the Iron Ores of Great Britain, *Journal of the Iron & Steel Institute* 1870, p. 387, *ibid.*, 1871, pp. 7–26. S. Timmins (Editor) *The Birmingham and Midland Hardware District* 1866, pp. 35–37. *Iron* 29 September 1882, p. 277. *Report of the Commission on the State of Population in Mining Districts* 1847, pp. 12–13.
14   H. Scrivenor, *History of the Iron Trade* 1854, p. 301.
15   S. Bailey, 'On the advantage and necessity of the introduction of steam power for the purpose of underground conveyance in the coal and ironstone mines of South Staffordshire', *Transactions North of England Institute of Mining Engineers* X, 1861, pp. 25–39.
16   *Iron and Coal Trades Review* 9 April 1875, p. 429.
17   G. K. V. Gale, *op. cit.*, p. 56. H. Scrivenor, *op. cit.*, p. 304. J. Jones in S. Timmins, *The Resources, Products and Industrial History of Birmingham and the Midland Hardware District* 1866, p. 64.
18   F. P. Mackelcon, *Suggestions to Ironmasters on increasing the demand for iron; also to the ironmasters of Staffordshire on competing with those of Scotland and Wales*, A pamphlet, 1843.
19   W. Truran, *op. cit.*, pp. 140–141.
20   E. Williams, *Report on Northern and Midland Ironworks* 1859. Dowlais Company Records. Box 8, Section C (available in Cardiff record office).
21   S. H. Blackwell, *Midland Counties Herald* June 1861. Quoted S. Bailey, *op. cit.*, pp. 26–27.
22   E.T. of Tipton, The Iron Trade of South Staffordshire Past and Present. *Mining Journal* 23 November 1850, p. 561 and Williams, *op. cit.*
23   *Engineer* 14 January 1868, p. 122. S. Timmins, *op. cit.*, p. 615.
24   R. Heathfield, Minutes of Evidence. *Select Committee on Railways* H.C. Papers 1881, 13, p. 493.
25   R. K. Dent, *Old and New Birmingham* 1880, p. 613, *The Making of Birmingham* 1894, pp. 93, 257. William Pitt, *General View of the agriculture of the County of Stafford* 1794, p. 161.
26   There is a scattered literature on the japanned ware industry. On its products the catalogues of Victorian domestic hardware in the local collection of Birmingham Public Library are revealing. See also *Engineer* 1 September 1865, p. 128. J. T.

Jeffcock, *The Original Wolverhampton Guide* 1884, p. 103.   *Price and Beebe's History of Bilston* 1868, p. 85.   S. Griffith, *Guide to the Iron Trade of Great Britain* 1873, p. 94.   A. Briggs, *History of Birmingham* 1865–1938, p. 39.   On organisation and location see *Engineer* 2 May 1856, p. 342, 20 February 1857, p. 159. *Pigot and Co. Commercial Directory of Birmingham and its environs* 1829.   *Kelly's Directory of Birmingham* 1900 and 1910.

27   E. H. Brook, *Monograph of Tinplate Works of Great Britain* 1932. W. E. Minchinton, *The British Tinplate Industry: A History* 1957. Minutes of Evidence, *The Oxford, Worcester and Wolverhampton Railway Bill* 1845, Vol. 11, p. 186.   Statistics of finished iron production and disposal.

28   *Engineer* 1 June 1877, p. 384.   *Iron* 16 February 1878, p. 210.

29   *Journal of the Franklin Institute* Vol. XII, 1833, pp. 43–45 quoting Mechanics Magazine and Vol. XI, 1833, p. 209.

30   *ibid.*, XI, 1833, p. 209, XVI, 1835.

31   *Engineer* 26 October 1866, pp. 306–307 article 'Galvanising'. See also *Journal of the Franklin Institute* 1838, pp. 52–56.   A. Ure, *Dictionary of Arts. Manufactures and Mines* 1843, p. 544. *Mining Journal*, 14 June 1845, p. 298.   H. Bablik, *Galvanising (Hot Dip)* 1950, p. 1.

32   *Engineer* 26 October 1866, pp. 306–307.

33   *Mining Journal* 14 February 1846, p. 45.

34   M. E. Seebohm, *The Evolution of the English Farm* 1927.   *Journal Royal Agricultural Society* 2nd Series, Vol. 2, 1866, p. 140.

35   Quoted *Journal Society of Arts* 10 July 1857, p. 487.

CHAPTER 2

Black and Galvanised Sheet Works in the Black Country and other districts to the 1870s

THE ESTABLISHMENT OF GALVANISED SHEET IRON PRODUCTION

The first big galvanised iron firm was formed in 1837, with a capital of £400,000 and directors who included such a renowned ironmaster as W. Crawshay of Cyfarthfa. Divisions in the board led to its dissolution, and patent rights were bought in 1839 by the Patent Galvanised Iron Company, which overextended itself in both areas of interest and finishing lines, and was wound up in 1850. Among its activities it had galvanising works in Birmingham, at the Leabrook Works, West Bromwich, and near the West India Docks, an excellent market location. In the first half of 1846 the company produced 40 to 50 tons of galvanised iron a week, but it had already been far exceeded in the trade.[1] Two Derbyshire merchants, E. Morewood and G. Rogers, took out a series of patents, which led them into legal conflict with the Patent Galvanised Iron Company, and set up galvanised iron works in Broad Street, Birmingham, in 1843. They bought their black sheet from the Tipton and Gospel Oak works of the long established firm of J. and E. Walker, which had helped to finance them. Walkers themselves then began galvanising and brought some Broad Street plant to Gospel Oak. By 1845 their other works, the Tipton Old Church works, was said to be capable of 120 tons galvanised iron a week. Meanwhile Morewood and Rogers retained the Broad Street premises.[2]

The centripetal force that brought Morewood and Rogers to the West Midlands also affected a Southwark railway firm. J. H. Porter brought skilled galvanisers from Paris in 1842 and extended the use of galvanised sheet to cotton mill construction and bridge work. On gaining control of the business, he moved it to Gas Street, Birmingham. In an area surrounding Porter's works, occupying less than one square mile, and delimited by a line from Shadwell Street to New Street, Broad Street and Sand Pits, there were, by 1854, four galvanised iron works, two galvanised plate works and two other iron roofing firms.[3] These were the only Birmingham works of this nature, the strong localising agent being the Birmingham Canal which provided a link with the sheet mills of the iron district to the west.   Between the transfer of part of More-wood's plant to Gospel Oak and the early twentieth century, there was to be not only a flow of material but an interplay of ownership patterns, sometimes involving removal of plant, between this canal belt of Birmingham and Smethwick and the bigger industrial area of the Black Country beyond.

At the other end of the Black Country, in Wolverhampton, galvanised sheet iron manufacture, destined to become even more important, made a slower start.   There Edward Davies, a tinplate worker, began galvanising in 1838 though he was concerned only with bucket production and jobbing work. Sixteen years later his works on Snow Hill, south of the town centre, seems to have been the first to produce galvanised corrugated sheet.   In 1859 two other tinplate workers, John and Joseph Jones, began works only a few hundred yards away from Davies, in Church Lane, as the Wolverhampton Corrugated Iron Company.[4] Both sites were well away from both canals and railways and neither was to prove suitable for a heavy, rather low value and noxious trade.

While galvanised sheet manufacture was invading the metalworking structure of the West Midlands, black sheet production was gradually becoming a more prominent trade, so that by the early 1860s, and apparently for the first time, it attracted comment as the most actively in demand of all the district's finished products.   The biggest and most renowned firms, W. T. and J. Barrows, John Dawes of West Bromwich, the New British Iron Company, the Earl of Dudley or the two biggest Wolverhampton firms, the Chillington Iron Company and G. B. Thorneycroft and Company, had their whole or chief interest in other lines, but some smaller firms already concentrated on sheet iron, and certain areas, particularly around Bilston and Wolverhampton, were specialising in sheet.

The extension of railways at home and abroad, expanding warehouse facilities, the Californian and Australian gold rushes, all increased the demand for galvanised iron, while the prospector grilling under a Staffordshire 'tin roof' probably kept his water in a bucket, had a frying pan, a billy can or that most vital item of his equipment, his pan for work in the placer deposits, made from black sheet from the same district. Just as railway extension anywhere in the world was significant to the mills of Cleveland or Glamorgan, so world economic growth stimulated the hardware trades and so the sheet mills of the West Midlands. Soon the mail boat from California, from southern Africa, from Latin American ports brought intelligence vital to the district. Iron roofing for the West Indies became important, and in the late 1860s and early 1870s warehouse construction in India opened an almost completely new outlet. Failure of the monsoon, drought in the pasture lands of New South Wales, or a hurricane in Jamaica now brought consternation to the iron trade, and distress to hundreds of poor homes in Birmingham, in Bilston and in the east end of Wolverhampton.

OUTLYING SHEET IRON & GALVANISED IRON PRODUCTION

In spite of the pre-eminence of the Black Country, both black sheet and galvanised sheet were produced on a considerable scale in other districts, although the latter frequently involved purchases from West Midland black sheet mills. This connection was usually simply a close commercial link, but common ownership was not unknown and there was some backward integration by outlying galvanisers which brought them into the Black Country as operators of black sheet mills. Midland managers and workers were key men in the trade in all districts. (Figure 1.)

London was an important early centre of galvanised sheet production although its relative importance soon declined. Some locations there seem to have been haphazardly chosen, as in Clerkenwell and Moorgate, and sites near the railway lines were sometimes used. Other locations, like those in the Broad Street-Gas Street area of Birmingham, were linked

Figure 1.   This was the high point of Black Country domination.   Th
were no combined black sheet and galvanised sheet works outside that distri

with their Black Country sheet suppliers by canal. Sites
near the outfall of London canals into the Thames were
well placed also for dock and export markets. Tupper and
Company of Berkeley Street, Birmingham, also had a works
in Limehouse near the Regents Canal. The Gospel Oak
Iron Company of Wednesbury and Tipton operated the
Regents Canal Bridge works in Limehouse, which made roofing
and tanks from galvanised sheet iron, and in another favourable
location, which survived into the mid-twentieth century,
the Blackwall Galvanised Iron Company had works in Orchard
Place, hemmed in between the East India Docks, Bow Creek
and the Thames. Frederick Braby, from the Wolverhampton
works of Davies Brothers, built galvanising works in Euston
Road about 1860, but later moved to the wharf at Deptford
on the Grand Surrey Canal, well located for the export
business and accessible to the Regents Canal and so to the
Black Country.[5] Although Belgian nail sheet was soon a
troublesome competitor in the London area, home supplies
of galvanising sheet were still dominant.

Merseyside also became an important galvanised iron sheet
district, and for the same reasons as the port of London.
Here, however, on the foundations established in the 1860s
and 1870s, was later to be built an important black sheet
production. There were two galvanisers and another three
galvanised sheet iron makers in Liverpool in 1873, and at
Garston was the Hamilton Galvanised Iron Works.[6] The
Shropshire Union Canal brought Staffordshire iron, their
chief supply, but there was already local material as well.
The wire firm of Rylands, to reduce its dependence on Shropshire and Staffordshire wire rod, in 1863, with the Dallam
Forge, formed the Warrington Wire Iron Company, which
also built sheet mills. Ten years later Warrington Wire
merged with the Wigan colliery firm of Pearson and Knowles
to form the Pearson and Knowles Coal and Iron Company
Limited.[7] In the late 1870s the railway companies charged
more for transport of galvanised sheet than for black sheet, and
this encouraged a new interest in coastal locations, from which
Liverpool benefited. Of eleven new galvanised sheet works
built in Britain between 1876 and 1881 five were in Liverpool and one in Warrington. Minor additional locational

D

advantages of this area were proximity to the point of import of foreign spelter and to hydrochloric acid from the Leblanc alkali works of St. Helens and Widnes.[8]

The galvanising business of the Clyde was supplied in the mid-1860s by large tonnages of black sheet from Staffordshire. The failure of two Scottish galvanisers in 1870 revealed debts to one Black Country sheet firm alone of £6,000, and similar links were indicated by later failures.[9] Black sheet was naturally dearer than on Merseyside, for it involved either an extra break-of-bulk from barge to coasting vessel or a very long rail haul. Accordingly the Scottish galvanisers sought sheet supplies from the mills of Lanarkshire. The firm of Smith and McLean had built a galvanising works at Mavisbank on the Clyde in 1862, but within ten years had taken over sheet and bar mills at Gartcosh in northern Lanarkshire. In 1882 George Beard, Black Country mill man and entrepreneur, went to manage the Gartcosh works, taking with him Staffordshire workers whose distinctively Midland names still survive in the area.[10]

The North-East Coast, in spite of its leadership in pig iron production and its important position in many finishing trades, had little part in sheet iron. The Bowesfield and Ayrton works, in Stockton and Middlesbrough respectively, rolled sheet grades by the late 1870s, but were essentially makers of light plate. The single galvanised sheet works built in Middlesbrough was wholly dependent on Staffordshire black sheet. On the North-West Coast the ill-fated West Cumberland Iron and Steel Works at Workington rolled a certain amount of heavy sheet in the 1880s.

Bristol had a substantial galvanised iron capacity, a much smaller part in black sheet production and a more significant role than either of these suggested by reason of the quality of entrepreneurship its firms were to show. At the Ashton Vale mills, Bedminster, the firm of Joseph Tinn operated puddling furnaces and sheet mills, and a relative, George Tinn, made galvanised iron at the Bristol Ironworks. By the early 1870s George Tinn had installed three puddling furnaces and a sheet mill. The Bristol Galvanised Iron Works in the St. Philips district obtained some of its iron sheet from Joseph Tinn.[11] In the mid-1850s a small works, largely engaged in the production of galvanised buckets, was established in Temple Backs. In 1857 the works was taken over and turned to the production of galvanised sheet iron by John Lysaght, who from the earliest days concentrated especially on the Australian trade. Economic growth was already rapid there following the gold discoveries of Bathurst and Ballarat in 1851, with great crop and livestock developments and with responsible government granted in turn between 1857 and 1859 to Victoria, New South Wales, Tasmania, South Australia and Queensland. In the event John Lysaght overestimated the economic growth potential of Australia, but none-the-less prospered by equipping his works to supply the needs of pioneer districts—complete buildings, fencing, wire netting and especially galvanised corrugated roofing. Lysaght's exports of galvanised sheet iron in 1869 were only 2600 tons, but the firm moved in that year to bigger premises on the banks of the Avon Feeder canal in the St. Vincent's district, a site convenient for obtaining its black sheet, which still came wholly from Staffordshire, and for shipping finished galvanised sheet either by water or by the Great Western Railway. Ten years later, when Lysaght made his first sales visit to Australia, two-thirds of a much expanded output from St. Vincent's works was sold there.[12]

THE SHAPING OF COMPANY LINKS BETWEEN THE BLACK COUNTRY SHEET TRADE AND OUTLYING FIRMS

Black Country men and managers built up the sheet trade of other British districts and indeed that of other countries, notably the United States. Staffordshire black sheet was the essential supply of most of the galvanising plant in Britain in the 1860s, but supply, quality and price could better be controlled by a more tightly drawn company organisation than by either traditional trading links with Staffordshire firms or by open market purchases of black sheet. Most firms lacked the resources for such a development. Others chose alternative local linkages. The initiative in backward integration into the Midland sheet trade came from George Tinn.

Tinn had tried to make puddled iron in the Bristol area,

but in 1875 bought the Deepfields Ironworks, Bilston. The 12 puddling furnaces and 2 mills were in partial operation in 1878, and by 1880 Deepfields had 20 furnaces and 7 mills. Tinn retained control, but the works seems not to have been steadily employed throughout the 1880s and it never became a galvanising plant.[13] Tinn's action provided the model for the more important move by his Bristol contemporary, John Lysaght.

Lysaght already had close links with Staffordshire. By the 1870s his galvanising works was a good customer for several black sheet works, notably those of Wolverhampton, and in 1874 his nephew, William R. Lysaght, was sent for a three-year apprenticeship to the sheet iron business at the Gospel Oak works. The failure of the Wolverhampton house of G.B. Thorneycroft provided an opportunity for backward integration. Founded in 1824, Thorneycrofts had expanded output from 8 tons a week to a record 800 tons in one week in 1851. By the mid-1870s they employed some 1000 men at the Shrubbery works and at Swan Garden works. They were renowned for plate and bar iron but also had a considerable interest in sheet, in which trade they had pioneered important technical advances in the 1850s. Their heavy trades suffered severely in the depressed conditions of the mid-1870s. In the spring of 1877 they served notices on their salaried employees and at Christmas, after their men had refused to accept a wage reduction, closed both works and dismissed their labour, while representatives of the firm made it clear that they saw no hope for the trade.[14]

A local agent purchased both plants for £45,000 but within a month had sold Swan Garden, the smaller of them, to John Lysaght for £22,000 or £23,000. Galvanised iron demand had remained buoyant in 1877 in spite of the depression of other lines and Lysaght had been short of sheet supplies. Looking over Thorneycroft's works he formed the impression that they had now fallen behind good current practice in finished iron and sheet production. At the end of January 1878 Lysaght met 300-400 former Thorneycroft men and spoke to them of the expansive prospects for sheet. He concluded by saying that in wishing them 'Good morning' he hoped that when he saw them again . . . 'they would have their jackets off and a good heat before them'. Soon the works was busy on the gauges the St. Vincent's galvanising works required. Lysaght chose to leave the running of the business to Staffordshire trained men. Richard Dodd, formerly one of the proprietors of the Monmore Ironworks, Willenhall, was general manager at Swan Garden until his death in 1893, when he was succeeded by W. R. Lysaght.[15]

The puddling forge at Swan Garden was reorganised, more of the mills were converted to sheet so that the number of sheet mills went up from 6 in 1878 to 11 by 1881. Demand for Lysaght's renowned 'Orb' brand of galvanised sheets continued to grow, and Swan Garden proved unable to supply all the black sheet needed, so that outside purchases had to continue. Nearby, William Sparrow, of the Osier Bed Iron Works, was making losses on tinplate as locational advantages in that trade swung heavily and quickly in favour of South Wales when steel replaced iron as raw material for blackplate manufacture. The Osier Bed tinplate department closed in 1882, the whole works in the summer of 1884, and in 1885 Lysaghts acquired the plant for black sheet production to make good the shortfall from Swan Garden.

LOCATIONAL CHANGE & LINKAGES WITHIN THE WEST MIDLAND INDUSTRIAL AREA

Although there was certainly growth, contrasting sharply with depression in other trades, the geographical character of that growth in the West Midlands sheet business is confused by kalaedoscopic change in the organisation of the trade. Firms came and went, new works were established, changed hands or function, galvanisers bought black sheet mills, sold them, bought others or built their own, or the black sheet makers integrated forwards to control their own galvanising operations. These characteristics are all a reflection of the relative ease of entry to the sheet trade.

A sheet mill had a small capacity and successful operations did not require control over coal pits, ore mines or iron furnaces, as did the big output and lower value products of most iron firms in Cleveland or Lanarkshire. Indeed by the mid-1870s local pig iron, made from Staffordshire 'mine' or

Northamptonshire iron ore, was too poor for most sheet, and pig iron from Barrow, Yorkshire, the Forest of Dean and Shropshire was used instead. Consequently, and in such a concentrated metalworking district, there were always enterprising mill managers who, having saved carefully, could become entrepreneurs, or, alternatively, entrepreneurs from outside the iron trade altogether who could hire a competent mill man to run a sheet mill acquired cheaply on the failure of its previous owner. W. R. Lysaght recalled that in the mid-seventies a four-mill plant, complete with puddling and ball furnaces, could be built for £20,000. 'Many managers and foremen who had saved a little money joined hands with the local grocer and butcher and started works. Brothers, uncles and cousins held all the principal posts. Even the roller was often a relation, who made substantial sums by subletting the work at less than the so-called country rates'.[16] Nepotism was scarcely an augury of success, and small, inadequately capitalised operations, tossed about by every change of fortune in the sheet market, constantly failed in spite of the skilled labour, good iron and high reputation of the district. Some indeed succeeded in spite of amazing inadequacies of business organisation. O. S. Walsh, iron plate worker and galvaniser of Dudley Road, Wolverhampton, and with branches in London and Liverpool, had carried on business for 25 years before he failed in 1881. It was then shown that he had neither purchase ledger nor cash book![17] Each failure gave the possibility of a new start to someone else and so contributed to the confusion which a study of industrial change in the district reveals. A sample of the changes linking a group of sheetmaking enterprises may show this more satisfactorily.

In 1866 Arthur Wright, of the Grove Ironworks, Smethwick, suspended payment with liabilities of £10,000. The *Engineer* commented: '. . . Mr. Wright has been an ironmaster only 12 months. Previous to that time he was keeping a well frequented public house in the Bradley district near Bilston, and had made a very profitable purchase of some mineral property which he was successfully working up to the time at which he entered the iron trade'.[18] Nearer Birmingham, J. Fletcher had operated sheet mills in Eyre Street, Winson Green, through to at least 1865. When trade revived, both the

Grove Works and the Eyre Street mills were taken over by Eberhard and Beard. George Beard was then recovering from a disastrous failure. As a lad of very tender years he had begun work as a plate roller's helper, but in 1858–1859 entered the trade as a partner in the firm of Ambrose, Beard and Sons of the Regent Ironworks, Bilston, whose annual profits were £3,000–£4,000. By 1867 he was also connected with four other concerns, three of which were ironworks, but he failed with liabilities of over £70,000. In his defence at the creditors' meeting it was said, with some exaggeration, that his was the plight of thousands. 'Successful in their early career, they forgot that the sun did not always shine upon them, and an overweening confidence in the future had extended their operations to concerns that they could not manage together, and a breakdown resulted.'[19] In less than four months from this catastrophe, however, Beard was willing to try again, and the *Engineer* was prepared to give full endorsement to his re-entry to the sheet trade. '. . . we have no doubt (Mr. Beard) will soon be again producing iron of a quality which reflects credit upon the district in which it is turned out.'[20] Rather than the small Cape Ironworks, Smethwick, with which rumour had connected his name, Beard and Eberhard took over the rather larger Grove Works and Eyre Street mills. Meanwhile, as trade revived, others with money and enterprise were showing interest in Beard's old works. In August 1867 Stephen Thompson, a senior executive with Thomson Hatton and Company of Bilston, joined with C. Rollason to take over their Bilston works. The Regent works seems to have been idle for some years until it was acquired in 1878 by J. and C. Onions, who had suffered a grievous failure in 1871 in pig-iron manufacture. Failure in the mid-80s made Regent works idle yet again.[21]

Separate ownership of black and of galvanised sheet works persisted, but even when there was joint ownership separate locations were common, with exchanges along the canals, for possession of railway sidings was, until long after the third quarter of the nineteenth century, quite exceptional in the Black Country. Split operations of this type largely reflected piecemeal acquisition of plants formerly operated by others, but this was not the full explanation, as specially built sheet mills were frequently well away from the galvanising works. The large consumption of coal in puddling furnaces and the mills was undoubtedly a major factor here.   Gospel Oak, with sheet mills in the centre of the Black Country, had its galvanising plant in the Mitre Works, Wolverhampton, Israel Parkes of the Atlas Works, West Bromwich, rolled sheet iron which went by canal to the galvanising works in Rotten Park Street, Winson Green. By the seventies, Morewood and Company had moved their galvanising works from central Birmingham to Wiggin Street just across the Birmingham Canal from Parkes. At Ettingshall, west of Bilston, they had operated puddling furnaces and sheet mills, but in 1876 the lease expired on this plant and it passed to the Barbor's Field Company.   To replace it, Morewood's laid down the extensive Woodford sheet mills in Smethwick, much nearer but still requiring substantial cartage.[22] In 1878, at a time when Lysaght's were busily extending Swan Garden works, when the future of sheet manufacture in the Black Country seemed assured, Morewood's made an acquisition which must then have seemed of passing interest only but which perhaps presaged an eventual flight of the trade from the Black Country.   Securing control of the South Wales Works in Llanelly, they entered the tinplate trade and there, by 1881, also rolled thin iron sheets.   Before this two factors which were eventually to cause a much more substantial shift had already attracted attention : the problem of land freight charges on deliveries to the ports and, much less widely recognised, the threat from steel.

FREIGHT RATES & STEEL

The counterpart to the advantages of central position, which Blackwell in 1861 judged a major advantage of the Black Country, was the problem of freight charges, a problem which increased for the sheet trade as exports became steadily more important.   Eight years earlier William Matthews of Corbyn's Hall had stressed to the Select Committee on Railway and Canal Bills that with increasing competition '. . . it has become indispensably necessary for South Staffordshire to effect the greatest possible economy in the transport of its raw material for the manufacture of iron' and he recalled that previously ironmasters had played one canal company off against another, or even had promoted another canal. As early as 1825, frustrated in a meeting with the Staffordshire and Worcestershire Canal, the ironmasters had met in a Wolverhampton hotel and projected a railway to Liverpool. The London and Birmingham Railway had been a help but as early as 1845 the railway company and the Birmingham Canal Company were said to have an understanding, and Matthews observed that whenever he applied for a reduced canal charge he was told 'We are very sorry we cannot reduce our tonnages without first consulting the London and Northwestern Railway Company . . .'[23]   At the end of the 1850s there was a brief period of keen competition between the Midland, London and Northwestern and Great Western Railway for Midland traffic in which the carriers were said to be making heavy losses.   Eventually the companies adopted agreed rates and after 1861 the reply given to Matthews by the Birmingham Canal Company became the common one when application was made to any one of the three railway companies.   Landlocked, with almost all its canals under railway control, Birmingham and the Black Country had no redress.   It could promote its own railway, canal, or, a more common ambition after 1880, a so-called ship canal, but it was always difficult to decide which of four possible estuaries would provide the best outlet, and in any case the host of small firms could never agree on such a major project.   Almost 100 years after the Wolverhampton hotel meeting to which Matthews referred the West Midlands still entertained hazy ideas of easier access to the coast, this time by improved canal to the Severn estuary.   Not surprisingly little was done.[24]   In the mid-nineteenth century the problem was one for the low-grade ironmakers; when almost all galvanised sheet was made from Black Country iron the freight problem was of little moment to the black sheet mills or to Midland galvanisers.   As distant ironworks improved their iron quality the problem increased, and when steel ousted wrought iron it became serious.

By the 1850s there was an impressive body of evidence concerning the lack of scientific knowledge, unwillingness to introduce improvements and what the metallurgist, Percy, called 'mere dilatoriness' of the Staffordshire ironmasters.[25]   It was scarcely a favourable setting for consideration of the Bessemer process. By removing the need for most of the fuel used in iron puddling, Bessemer's process lessened the advantage of a coalfield location for the finishing trades. At the same time it favoured bigger units capable of dealing with the output of its highly productive operations. The first characteristic injured a coal-based industry such as that of the Black Country, the second suited neither the company structure nor the specialisms of the area. In an acrimonious correspondence, the attack on the Bessemer process made by Joseph Hall, himself an innovator 30 years before in the introduction of wet puddling, is notable.[26] The *Birmingham Journal* spoke of the inability of the process to eliminate phosphorous and therefore its practical failure. 'In taking leave of this subject, we think we may safely predicate that the iron manufacture will remain unaffected in any essential respect by anything which Mr. Bessemer has done. No one will more sincerely rejoice at any real improvement in the iron manufacture than we shall, although we admit a preference for such improvements as are not heralded by announcements of "revolution", but are modestly propounded, and left to demonstrate their importance by that quiet and cautious introduction into practice which generally characterises really meritorious inventions.'[27] For the sheet trade there proved to be a good deal of truth in this conclusion even after Bessemer had overcome the phosphorous problem, but already when his process was being widely taken up and tested, steel had been tried in the district. On 16th September 1856 a piece of Bessemer's own steel from Woolwich was rolled into a thin sheet at the Chillington works, and finally, after annealing, was made into a tobacco box at another Wolverhampton works.[28] A few years later William Siemens made openhearth steel at his Sample Steel Works in Birmingham but again there was no substantial impact on the Black Country and certainly not on its sheet trade. In 1876 a shipment of Siemens steel from Panteg, Monmouthshire, was rolled down into sheet at Bilston, but suggestions that eventually the Midlands would commonly use this material still seemed wild surmise.[29] Even if steel sheet might be used with profit by the holloware stampers, the opinion of all concurred that for galvanising a smooth steel sheet was much less suitable than the rather rougher iron sheet. The trade in black and galvanised sheet was still expanding at the end of the 1870s, and amidst all the ruin of its other trades the Black Country seemed to hold an unassailable position in their production. The 1880s were apparently to confirm the optimism which saw the district as the natural centre of sheet manufacture.

REFERENCES

1 *Mining Journal* 27 September 1845, p. 501, 4 April 1846, p. 143, 24 October 1846, p. 447.
2 *Mining Journal* 12 December 1846, p. 530. W. H. Jones, *Story of the Japan, Tinplate working and other trades of Wolverhampton and District* 1900, pp. 163–164. *Shadler's Birmingham Directory* 1854. *Oxford, Worcester and Wolverhampton Railway Bill* 1845, Vol. 11, p. 186.
3 Obituary of J. H. Porter, *Procs. Institute of Civil Engineers* 124, 1896, pp. 441–442. *Shadler's Directory* 1854.
4 W. H. Jones 1900, *op. cit.*, pp. 171–173.
5 Mr. F. C. Braby kindly supplied information on his firm.
6 *Post Office Directory of Liverpool* 1873.
7 H. Jones, *Rylands of Warrington 1805–1955*, pp. 35, 46, 47.
8 R. Heathfield of Morewood and Company, *House of Commons Papers* 1881, 13 pp. 491–501.
9 *Engineer* 5 June 1868, p. 423, 1 April 1870, p. 197, 4 November 1871.
10 G. Beard, Obituary notice, *Journal of West of Scotland Iron and Steel Institute* XX 1912–1913, p. 241.
11 S. Griffiths, *op. cit.*, p. 277. *Mineral Statistics of the United Kingdom* 1869. *Engineer* 22 March 1878, p. 207.
12 *The Lysaght Century 1857–1957*, 1957 passim. *Engineer* 5 June 1867, p. 21.
13 *Mineral Statistics of the United Kingdom.*
14 G. Beard, 'Sixty Years in the Ironworks', *Journal West of Scotland Iron and Steel Institute* 1899–1900, p. 16, recalls Thorneycroft's innovations. *Engineer* 13 April 1877, p. 263, 28 December 1877, p. 465. *Iron and Coal Trades Review* 28 December 1877, p. 716.
15 *The Lysaght Century* 1957, p. 50, *Iron and Coal Trades Review* 25 January 1878, p. 93. *Engineer* 15 December 1893, p. 579. *Wolverhampton Chronicle* 2 October 1895.
16 W. R. Lysaght, Presidential Address, *Iron & Steel Institute Journal* 1933, 1, pp. 35–36.
17 *Colliery Guardian* 11 March 1881, p. 383, 8 April 1881, p. 546.
18 *Engineer* 21 September 1866, p. 225.
19 *Engineer* 31 May 1867, p. 501.

20 *Engineer* 20 September 1867.
21 *Engineer* 9 August 1867, p. 123, *Iron and Coal Trades Review* 22 February 1871, p. 124. *Engineer* 17 May 1878, p. 359. *Mining Journal* 2 April 1887, p. 425.
22 *Iron and Coal Trades Review* 5 April 1878, p. 385.
23 Minutes Evidence, *Select Committee on Railway and Canal Bills* 1853, pp. 116–118.
24 See Minutes Evidence *Oxford, Worcester and Wolverhampton Railway Bill.* Minutes Evidence *Royal Commission on Railways* 1867 passim. *Select Committee on Railway Company Amalgamation* 1872. Evidence of E. J. Lloyd, p. 481. S. Timmins, *op. cit.*, 1866.
25 The Iron Ores of Great Britain, *Memoirs of the Geological Survey* 1856, p. 8. *Colliery Guardian* 4 May 1861, p. 278. *Report of the Select Committee on Scientific Instruction* 1868. Minutes of Evidence, p. 79, *Colliery Guardian* 8 November 1872, p. 522. *Minutes of Evidence to Coal Commission* 1871, Vol. II, p. 238, 277.
26 J. Hall, *The Iron Question—Considered in connection with theory, practice and experiment with special reference to the Bessemer Process,* London 1857.
27 *Birmingham Journal* quoted *Mining Journal* 6 December 1856, p. 833.
28 *Engineer* 19 September 1856, p. 521.
29 *Engineer* 16 November 1877.

CHAPTER 3

Black Country Apogee and Decline: Sheet Iron Production in the Eighties and Nineties

'Staffordshire,' wrote the journal *Iron* when reviewing the trade of 1881 '. . . shows a decadence in all the heavier classes of iron, and only maintains a supremacy for the small sizes of bar iron, and fine iron such as hoops, sheet, wire, etc. . . .' It was the 'nursery' or centre of the sheet manufacture, which within a few years was generally quoted as the mainstay of the district. Yet by the mid-1890s there was a sharp decline. The 1880s were the peak years of prosperity and expansion for both black and galvanised sheet in the West Midlands.[1] (Figure 2)

The activity of the local finished ironworks had fallen much less rapidly than that of the blast furnace plants (Table 8), but now, with the decline of heavy lines, the puddled ironworks also decreased while the sheet mills continued to increase. In the ten years following the Franco-Prussian war 30 out of 123 finished-iron works in the Black Country closed permanently.[2] The buoyancy of sheet iron, however, lengthened the life of the survivors and kept production at a higher level than in most other districts (Table 9).

There were 51 iron sheet firms in the West Midlands in 1881 but 59 in 1890. Twenty years later sheet firms numbered under 20 and a further sharp contraction of iron puddling had occurred.

Growth in the sheet iron trade was supported by continuing activity in holloware, japanning and other traditional trades, but increasingly it was dependent on galvanised sheet production for home consumption and for export. In the early 1880s the black sheet capacity of the area was some 100,000 tons a year but within 10 years it had increased to between 200,000 and 300,000 tons. As in the seventies, outsiders were willing to buy up and restart old works, completely new plants were also built, while the distress in other iron trades encouraged conversion of mills to sheet production.

Best marked bars, once £20 a ton, could be bought for £7 by 1888. Long before this Potteries' firms could produce bars at

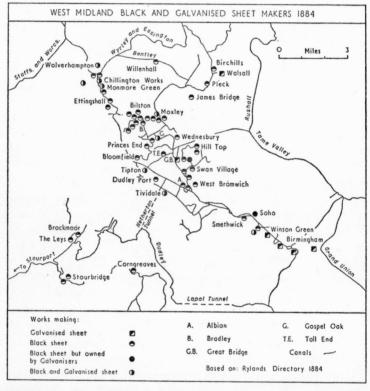

Figure 2.   Within the Black Country the industry was concentrated north of the central ridge and along the Birmingham Canal.   The prominence of the Bilston area, of Wolverhampton–Ettingshall and of the Birmingham–Smethwick industrial belt was marked.

lower cost, and with freight advantages on export orders their trade continued to grow at the expense of the Black Country.[3] Meanwhile, as earlier in the rail trade, local firms declined to debase the quality of their product in the face of the high cost of raw materials.   They tried to cut wages and thereby lost

TABLE 8

Number of Blast Furnaces and Puddling Furnaces at work 1865,
1871, 1879, 1884, 1910

| | South Staffordshire & Worcestershire | | United Kingdom | |
	Blast Furnaces	Puddling Furnaces	Blast Furnaces	Puddling Furnaces
1865	114	2116	659	6407
1871	103	1934	688	6699
1879	44	1589	496	5149
1884	36	1596	475	4577
1910	—	289	—	1261

Sources: various

TABLE 9

Output of puddled iron South Staffordshire, Cleveland and United
Kingdom 1882, 1885, 1890, 1895, 1900, 1905 (thousand tons)

	South Staffordshire	Cleveland	United Kingdom
1882	660	852	2841
1885	585	394	1911
1890	534	420	1923
1895	240	186	1148
1900	265	198	1163
1905	242	111	938

Source: British Iron Trade Association statistics

many of their better men to other districts or to overseas firms.
Disastrous failure of once famous houses became common news
in the local press.   Early in the 1880s forges and mills which
had cost the Darlaston Steel and Iron Company £25,000 were
knocked down for £3,750, and in 1887 the Bromford Ironworks
of John Dawes in West Bromwich, which it was said could not
be duplicated for less than £120,000, was withdrawn from
auction when bidding reached only £11,000.[4]

W. T. and J. Barrows had long been one of the most renowned
finished-iron firms, having the largest concentration of puddling
furnaces in the district in three works at Tipton.   In 1877 their
Factory Works closed, but after 10 years of idleness it was
acquired by a galvanising firm and converted from bars to
sheet.[5]   In the early 1870s the large Chillington Iron Company

produced mainly boiler plate, nail rods, angle, hoop and bar iron and rails. By 1880 they already had some interest in sheet, but the sharp decline in demand and in prices for bar iron caused them to enter the sheet trade in a much bigger way. During 1880 and 1881 bar iron prices fell by £3 a ton, and the firm built a new edge tool works and started to make galvanised iron sheets, for which an outlet was available.[6] Elsewhere there were new works. In 1882 Hill and Smith, with puddling furnaces and mills in the Delph area of Brierley Hill, built new galvanising works across the central ridge of the Black Country at Tividale but linked with Delph via the tortuous canal route and the Netherton Tunnel. In 1883 the new Greets Green Sheet Iron Company and the Wednesfield Galvanised Iron Company both began work.[7] In the north east, the Walsall Ironworks was converted from strip to sheet after 1878, while in Wolverhampton Lysaghts reopened Sparrow's Osier Bed works. Yet amidst all the growth, other firms, also with a large interest in sheet, were failing—David Rose in 1881, Samuel Groucott in 1884 and the New British Iron Company in 1887. Despite early success the Chillington Works closed at Christmas 1884 leaving only its edge tool manufacture to preserve its name into the twentieth century. The reasons for such failure were complex.

Perhaps decisive was the quality of management   Whereas men of drive and vision, welcoming new opportunities and techniques, like Lysaght, the Jones brothers, Sankey or Stephen Thompson, could do well, others were more the traditional ironmasters. Such men were also frequently burdened by material as well as mental legacies. Possession of other finished iron lines, of ironmaking plant and mineral properties could be a distinct disadvantage. When Lysaghts took over the mills of Thorneycroft and Sparrow, they did not acquire the two blast furnaces of the one or the three of the other. At the meeting of the Chillington Iron Company in 1881 it was said that their collieries in Bilston were worked out and their blast furnace operating costs were so high that it was cheaper to buy iron. A shareholder in Chillington, Alfred Hickman, of the large Springvale Ironworks, reckoned the Chillington blast-furnace plant worth only its price as scrap iron.[8]

Other difficulties in the sheet business could easily trap the unwary management and bring it to the Queens Hotel, Birmingham, for one of the all too frequent and doleful meetings with creditors of the local iron trade. Prices fluctuated wildly, to the discomfiture of firms which had to buy most of their materials, were increasingly dependent on a still largely independent galvanised iron trade and whose financial resources were exiguous. In 1887 E. Gittings of Bradley Works bought the old Ettingshall Road works of J Yorke. When his firm failed only two years later he had liabilities of £18,000, mainly for purchases from local, Northamptonshire or North West coast ironmasters [9] Association of sheet producers to lessen their risks was made difficult by the large number of firms and the ease of entry to the trade. These aspects, however, are characteristic of other periods besides the 1880s and deserve separate treatment as factors in the locational change of the industry. In the confusion of growth and change in the Black Country at this time one or two distinctive themes may be discerned.

Backward integration of galvanisers and forward integration in the black sheet mills continued. For the galvanisers control over quality was an important motive as well as desire to ensure supplies and to contain price fluctuations. James Davies, managing partner of a large galvanising works in the Midlands, later recalled that only six of the black sheet mills in the district could guarantee a regular, uniform quality of black sheet.[10] To ensure uniform quality Davies Brothers bought the Ettingshall Ironworks, which they operated until 1899.[11] Between 1881 and 1890 Lysaghts extended their mill power in Wolverhampton from seven to sixteen. By the early 1880s the Church Lane premises of the Wolverhampton Corrugated Iron Company were too congested for their growing business and they began to produce galvanised sheet in Thorneycroft's old Shrubbery Works. In 1885 they bought the Stour Valley side of this works and with Ernest Farnworth, from Baldwins, as managing partner, established the Shrubbery Steel and Iron Company, whose 12 puddling furnaces and four mills gave them a black sheet capacity of 120 to 150 tons a week. It was noted that the new works was exceptionally favoured by having direct rail as well as canal communications.[12]

As galvanisers extended backwards, so the prudent sheet

maker was encouraged to enter galvanising. George Adam
had been manager to Rose, Higgins and Rose of Bilston and
then to Wright and North of Wolverhampton, before he started
his own business at the Mars Ironworks, Priestfields. By 187.
he had established a reputation for quality and in 1881 had a
finished iron capacity of 300 tons a week, of which sheet iron
was a leading member. In 1886 he put down a galvanised
sheet plant of initial capacity 150 tons a week, linked to hi
sheet mills by a short railway.[13] These developments and
those of important black sheet makers who did not integrate
forwards, such as Isaac Jenks of the Minerva and Beaver works,
made the east end of Wolverhampton easily the biggest centre
of black sheet production in the country in the late 1880s.
(Figure 3)

The canal belt of Birmingham and Smethwick developed
rather differently. Here there was less room, the extra cost of
hauling coal from the pits and the problem of city rates on
industrial premises. For coal deliveries within the Black
Country the Birmingham Canal Company operated a uniform
delivery charge, 3d. a ton in 1870, but into Birmingham 1s. 5½d
a ton. A. T. Beck, a Birmingham black sheet maker, showed
that he was already burdened with freight charges £525 more a
year than if his works had been outside the town.[14] There
were ownership changes, as when Beard and Eberhard sold
Regents Grove works to Phillips Punnett & Co. Morewood's
properties were falling on evil times. Their Woodford sheet
mills were closed in 1888, though the Lion Galvanising Works
in Wiggin Street survived and for a short period Morewood's
operated the St. George's Galvanising Works in Darlaston.[15]
More common and understandable than such changes, which
probably reflected no more than managerial deficiencies, were
the acquisitions of galvanised sheet and black-sheet mills in the
Black Country. Ash and Lacey, long-established galvanisers
of Meriden Street, now acquired galvanising works at Great
Bridge, while Tupper and Company, who had galvanised for
even longer in Berkeley Street, acquired interests at the Bradley
Works near Bilston for galvanising, and by 1890 had also
acquired the black sheet mills of the Albion Ironworks, West
Bromwich, 5 miles by canal from Bradley and 5½ from the
Berkeley Street Works.[16]

Within the Black Country the high-quality sheet trade, catering for the holloware manufactures, remained prosperous. In the Bilston area Joseph Sankey, Hatton Sons and Company

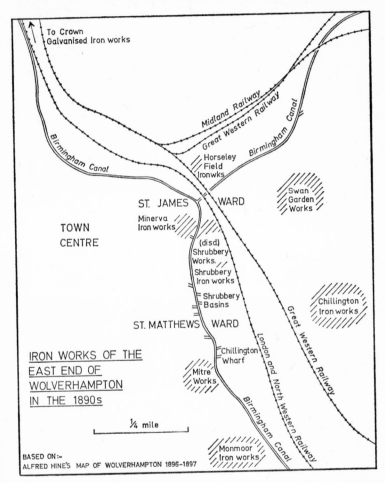

Figure 3. The significance of the canal is indicated in this area of major sheet capacity.

and Stephen Thompson, who left Hattons in 1876 to manufacture on his own account, were important representatives of this group. Beyond the district, but closely associated with it, the quality sheet business of the Stour Valley was growing.

Baldwins were undertaking their first tinplate developments in Monmouthshire but their sheet trade remained at the Wilden Works, Stourport. The firm of John Knight had been at Cookley, north of Kidderminster, for 200 years, but by the 1880s this location had become much less suitable. Shropshire pig iron, the traditional material, accessible by the Severn and the Stafford and Worcester Canal, was being replaced by steel for their products, fuel supply was easier in the Black Country and the west Midlands market was attractive. Finally, from Cookley rail dispatch involved a preliminary cart or canal haul to Kidderminster. At a cost of £14,000 Knights moved in 1886 and 1887 to the site of the old Brockmoor Iron and Tinplate Works at Brierley Hill.[17] The movement witnessed the continuing attraction of the Black Country for sheet production, especially as Knights had earlier considered a move to Middlesbrough, but that a quality producer found it necessary to move at all indicated how serious the difficulties of common sheet producers might become if conditions moved against the district as a whole.[18] The general use of steel in sheet manufacture, although long delayed, set in train such a process of adjustment.

STEEL & THE SHEET TRADE

In the early 1880s steel became the chief raw material in tinplate manufacture. Its progress was marked by the establishment of open-hearth steel plants in the tinplate districts of South Wales and a further contraction in the tinplate production of the West Midlands, where the trade was not sufficiently large to justify such installations in its own right. According to John Saunders of Cookley, the West Midlands had made 25 per cent. of the country's tinplate in 1858 but by 1880 it had only 5 per cent. of the capacity. Tinplate works in the area fell from twelve in 1875 to six by 1891.[19] The sheet trade was little affected, but uncomfortable questions bubbled below a generally calm surface. If steel sheets were better for a tin coating, why should they not eventually supersede iron sheets also when a zinc cover was used? If that happened could not possession of steel capacity and bar mills supplying the producers of flat-rolled steel affect the location of the industry? One further great attraction of South Wales for tinplate manufacture stemmed from the overwhelming impor- tance of export markets. Galvanised sheet exports were grow- ing rapidly and concentration in the West Midlands exposed the galvanisers to all the cost disadvantages and irritations of dependence on substantial land hauls, subject to the established understandings among the three big railway companies. A seaboard location enabled the producer to avoid these controls. Steel intruded into the sheet business, but for years the general upward movement of the trade and the continuing faith in wrought-iron sheet retained the industry amidst the wrought- iron works and the increasingly idle coal and iron pits of the Black Country.

In 1873 the Darlaston Steel and Iron Company advertised Bessemer steel sheets rolled from purchased billets. Their price was much higher than that of even high-quality iron sheet. Steel sheets down to 20 G were £22 a ton when even lattens of iron were only £18 10s.[20] The steelmaking prospects of Staffordshire seemed to be considerably improved with the introduction of the basic process, which made it possible to use iron made from local or Jurassic belt ore and to work the large heaps of 'puddlers tap', cinder from the wrought-iron works which had a substantial iron content but had previously been a costly embarrassment.[21] In the spring of 1882 the Chillington Iron Company was discussing with other firms the possibility of basic steelmaking to serve the needs of the district, and a little later Gilchrist made trials in the district at Alfred Hickman's expense. The 70 tons of ingots produced were rolled into slabs and billets and distributed to some 15 finished ironworks in the district for test rolling into plates, bars, sheets and other products.[22] Early in 1884 the new Staffordshire Steel and Ingot Iron Company began to make basic Bessemer steel at Bilston. By the mid-1880s steel sheet making was progressing, notably in stamping sheets, as Knights developments at Brierley Hill showed. The Bilston steel works rolled some thin steel sheets, at Corngreaves the New British Iron Company made steel and steel sheets, while Hatton Sons and Company at Bilston, with side-blown converters, made 250 tons ingots a week which they worked up into sheets, bars, plates and forgings. At Oakengates, in the Shropshire outlier of the industrial West

Midlands, the Snedshill Iron Company was rolling Bessemer steel sheets.[23]

Even before their local steelworks were built, the Black Country mills were buying increasing tonnages of steel from elsewhere, and, although an informed local manager had claimed that the Bilston steelworks would produce at a price and of a quality '. . . that will prevent competition from the north', the impact of new local supplies of steel was small.[24] The steel makers, notably the Staffordshire Steel and Ingot Iron Company, soon moved into more remunerative lines than semi-finished steel, undertaking the manufacture of plate, girders and channels. The opening of the Aireside Steelworks, Leeds, in 1887, to manufacture blooms and billets only, was noted as important to the Black Country trade.[25] In 1888, when local material cost £5 a ton, northern blooms and billets were selling in South Staffordshire for between £4 7s. 6d. and £4 15s.[26]

For high-quality sheet, used for stamping or working up, steel was quickly recognised as a superior material, permitting more severe manipulation than wrought iron. Knights made sheets and bars in all classes of steel by 1884, and a little later Hattons were endorsing its superiority for the better sheets.[27] For the much larger output of black sheets of galvanising grade, iron was still considered superior. The open surface of iron sheet was said to provide a better base than the smooth surface of steel sheet for the cover of spelter. Moreover material cost per ton of product was much higher with steel. This partly reflected its higher cost per ton and partly the lower output of plants rolling the harder steel in mills designed for wrought iron. Apparently not unreasonably, it was concluded in 1888 '. . . the puddling furnace in South Staffordshire has still, therefore, a long life before it'. Within six or seven years steel was displacing iron in the production of galvanising sheets with startling rapidity.[28] It was now shown that the finer surface and closer grain of steel lessened the amount of spelter employed and new mills were designed to roll the tougher material. Contemporary American experience showed that first-class sheets could be made at about the same cost as formerly with common sheets.[29] Once the technical problems of using steel had been overcome substitution depended only on a price fully competitive with wrought iron. In June 1893 iron sheet singles were

£6 to £7 10s. on the Swansea Metal Exchange when steel singles ranged from £7 to £8 a ton. By the end of 1895 makers were asking only 5s. and sometimes as little as 2s. 6d. a ton more for steel sheets than for iron ones.[30]

1894 and 1895 were transition years from iron to steel in the sheet trade, and not surprisingly not all the firms agreed in their assessment of the prospects. In the spring of 1894, although steel was already cutting into the galvanising sheet trade, Joseph Tinn of Bedminster was leasing Rose's old iron sheet mills at Moxley, and soon after the Wolverhampton Corrugated Iron Company enlarged its puddling forge.[31] John Lysaghts had greatly expanded their wrought-iron capacity at Swan Garden and Osier Bed in the previous few years, but by mid-1894, when northern billets were undercutting sheet bar prices in South Staffordshire, it had laid off almost all its furnaces while the mills were fully employed rolling steel.[32] After considerable experimenting with steel sheets in their galvanising departments, Lysaghts put down a new mill expressly to employ steel, and within two years the new material had almost wholly replaced the 1,000 tons of iron previously used each week.[33] High-quality iron, the chief reason for the localisation of an export trade in the Midlands, was soon no longer important and centrifugal tendencies began to appear. In a darkling setting, competition from other districts, freight rate burdens and countless other irritations of an earlier period began to assume the dimensions of insoluble problems. In this difficult period Staffordshire again proved incapable of producing its own steel.

The ranks of local steel producers were increased in the mid-1890s by the Earl of Dudley's open-hearth steel works at Round Oak, Brierley Hill, but, like Staffordshire Steel at Bilston and the Patent Shaft and Axletree Company at Wednesbury, this concentrated on finished products (Table 10). By 1898, though having a combined annual capacity of 100,000 tons steel, none of the three seems to have rolled sheet bars. Local, independent steel firms occasionally made semi-finished material for the rerollers, but they were prospering on finished material—in 1897 Staffordshire Steel and Ingot Iron Company £5 shares stood at £18 to £20—and this was not likely to be a reliable base.[34] At this time some 3,000 tons steel a week was brought into South Staffordshire, with freight charges on Welsh or northern semis of 10s. to 12s. 6d. or even more a ton.[35] Such suppliers were also unreliable, especially when their own local mills were busy. In 1898 a Welsh strike cut off that supply and gave a passing fillip to Staffordshire puddled iron-works.[36] An obvious remedy was for the rerollers themselves

TABLE 10

Prices for finished and semi-finished material from Bilston steel works, 1909 (per ton)

	£	s.	d.	£	s.	d.
Bars suitable for galvanising sheet	4	10	0 to	4	12	6
Angles	5	15	0			
Flats	6	0	0			
Tees	6	2	6			
Girder plates	6	2	6			

Source: Engineer, 19 March, 1909, p. 302

to make steel. Given the contrasts between the techniques of puddled iron and of steel production a melting shop would need to be on a bigger scale and would therefore require co-operative action. That single requirement rendered success unlikely in view of the individualism and small capital resources of most Staffordshire sheet-making firms, and in fact project after project foundered.

By the late eighties it seems that an openhearth furnace of 15 to 25 tons capacity could be built in South Staffordshire for as little as £1,500, after allowing for all the materials obtained in dismantling puddling furnaces. Several projects were abandoned in 1892 when steel came in from other districts at very low prices, and although after that there was substantial technical progress, including alleged production in 1895 of small ingots for rolling directly into sheet, nothing had been done by 1897 when T. Hughes of Birmingham urged the construction of co-operatively owned works operating either the basic Bessemer or the open-hearth process, equipped with every labour-saving device and located in the various steel-using neighbourhoods.[37] As opposed to this dispersed pro-duction, Toy held that monopoly in sheet production would go to integrated plants, and Le Neve Foster was edging towards the idea of larger, centralised operations. He recommended the use of hot-metal operations and of a basic open-hearth plant with an output of 1,000 tons a week. Although the construction of blast furnaces would increase the capital outlay and raise again the problem of the high cost of ironmaking in South Staffordshire, he made valuable suggestions in that regard too. Two years later he showed that the numerous small ironworks could not be reconstructed to produce steel cheaply, and prescribed a remedy very similar to that urged over 30 years later in South Wales. 'What is required is a large central works which will make steel billets on the most economical principles; this steel can then be delivered to the smaller works and they can finish it themselves.'[38]

Periodically the idea of a central steelworks to serve the finishing mills was revived. In 1902 the Wolverhampton Corrugated Iron Company actually promised its custom to promoters of such a scheme, and at the end of 1903 Ebenezer Parkes of Birmingham Corrugated Iron Company raised the whole question again. There was never much chance of success. If a sheet firm had capital resources of a few thousand pounds, it was clear that it could much better spend it in moving to the coast where steel could be obtained more cheaply and haulage to the port cost less. Already the change from puddled iron to steel had made freight charges a critical problem of the Black Country firms.

FREIGHT RATES & OTHER PROBLEMS

Not surprisingly, accusations of freight rate discrimination had been frequent in the development of this inland district. In 1861 Blackwell had claimed that some finished iron trades were going to districts where costs of carriage were 15s. to 17s. 6d. a ton more favourable. Through evidence given to the Royal Commission on Railways in 1867, agitation that Belgian nail sheet was competitive in London by 1868 and even in the Midlands eight years later, feelings grew stronger, as is shown by evidence to the Royal Commission on the Depression of Trade and Industry in 1886. In 1866 government control of freight rates was urged, and by 1884 Smith-Casson had even recommended nationalisation of the railways.[39]

In the 1870s the railway companies quoted a lower rate on black sheet than on galvanised sheet, which, as Heathfield pointed out, enabled coastal works to save about 2s. 6d. a ton on galvanised sheet even though their material came from Staffordshire. This, he claimed, had encouraged the growth of galvanised iron works on the coast and, although the pressure was eased with equalisation of the rates on black and galvanised sheet, the new firms sought local supplies in Warrington or in Lanarkshire.[40] In 1877 Lysaghts had made their first direct exports of galvanised sheet from Bristol rather than as previously via Liverpool or London. This put Staffordshire firms, with their rail freight of 17s. 6d. a ton to London and 10s. to Bristol, at a disadvantage.[41] In this case the Black Country petition for a concession rate succeeded, and the Freighters' Association had some success in 1885, but redress was not always adequate. Apart from the Grand Junction Canal the waterways were railway-controlled and canal improvement or ship-canal proposals proved abortive.[42] The position of the Black Country trades in bargaining for rate reduction was on all counts weak.

In the first place high per ton mile rates were in part a reflection of the relatively short hauls to the ports. Secondly, they reflected the strength of railway companies in a district which had no alternative means of transport. Numerous small firms treating with three big railway companies, which had already correlated rate policy for many years, were inevitably in a weak bargaining position. Before the Select Committee of 1881, while Midland firms petitioned for lower rates, William Menelaus of Dowlais spoke with brutal frankness of the advantages of bigness in bargaining, although he did not recognise that failure of ironworks in South Wales meant a far bigger loss to the railways than did failure in the continuously expanding West Midlands. 'As far as we are concerned,' he said, 'we do not care anything about the Railway Commissioners; we are strong enough to fight the railway companies ourselves; we appeal to their selfishness; but I can quite understand that there are weak people to whom the Railway Commissioners would be invaluable; that is to say, strong companies like ourselves get concessions which would put the small people to a disadvantage, whereas the Railway Commissioners might compel the railway companies to equalise the rates.' Thirty years later, in evidence before the Departmental Committee on Railway Rates and Agreements, two others agreed that the small traders were suffering more severely than the bigger ones. H. W. Edmunds of the Birmingham Chamber of Commerce Railway Rates Committee observed that whereas concerns of the size of Nettlefolds or even Hickmans could look after themselves, the small firm could not afford the thousand pounds or so which might be needed to take a case to the Railway and Canal Traffic Commission. He recalled, 'We have always received, with regard to the North Western Railway Company for instance, the very greatest civility possible, but when we come to business, when we try to get them to talk to us, we are always dealt with in too much of a red-tape manner . . . they always hold us as it were at arms length, and fight us in that way.'[43]   A third weakness was the economic buoyancy of the West Midlands, which enabled the railway companies to regard the decline of the basic industries with equanimity. As James Grierson of the Great Western said when discussing an application for a low local rate from Hickmans' in 1881 'I said it would not answer to carry traffic at $\frac{1}{2}$d. per ton over the Dudley Bank; it would not suit our purpose to block an important district by carrying a traffic which did not pay.'[44]

No doubt complaints about freight rates were sometimes used as a scapegoat by Midland iron companies and blinded them to much else that was wrong. The British Iron Trade Association report on continental competition, published in 1895, showed that black sheet prices in Germany were £1 a ton lower than in the Midlands while, more understandably, Silesian spelter was also £1 a ton cheaper and the Germans had also cheaper chemicals and packing boxes. Wage rates were 30 to 40 per cent. below Midlands level. In Belgium the gap was much wider still, for there the roller of finest quality sheet was paid only 36s. a ton as opposed to 120s. in Staffordshire. Railway rates were also lower on the continent.[45] The local iron exchanges regarded the report as '. . . a colourless document, too much being made of railway rates and rolling mill equipment and too little of the wages matter.'[46] Sir Benjamin Hingley, Chairman of the Midland Iron and Steel Wages Board, argued, however, that German wages were much in line with those in Britain and stressed the great superiority of German mills. I. J. Jenks of Minerva and Beaver Works, Wolverhampton, was more willing to sympathise with the local firms—'He thought they were suffering from three things— heavy railway rates, trades unionism and grandmotherly legislation—which were prejudicing them in the markets of the world, and they needed looking to.'[47]   In 1898 attempts were made to lower wages and to obtain freight rate concessions.[48]

In the spring of 1898 local Chambers of Commerce, and mayors from the Black Country and from Birmingham, petitioned the three railway companies for lower export rates. Although the meeting which followed left a favourable impression, the railway companies' reply, delivered a few weeks later, was negative. They added that other factors must account for the troubles of local industry for freight charges had already been going down for many years.[49]   Nevertheless, it was clear that, in the new competitive framework shaped in part by the continuing growth in the export trade, and, more particularly, by the switch from iron to steel sheets, transport costs had become critical. Greater growth in the coastal districts, along with some removal of firms from the West Midlands, was to result. Developments of this nature built on an already substantial black and galvanised sheet industry in these outlying areas.

REFERENCES

1   *Iron* 6 January 1882, p. 9, 4 January 1884, 2 February 1885, p. 12.   *Select Committee on Railways*, House of Commons Papers 1881, 13, p. 491.
2   *British Iron Trade Association. Report for* 1882 p. 27.
3   *Select Committee on Railways* 1881.   Evidence of B. Hingley, Chairman of the Ironmasters Association of South Staffordshire, *Iron* 2 November 1888, p. 390.
4   *Engineer* 11 January 1878, p. 33.   *Mining Journal* 1 September 1888, p. 991.   *Colliery Guardian* 3 March 1882, p. 333, 30 September 1887, p. 449.
5   G. K. V. Gale 1966, p. 121.   *Iron* 26 August 1887, p. 206.
6   *Colliery Guardian* 8 April 1881, p. 544, 22 April 1881, p. 627.
7   *Iron* 7 November 1882, pp. 426–427, 21 December 1883, p. 557, 28 December 1883, p. 575.
8   *Colliery Guardian* 14 April 1881, p. 583, 22 April 1881, p. 627.

9 *Colliery Guardian* 30 September 1887, p. 449, 8 November 1889, p. 660.

10 J. Davies, *Galvanised Iron; Its Manufacture and Uses* 1899, pp. 6–7.

11 *Wolverhampton Chronicle* 22 May 1901.

12 *Mining Journal* 19 September 1885, p. 1061, 12 December 1885, p. 139. *Iron* 23 April 1886, p. 361.

13 S. Griffiths 1873. *Rylands Directory* 1881. *Iron* 4 June 1886, p. 507.

14 G. H. Wright, *Chronicles of the Birmingham Chamber of Commerce* 1813–1913, 1913, pp. 232–233.

15 *Rylands Directory* 1881, 1890. Griffiths 1888.

16 *Rylands Directory* 1890.

17 *Colliery Guardian* 5 August 1887, p. 161. *Mining Journal* 17 April 1886, p. 454, 6 August 1887, p. 958.

18 *Iron* 17 October 1884, p. 364.

19 W. E. Minchinton, *The British Tinplate Industry* 1957, pp. 36–39. E. H. Brook *Monograph of Tinplate Works of Great Britain* 1932, pp. 131–132.

20 S. Griffiths 1873.

21 Recollections of W. R. Lysaght, *op. cit., Journal of the Iron and Steel Institute* 1933, 1, p. 38.

22 *Colliery Guardian* 14 April 1882, p. 583. *Iron* 23 June 1882, p. 498, *Journal of the Iron and Steel Institute* 1882, 1, pp. 193–197.

23 *Mining Journal* 17 October 1885, p. 1179, 15 January 1887, p. 90.

24 *Iron*, Review of 1883, 4 January 1884. A. Smith-Casson (Manager of Round Oak Ironworks), *Transactions National Association for the Promotion of Social Science* 1884, p. 651.

25 *Iron* 5 August 1887, p. 139.

26 *Mining Journal* 14 April 1888, p. 427.

27 *Iron* 14 January 1887, p. 27.

28 *Colliery Guardian* 13 December 1895, p. 1122.

29 A. Beard, *Iron Age* 1894 quoted *Journal of the Iron and Steel Institute* 1894, 1, p. 541.

30 *Iron* 9 June 1893, p. 497. *Engineer* 3 January 1896, p. 21.

31 *Engineer* 9 March 1894, p. 208, 16 March 1894, p. 232, 4 May 1894, p. 382.

32 *Colliery Guardian* 8 June 1894, p. 1090. Reference is to one large Black Country firm but Lysaghts is clearly intended.

33 *Engineer* 19 October 1894, p. 350. *Iron and Coal Trades Review* 11 September 1896, p. 354.

34 *Engineer* 2 April 1897, p. 354, 29 April 1898, p. 753.

35 *Rylands Directory. Iron and Coal Trades Review* 7 January 1898, 11 September 1896, p. 354. H. Le Neve Foster in *Proceedings South Staffordshire Institute of Iron and Steel Works Managers* 1898–1899, p. 39. H. B. Toy, 'Iron and Steel Works Plant', *ibid*, 1899–1900, p. 44.

36   *Engineer* 12 March 1897, p. 278.
37   *Iron* 2 August 1889, p. 92.   *Colliery Guardian* 29 July 1892, p. 199.
     Wolverhampton Chronicle 20 November 1895, p. 8.   *Engineer* 26
     February 1897, p. 226, 3 December 1897, p. 558.
38   *Proceedings S. Staffordshire Institute Iron and Steel Works Managers*
     1898–1899, pp. 39–40, 1901–1902, p. 101.
39   J. Jones in S. Timmins, *op. cit.*, Smith-Casson, *Trans. National
     Association for the Promotion of Social Science* 1884, p. 652.
40   *Select Committee on Railways* 1881, pp. 491–492, p. 435, p. 254,
     p. 496, 501.
41   *Engineer* 20 April 1877, p. 279.
42   *Select Committee on Canals* H. C. Papers, 1883, Evidence of E. J.
     Lloyd.   *Transactions National Association for the Promotion of
     Social Science* 1884, pp. 649, 652.   *Industries* 2 March 1887, p.
     257, 23 March 1888, p. 287.   C. A. Vince, *History of the
     Corporation of Birmingham* 3, 1885–1899, 1902, p. 364.   *Pro-
     ceedings of the Council, Borough of Birmingham* 1887–1888, pp.
     295–321, 503–507.   *Journal of the Society of Arts* 1887–1888,
     Proceedings of Canal Conference, May 1888.
43   *Departmental Committee on Railway Agreements and Amalgamations*
     Cd. 5927, 1911.   Evidence of W. A. Walber and H. W.
     Edmunds, p. 178 and pp. 238–239.
44   Mins. Evidence, *Select Committee on Railways* 1881, p. 650.
45   *Wolverhampton Chronicle* 20 November 1895, 20 May 1896, p. 7.
46   *Engineer* 24 January 1896, p. 98.
47   *Engineer* 21 February 1896, p. 202.   *Wolverhampton Chronicle* 20
     November 1895.
48   *Engineer* 18 February 1898, p. 298, 2 September 1898, p. 239.
49   *Wolverhampton Chronicle* 9 March 1898, 30 March 1898.   *Engineer*
     11 March 1898, p. 242, 18 March 1898, p. 267, 6 May 1898,
     p. 438.

CHAPTER 4

The Emergence of New
Sheet Making Districts

The crisis in the Black Country sheet trade was deepened by aggressive competition from expanding districts. This point is vital, for the market was still growing very rapidly, so that a major locational adjustment rather than the decline of an industry was involved. The predominance of exports in the growth of demand naturally assisted the development of black and galvanised sheet production nearer the ports, although in the nature of the geography of the country any area was more favoured in this respect than the West Midlands (Table 11).

TABLE 11

Exports of Galvanised Iron and Steel Sheets, 1885–1913
(thousand tons)

To	1885	1895	1900	1907	1913
Colonies	88	122	147	256	480
Foreign countries	43	82	100	211	281
Total	131	204	247	467	761

There were other substantial advantages in these areas as well as saving in freight charges, but in difficult years such as 1895, when galvanised corrugated iron sheets reached a nadir of £9 17s. 6d. a ton, a saving of perhaps 15s. in overall transport charges was itself a very considerable boost.

The London area declined in relative importance. There was a temporary increase in galvanising plants helped by the differential freight rates on black and galvanised sheet at the end of the seventies, but no black sheet mills were ever established there. By the 1890s production of galvanised sheet was giving way to odd-job galvanising, as for instance at the still important

Blackwall works.   A strongly contrasting area, the North East Coast, with raw material rather than market advantages, failed to become an important sheet and galvanised sheet district— which was to have great significance for its long-term metallurgical future.   Although many of the plate mills produced the thicker sheet gauges, poor iron prevented success with the finer grades, so that, to Heathfield's surprise in his examination before the Select Committee on Railways in 1881, he was told that the sheet iron for the new Middlesbrough galvanising works came from Staffordshire.[1]   However, the quality of iron produced in the area was steadily improved, and the rapid decline of the iron ship plate trade in the mid-1880s provided an incentive to roll more iron of sheet gauge.   The advance of steel for the first time provided advantages over the Black Country in access to raw material for the black sheet mills. By 1888, at the Low Walker works on the Tyne sheet was the only trade, two years later five of the seven sheet producers in the area rolled in steel as well as iron, and at Jarrow, Tudhoe and Stockton steel manufacture and sheet rolling were conducted on the same site.   The Bowesfield Iron works, Stockton, and the Ayrton mills in Middlesbrough were the chief producers of sheet.   For the North East as a whole, however, success in traditional heavy lines such as plate, angles and rails, or in new heavy trades, notably the production of structural steel, worked against a bigger entry into sheet.   The only two galvanising works in the area were at Ayrton and at Battle House Point, Middlesbrough.

By 1881 there seem to have been seven black sheet works in Scotland.   There had been a reduction in producers of galvanized sheet since the late 1860s, and by 1890 only two firms remained (Figure 4).   Smith and Mclean galvanised both at Port Glasgow and in Hyde Park Street, Glasgow. They obtained their black sheet from Gartcosh, Lanarkshire, now under George Beard's management, and also by the early nineties from the newly acquired Milnwood Works.   Braby's galvanised at the Eclipse Works in the Petershill district but at this time bought all their black sheet from independent firms in Scotland.[2]   Apart from Braby's links with galvanising in London and Liverpool, the Scottish industry, like that of the North East, was self-contained and separate from that of other

British districts. In the three other growth areas for black and galvanised sheet production, the Bristol area, the Mersey and Dee basin and South Wales, there were more important links with the Midlands.

Although earlier the most illustrious member of this group, the Bristol area was now growing least (Figure 5). Its great

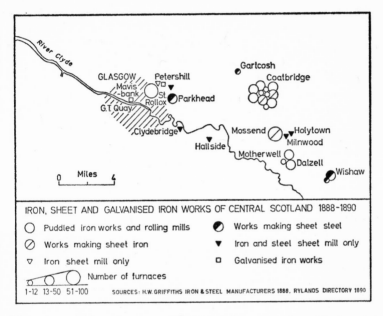

Figure 4. Although not as marked as in some other districts the port orientation of the galvanising section of the industry was discernible.

weakness was lack of an adequate resource base of coal and iron. Joseph Tinn retained the Ashton Vale rolling mills at least until 1890, although they were sometimes idle, as for instance in 1886. As with George Tinn's acquisition of Deepfields works in 1875–1876, Joseph Tinn also paralleled Lysaghts in backward integration for control over black sheet capacity from outside the district. The link took a rather different form, a form indeed which foreshadowed later developments in the Lysaght organisation. The Pontnewynydd works near Pontypool, noted for the quality of its iron and its sheet, but idle from

F

September 1876 to 1881, was acquired in 1882 and two years later was back at work presumably supplementing Tinn's supply of galvanising sheets from Ashton Vale. As noted earlier, in 1894 Tinn still found it desirable to acquire the sheet mills at Moxley, between Bilston and Wednesbury.[3] By the mid-1880s Lysaghts rolled up to 40,000 tons black sheets a year

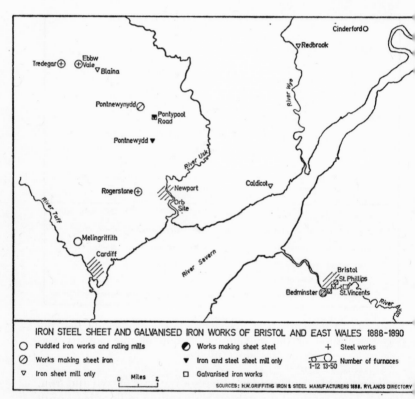

IRON STEEL SHEET AND GALVANISED IRON WORKS OF BRISTOL AND EAST WALES 1888-1890

○	Puddled iron works and rolling mills	◑	Works making sheet steel	+	Steel works
◐	Works making sheet iron	▼	Iron and steel sheet mill only		Number of furnaces 1-12 13-50
▽	Iron sheet mill only	☐	Galvanised iron works		

0 Miles 2

SOURCES: H.W.GRIFFITHS IRON & STEEL MANUFACTURERS 1888, RYLANDS DIRECTORY

Figure 5.   As a legacy of its former eminence as a port Bristol still had a large role in galvanised sheet.   Except in the case of Pontnewynydd there was little link with South Wales works.

in Wolverhampton.   Some of this was locally galvanised, but most of it was sent by canal boat to Sharpness and then on down the Severn estuary and up the Avon to St. Vincent's Works.   After galvanising the sheets were exported through Bristol docks.[4]

The sheet and galvanising industry of the Mersey basin contrasted with that of Bristol in its larger number of units, its prolonged lack of integration, the changing associations and locations of firms within it and its obviously greater growth potential (Figure 6). The port industries and foreign business of Liverpool, long attractive to the trade, were increasingly significant as exports grew still more in relative importance. A 10s. a ton freight rate on black sheet when the galvanised rate from the Black Country was 12s. 6d. assisted growth, and from 1876 to 1881 five new galvanised sheet works were established in or near the port.[5] By 1890 there were six galvanised corrugated iron works in Liverpool and one each in Birkenhead and Ellesmere Port. There was good rail and canal access to Staffordshire sheet and an expanding regional supply as well, from Pearson Knowles in Warrington, John Summers of Stalybridge, the Bolton Iron and Steel Company and at Huyton Quarry, just east of Liverpool, the sheet mills of Maybury, Marston and Sharpe of Pendleton, Manchester.

The attraction of the area for finishing operations was indicated by the interest that West Midland firms were beginning to show in it. At a time when the differential freight rate on black and galvanised sheet existed, the Chillington Iron Company, then entering the trade on a bigger scale, bought old-established galvanised sheet works in Spekeland Street, Liverpool. After the failure of Chillington in 1884, these were sold to Briggs and Horsfall who carried on under the trade name, the Chillington Galvanising Company.[6] In the eighties, Phillips and Punnett, black and galvanised sheetmakers of Birmingham, also acquired the galvanised sheet works at Bank Quay, Warrington. Connections with the Black Country were later to take place in very different circumstances and involved complete operations.

As finishers the galvanised iron firms of the Mersey basin seemed to have the initiative in dealing with the black sheet makers, but in fact their lack of control of raw materials and the smallness of their operations and of their capital resources made their position weak. Like the galvanisers and small sheet mills of the Midlands they frequently failed, were bought up only to fail again, until their exits from the business were made. Henry Summers, who sold black sheets to them, knew both

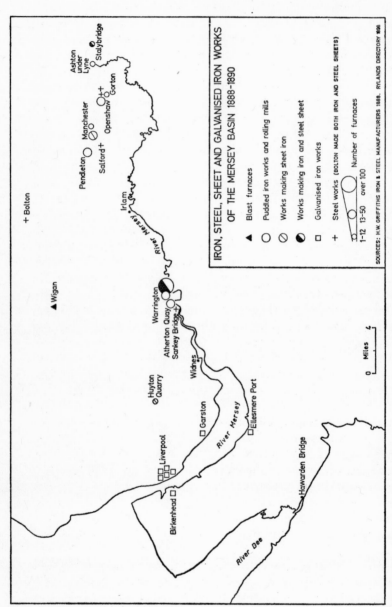

Figure 6. This was the clearest case of port orientation of galvanising. Black sheet supplies still came largely from Staffordshire via the Shropshire Union Canal and through Ellesmere Port.

their outward haughtiness and their inner emptiness, which he recalled long afterwards. 'They were all run by people of straw who bought their sheets through merchants who gave them credit. Failures and bad debts were not uncommon, but when one went another bought up the place at scrap price and the thing went on again. I used to go round these places and to the merchants touting for orders. They were always the top dogs and we seem to have lived only to be squeezed.'[7] Profit margins narrowed in the nineties and lack of control over raw materials, and presumably also the high costs of their central city locations, caused further failures and elimination of producers. Bruce and Still and the Chillington Galvanising Company and in Birkenhead the firm of Skidmores went.[8] The bigger firm of Burnell, however, which had already shown exceptional enterprise, survived and expanded. With properties in Tabley and Bentinck Street, Liverpool, Burnells broke new ground in the 1880s by building a works at Ellesmere Port. The Shropshire Union Canal brought Staffordshire black sheet to their wharves, and along the Mersey, and soon also via the Manchester Ship Canal, galvanised iron could easily be delivered to the docks or directly to ships in Liverpool roads.[9] By 1890 Burnells were capable of 200 tons galvanised products a week and six years later of the considerable figure of 500 tons.[10] The greatest growth, however, was taking place in a less favourable location, at the works of John Summers in Stalybridge. In 1890 Summers had a weekly black sheet capacity of 300 tons, but was soon to rise to joint leadership with John Lysaghts. The background to this development justifies examination for it shows how locations for growth were sometimes sifted out by peculiar factors and yet those locations were perpetuated as scale of production and size of capital investment grew.

Son of a Bolton weaver, John Summers was making clogs at Dukinfield in the cotton textile district east of Manchester by 1842.[11] Like many other small manufacturers of enterprise in an era of self-help, he visited the Great Exhibition, and there, for £40, bought a nail-making machine to use in his trade. Shortly afterwards, however, he abandoned clog manufacture to concentrate on the manufacture of nails, from purchased iron sheets, for sale to Lancashire buyers. By 1856 he had moved to an old engineering works in Stalybridge, where by 1860 the firm was rolling iron. Although much of the output was boiler plate for local works, nail sheets were also rolled. By 1873 there were six puddling furnaces at Stalybridge and two years later eleven furnaces and two mills.[12] John Summers died in 1876, and soon after steel ousted iron from the boiler-plate business, the Bolton works a few miles away being important in the new product. This was a crisis and the company nearly succumbed. A new mill to increase the output of nail sheet was never even nearly fully employed, so that its operating costs proved too high. In the 1880s this plant was replaced by standard sheet mills whose product was largely sold to the galvanisers of the Liverpool area. Over the whole 14 years after the death of John Summers the firm lost apparently well over £1,000 a year on average. In 1889 the youngest son of the founder, Henry Hall Summers, joined his brothers in the business.

Faced with the risks of selling black sheet to the galvanisers, Henry Summers pressed his partners to consider galvanising themselves. Guided no doubt by what they saw among their customers, they considered galvanising a dangerously speculative business. Eventually an experimental galvanising plant and corrugating machinery was ordered from a Midlands supplier, news of which aroused much discussion in South Staffordshire.[13] Even then the galvanising plant was not employed, but in 1894, short of orders, Henry Summers pressed Burnell to buy black sheet. Otherwise he threatened to galvanise, and, when Burnell still refused to move, the Stalybridge galvanising pots were at last put to work. The operations proved successful and the galvanising plant was soon increased to six units, in which most of Summers's black sheet was further processed. By 1896 Stalybridge was capable of 400 tons iron sheets and 150 tons iron bar and strip a week. It had equal capacity for rolling steel. Expansion in steel was to render Stalybridge an unsuitable location, and the growth of the firm was a major factor in causing disturbance in the Midland trade and further adjustment among the firms Summers had previously supplied with black sheets. Although no one project of equal size was involved, developments in South Wales were collectively still more disturbing for Staffordshire.

THE EXPANSION OF SHEET MANUFACTURE
IN SOUTH WALES

The development of tinplate manufacture in South Wales gave it a large footing in a trade with many similarities to the sheet and galvanised sheet industries, but in these latter lines of production it was of relatively minor importance until the 1890s (Figure 7). The Aberavon works at Port Talbot had been associated with the short-lived Patent Galvanised Iron Company, at the end of the 1840s the Briton Ferry Ironworks were described as 'extensive' bar and sheet mills, and twenty years later the Garth Sheet Iron Company began work near Maesteg.[14] Although wage rates were lower and cost of transport to export points less, iron was poorer and the regional outlets few as compared with the West Midlands. After 1880, while iron remained dominant in the sheet mills, steel replaced it in the manufacture of black plate. More important, booming exports, which doubled in the 1870s and doubled again by 1891, diverted potential interest from sheet. Until 1890 the only galvanised sheet iron works in South Wales was at Pontypool Road. Some evidence suggests that preoccupation with tinplate possibly lessened concern with black sheet in the 1880s, although other indications suggest something of an increase in capacity. In 1878 T. W. Booker, of the Melingriffith Works near Cardiff, was noted as competing with Midland sheet firms, but gradually he shifted mills from sheet to tinplate, the number at work on these respective products changing from 6 and 6 in 1878 to 4 and 7 in 1884 and 2 and 8 in 1890. Between 1884 and 1890 the company's estimated weekly sheet capacity fell from 200 to 40 tons. On the other hand, whereas in 1881 Rylands Directory listed only 8 sheet makers in Glamorgan and Monmouth—and over 50 in the West Midlands—the 1890 issue indicated 13 producers of iron and steel sheet in South Wales. In the nineties the rivalry of Welsh works became a serious problem.

The switch to steel in the mid-1890s would inevitably have increased the advantages of sheet production near to the Siemens steel works of South Wales, but change was hastened by the disruption of the tinplate trade by the McKinley Tariff from the middle of 1891. Unlike the galvanised iron trade,

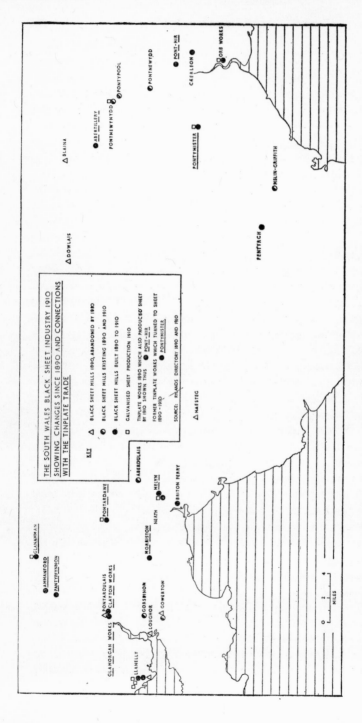

Figure 7. In this period, in reaction to the adverse effect of the McKinley Tariff Act on its tinplate trade, West Wales developed an important interest in sheet. The Orb Works, Newport, dating from 1898, was however the largest sheet works in South Wales.

that in tinplate was much more with foreign than with colonial markets, the share of the latter in 1894 being 59 per cent. for galvanised sheet but under 12 per cent. for tinplate. Subsequent events proved that even Empire markets were not inviolable, but they were not liable to such revolutionary change. The McKinley Tariff Act more than doubled the duty on tinplate brought into the United States, and although the Wilson Act of 1894 lowered it substantially the Dingley Tariff of 1897 raised it again to an intermediate but still troublesome point.[15] Meanwhile a large American tinplate industry was quickly built up. In 1894 and 1895 shipments of tinplate to all foreign markets were only 83.7 per cent. of the level of the years 1889–1891 and by 1898 only 64.0 per cent. of that level.

The change hastened the decline of the small Midland tinplate industry. Hattons closed their rather antiquated tinplate department and concentrated on quality sheet, and at the Manor Works, Ettingshall, Stephen Thompson contracted tinplate manufacture and expanded in steel sheet.[16] In South Wales reduced demand from local tinplate mills stimulated attempts to sell steel to Midland rerollers and hastened the contraction of the outlet for black iron sheets. Far more significant was the reaction of the Welsh tinplate firms. By March 1895 4,000 to 5,000 tinplate workers were out of work in Glamorgan alone, and steel works activity and employment were seriously affected as well. Fifteen months later, 26 of the 89 tinplate works in South Wales, Monmouthshire and Gloucestershire were wholly idle and another 17 only partially at work.[17] Conversion of tinplate mills to sheet rolling and entry to the trade in galvanised sheet began on a substantial scale. For these new trades the Welsh works had a number of assets.

In purchasing steel from local open-hearth plants a Glamorganshire works had perhaps 10s. a ton advantage in freight charges over Staffordshire mills, and some Welsh firms gained further from association with or part ownership of the steelworks. In mill fuel costs the Black Country probably had the edge on Welsh works, for slack there was at this time only 3s. a ton at the mine.[18] Although underhands were paid less in South Wales because of the mass of unemployed tinplate workers, wages for skilled men seem to have been higher, so that by 1899 some Midland firms were short of workers because of their migration for higher wages. Overall Welsh mill labour costs per ton were reckoned not to exceed those of Staffordshire.[19] Although there was a spelter works at Pelsall on the northern edge of the Black Country, Welsh works had direct access to cheaper continental supplies. However, although the cost of spelter was as much as £2 per ton of galvanised corrugated sheets the differential in favour of South Wales on this account can have been only a shilling or two.[20] For export the Welsh could ship directly through Swansea or send from there by water to Liverpool for 8s. a ton when the rail rate, dock and town dues on Midland sheet deliveries in Liverpool totalled 10s. a ton.[21] In processing and in sales the Welsh were also favoured.

Many of the Welsh tinplate mills had been rebuilt in the eighties to deal more effectively with the steel bars then replacing the softer puddled iron bars. The mill housings were strong enough to take the rolls for sheet steel, while many Staffordshire works were still rolling steel in mills designed for iron. In the narrower widths and thinner gauges to which blackplate rolling had accustomed them, lattens from South Wales mills were already selling at lower prices than Staffordshire houses were asking for doubles in the winter of 1894–1895.[22] After this more mills turned over to wider sheets, installing new plant. Some of their sheet was supplied to Midland galvanisers, over half of whose capacity was still owned by firms with no interests in black-sheet production, but increasingly it was galvanised in South Wales. Entry to this trade was still easy when a plant capable of turning out at least 10,000 tons a year of galvanised iron could be built for £4,000.[23] The widespread nature of the conversion to sheet and to galvanising is indicated in Figure 7, but some aspects merit further attention in the two chief areas of development, the metal-working districts centred on Pontypool and the hinterland of Swansea Bay.

In 1895 Baldwin's Panteg Tinplate Works, only seven years old, began to roll sheets, and their even more recently constructed Pontymoile Tinplate Works, a mile north of the steel and sheet mills, began galvanising, the whole representing a degree of integration unknown in the Black Country. Arrangements were made to restart the sheet mills at Pontnewynydd and in December 1895 a new company was registered as the Pontnewynydd Sheet and Galvanising Company to roll both iron and steel sheet and equipped with both galvanising and corrugating plant in place of former dependence on Tinn's Bristol galvanising works. A little later, Wright Butler and Company, a firm closely associated and soon to be merged with Baldwins, moved the whole of the plant of the Phoenix Galvanising and Corrugating Company from Aberavon, Port Talbot, to Panteg. In the spring of 1896 the tinplate works at Pontymister closed, but fifteen months later reopened as the Monmouthshire Steel and Tinplate Company, with two double sheet mills and producing galvanised sheet, while, to the north west, after three years of idleness, the Abertillery works was reorganised as the Glan Ebbw Steel Sheet, Galvanising and Tinplate Company Ltd.[24]

In 1896 the completely new Neath Steel Sheet and Galvanising Company was organised, and in 1897 Morewoods began galvanising in their already big South Wales works at Llanelly. Within a few years these developments, along with the decline of Staffordshire production, made South Wales the leading district for both black and galvanised sheet, but when tinplate exports revived a little, and by 1910 were higher than even in the years of dizzy expansion before the McKinley Tariff, there was new tinplate construction and indeed also reconversion from sheet back to the older staple. In Pontardawe, for instance, the Bryn Works Ltd. had converted two of its four mills from tinplate to sheet, and in 1894–1895 built another larger sheet mill and installed galvanising pots, but it was closed in 1895 and again in 1901. Reorganised then, the company dismantled the galvanising plant and one of the sheet mills and built a new tinning plant. Gilbertsons, a much more important firm in the same town, lost almost all their tinplate trade with the United States, or as much as 225 tons a week. In 1899 they converted their tinplate mills into sheet mills and began to galvanise, but in 1911, with the tinplate trade booming, built a new, 6 mill tinplate works. At the Eagle Tinplate Works, Neath, two sheet mills were added in 1896 but soon went out of production and were sometimes used for tinplate.[25] Nevertheless South Wales was now firmly established in sheet and new works continued to be established.

Six mills and galvanising plant were installed at the Bryngwyn siemens steel works, Gorseinon, 1908, the galvanising plant of the Wellfield Company at Llanelly in the same year, in 1909 the sheet mills at the new Whitford Works, Briton Ferry and 6 sheet mills and galvanising plant at the steelworks at Morriston of the Upper Forest and Worcester Company. In 1910 the sheet mills of the new Gorse Galvanising Company were built at Llanelly.

As with the galvanised iron trade of Staffordshire, Welsh production was largely for export. There was some development of a local market for stamping sheet along with that home growth in demand which was important in the tinplate trade in the 1890s—and which lessened the impact of the McKinley Tariff. The Welsh Tinplate and Metal Stamping Company already had a large output of tinned, enamelled, galvanised and japanned ware at Llanelly. This promising growth of metal fabricating, however, which might have saved South Wales serious distress some 30 years later was not carried very far, probably largely because of the expansion of traditional industries that was so characteristic of the period up to 1913. Already trading links with the Midlands were becoming important. As early as 1896 Welsh steel sheets were said to be competing strongly in South Staffordshire with locally made stamping and tray sheets.[27]

EXPORTS, STEEL SUPPLIES & COASTWARD MOVEMENT

Confident in its late Victorian values, the trade journal *Iron* noted how the export business was growing: '. . . the Chinese and Indian demand is improving as the nations are beginning to appreciate the advantages of iron roofing in place of tiles and thatch'.[28] Demand grew steadily until 1896; there was a slight decline in galvanised sheet exports till 1899 but then a revival, and in 1900 the export was almost 50 per cent. greater than in 1893. By 1906 the exports of British galvanised sheet iron and steel were 443,000 tons, compared with only 166,000 tons thirteen years before. In this period the change from iron to steel went on rapidly. There were some 103 concerns in England and Wales producing black sheet in 1890 and of these 35 rolled steel sheets only or steel sheets as well as iron ones. By 1910 there were only 50 units in production, of which 40 made steel or both iron and steel sheets.[29] The advantages of the coast for export business were thus reinforced, for these areas frequently had steel production, too, or could obtain steel coastwise from other British metal districts. Alternatively, foreign sheet bar—or tin bar as it was then frequently still called—could be used with little land haul. Use of foreign steel was already significant in the nineties, but after 1900, in very different trade conditions, consumption increased very greatly. Finally, the coastal districts gained increased attractiveness as locations for galvanised sheet production when Welsh mills began to cut into the markets and so made minimisation of costs still more desirable. Thereafter each new coastal plant rendered the position of remaining interior plants increasingly precarious. Contemporary descriptions of a flight to the coast exaggerated the significance of what was none-the-less an important new emphasis in the location of the sheet industry. The decisive development was the decision of John Summers to seek a coastal site.

Between 1890 and 1899 the weekly sheet capacity of John Summers went up from 300 to 1,200 tons, to equal that of John Lysaghts. The number of puddling furnaces remained at ten, the increase in sheet capacity being supported by purchases of steel. Some foreign steel was used, and some from north-west coast works, where both Workington and Barrow had large billet and bar capacity.[30] Rail freight became a significant item both in assembling material and in meeting export orders. At the same time the Stalybridge site was becoming congested. Search was begun for a new plant site, with good access to either Birkenhead or Liverpool. The banks of the recently opened Manchester Ship Canal were considered but rejected. Eventually 50 acres of land was acquired and an option taken on another 50 acres on the reclaimed marshland across the Dee from Queensferry, Flintshire.[31]

The area was an interesting one for the galvanised sheet trade. The North Wales iron and steel industry was passing through the same difficult adjustments as that of other districts. The great Ruabon Ironworks had closed in the late 1880s, but at Brymbo a new steel plant had been built, and was becoming an important supplier of billets and sheet bars to some of the most renowned sheet makers of the West Midlands. The pits of the Wrexham area provided an abundant local supply of fuel, and at Mold and at Bagillt down the estuary were spelter works.[32]   The site advantages were substantial. The land was acquired for as little as 1s. per square yard, and there was abundant water and plenty of room for disposal of effluent without offence to neighbours and for support of expansion beyond any reasonable expectation.[33]   This new Hawarden Bridge steelworks was indeed the first sheet works in Britain on a site which proved able to accommodate all the changes in scale of production and technique of the next 70 years.   There was also initially a reasonable hope of water access to the works, which the consideration of an alternative site on the Ship Canal suggests had been of importance to the company.   It was on this that the choice was subsequently shown to have been faulty.

In the 1840s Furness ore came to the Black Country through Ellesmere Port, in the seventies iron ore from Barrow went by rail to Staffordshire from wharves at Saltney on the Dee just below Chester, and from Connah's Quay Spanish ore was sent to Wrexham and other smelting centres.   One early report of the scheme for Hawarden Bridge indeed suggested that it was an extension of this trade, involving smelting at the transhipment point.[34]   Confining the Dee below Queensferry Bridge replaced the old mile-wide channel by a straight artificial cut 400 feet wide.[35]   Boats drawing up to 12 feet and carrying at the outside 900 tons brought iron ore, pig iron and bars up this channel and to the Summers wharves early in the twentieth century.   In 1905 28,277 tons materials were handled.[36]   Some of the galvanised sheet the plant produced also left the works by water, but by 1906 most of it, amounting to as much as 2,000 tons a week, went by rail to Birkenhead or to Liverpool docks.[37]

Henry Summers came from Stalybridge to take over management from his less dynamic brothers in 1907, and, when Liverpool port dues were increased to 10s. per ton, he built up a fleet of small coasters to take export material from the works wharves and to tranship without dues in Liverpool roads.[38]

Plans to provide the Dee with a navigable channel of 20 feet or more depth were not implemented and gradually it became clear that, in spite of its excellent site, Hawarden Bridge was essentially a landlocked plant, with a rail haul of fifteen miles from potential deepwater developments at Bidston at the head of the Birkenhead dock system.[39] Its long-term deficiencies notwithstanding the plant was a new and formidable competitor. By 1899 Summers had a black sheet capacity equal to over one fifth that of all the South Staffordshire mills. Stalybridge still made sheet, but most of their capacity was in the new and more efficient plant. They substantially increased the discomfiture of an already troubled district, and this encouraged the most enterprising Black Country sheet firms to consider removal to the coast in their turn.

REMOVAL FROM THE BLACK COUNTRY TO THE COAST

In the long conflict about canal or rail freight rates there had been many rumours or examples of removal of manufacturing operations. By the 1850s there were transfers of operations to Belgium, and the development by the West Bromwich nut and bolt firm of Weston and Grice of important interests in Cwmbran, Monmouthshire. In the mid-1880s, after sharp exchanges with the railway companies, Nettlefolds moved steelmaking and other operations from Wellington, Shropshire, to Rogerstone, Monmouthshire. Before building at Brierley Hill, Knights of Cookley had considered a plant at Middlesbrough, and in 1886 E. and P. Baldwin undertook their first South Wales development, moving their tinplate operations to a site beside the Panteg steelworks.[40] Their Swindon Works, in the upper Stour valley west of the Black Country, remained busy on sheet. Ten years later low grade sheet ironworks were much less secure. Besides high freight charges, the change from iron to steel sheets, Welsh competition and the competition of John Summers, there were, in a major industrial district, additional irritations, which were much less in small Welsh tinplate towns thankful to find any new employment, and almost completely absent in the sparsely populated lands along the Dee. These were not the cause of decline or removal from the Black Country, but they were sometimes the occasion.

Urban rates were naturally higher than those in the less mature, less populated manufacturing districts. More inflammatory was the problem of disposal of industrial effluent. As standards of public health improved, so the industrial communities of the West Midlands installed sewage disposal systems. This began conflict with the need of the local firms to dispose of the waste acid from their galvanising pots, or 'galvanisers' pickle', and to a smaller extent the 'bosh water', the acidic water left after washing the pickled sheets. In coastal districts concentrations of acid were rapidly dispersed by the tide, but as early as 1877 three Midland firms were said to have had to spend £1,000 to repair pumps and boilers damaged by polluted water drawn from the canals into which the galvanisers had discharged their waste. Already sewage works were adversely affected, although lime neutralised the acid. By the nineties the Crosbie Precipitation Process permitted the pickler to dispose of his acid without causing nuisance to others.[41]   Interesting differences of policy emerged among the local authorities of the West Midlands. In the Worcester part of the Black Country some galvanisers tipped their pickle onto the cinder heaps, others threw it down disused pit shafts, while yet others discharged it into the Stour '... which from time to time manifests a characteristic ochreous hue'. A little later the County Council appointed an Acid Waste Committee to meet the local firms to try to solve the waste-disposal problem without legal action. Birmingham Corporation permitted disposal of galvanisers' pickle into public sewers, but Wolverhampton Town Council, with a much bigger galvanising industry and a much smaller sewage system, did not.[42] The controversy which Wolverhampton policy aroused provides not only an interesting commentary on the relationship between private enterprise, even when comparatively enlightened, and local government, but also a sharp contrast with later developments. It is worth fuller examination because it was associated with the removal of John Lysaght from the district.

By 1896 John Lysaght and Sons employed about 1,500 workers in Wolverhampton, its rate contribution was £1,000

and its annual wage payments about £100,000. Lysaght
workers occupied about 1000 houses, mostly in the east end
of the town. Here the firm's arrival and expansion had
brought work again to an idle population, and the Council was
later glad to accept a clock and tower for the East Park as a
memorial to John Lysaght's influence on the town. But
neither he nor his immediate family had any large direct
connection with Wolverhampton, and the firm was con-
spicuously absent from discussions among local traders on wage
rates, railway freight charges or the analysis of the British Iron
Trade Association report of 1895 on continental competition.
In a memorial service to John Lysaght in the autumn of 1895,
the vicar of St. Matthew's, acknowledging his great contribution
through employment, yet took a text whose full import he
could not foresee, Psalm 39 verse 12, '. . . for I am a stranger
with thee, and a sojourner as all my fathers were'.[43]

By 1890 the St. Vincent's Works, Bristol, was unequal to
galvanising Lysaghts' increasing output, and it was decided
that, for the first time, some of their black sheet should be
galvanised in Wolverhampton. Galvanising plant was put up
at Osier Bed works and men were transferred from Bristol.[44]
In little more than a year, however, Wolverhampton Corporation was complaining about pollution and withdrew threat of
legal proceedings only when Lysaghts agreed to remove the
nuisance. Other local offenders were prosecuted.[45] Until
May, 1895, there was no further complaint against Lysaghts,
but then large quantities of acid discharged by them were
found in the Smestow Brook. The Sewerage Committee,
threatened with proceedings by owners of land alongside the
stream, in its turn brought the case before the Local Government Board in October. Throughout, Lysaghts adopted a
rather disdainful attitude to the case. They had solved the
pickling acid problem by selling it to the Crosbie precipitation
works, but their 3,000 gallons a day of bosh water could not be
dealt with satisfactorily, 'at least not in the commercial sense'.
If they had to build a works to deal with it they would shut
the galvanising plant, and the town would be the poorer. As
they put it, 'The firm took the works which were built in days
when people were not so careful in sanitary matters as now,
when the natural drainage went into the river Smestow

without anyone complaining. . . .' Capital cost of the necessary plant was put at £1,000, overall running costs at only 15s. a week, with lime to deal with the bosh water only 4½d. a day.[46] The problem came to a head again in 1896 and divided the council, some of its members being accused of acting as the mouthpiece of the firm. At this time it was decided to cease galvanising in Wolverhampton and move the plant back to Bristol. By September 1896 the controversy was taken to a completely different plane: the firm had bought 75 acres of Severnside farmland near the mouth of the River Usk and eventually all sheet mill operations would be moved there.

W. R. Lysaght had examined a possible site near Barry docks in 1895, and had also considered a location on the North East coast, but then proceeded with purchase of land south of Newport, with the encouragement of the Corporation. Negotiations had not been completed when newspaper reports revealed their existence to an apparently quite unsuspecting Wolverhampton. In reply to an urgent enquiry from the Mayor, Lysaghts noted that they had intended to inform the Corporation when the agreement with Newport was complete, and added that the tone of remarks from the Sewerage Committee and certain members of the Town Council suggested that not all would be sorry to see them go from Wolverhampton. Amid bitter recriminations among council members it was wisely argued that the basic causes of the move were the 1894 rate assessment and the troubles over railway freight charges. When a council deputation to discuss the move was suggested, Lysaghts' board wrote to 'intimate to the council that the arrangements for the removal of the works to South Wales are so far advanced that however much they would be pleased to discuss the matter with a deputation, they think that nothing would be gained by the interview'.[47] In March, 1898, with only three mills, Lysaghts new Orb works at Newport came into production. At the end of January, 1904, the 100 remaining men at Swan Garden works completed the removal to Newport, and a few months later the whole plant, except the foundry, was sold to the demolition firm of T. W. Ward of Sheffield. Even before the final stage of rundown, there was serious distress in the east end of the town and nearby Monmore Green. Now in January, 1904, before leaving, as the *Engineer* reported '. . . Mr. Lysaght gave instructions for each man to receive a gratuity of 5s., and he also forwarded a cheque for £50 to the East End Relief Fund, together with the indication that if more was needed the Committee were to let him know'.[48] With that the firm left Wolverhampton to its distress.

In all this Lysaghts were not acting harshly by the standards of the time. Indeed there is evidence of the liberality with which W. R. Lysaght habitually conducted relationships with the firm's employees, although these were tinged with a paternalism which may seem repugnant to modern judges of industrial relations.[49] The wider importance of the situation over these ten years lies in the contrast with later influences in industrial location. Forty years earlier Wolverhampton Chamber of Commerce had rejected a Birmingham suggestion of action to relieve local depression, arguing that the iron district of South Staffordshire was '. . . under the care of the ironmasters'.[50] Lysaghts acted with the very minimum of restraint from outside, and made locational decisions on grounds of business efficiency scarcely modified at all by social considerations. Forty years later Newport Corporation was exercising the utmost pressure to try to preserve what it now obtained from Wolverhampton, helped by a host of local organisations, sympathetically considered by central government and in the full glare of national publicity. The transfer of decision-taking to an arena in which there was conflict among many more contestants than merely those involved in narrow economic considerations meant that the changes of the last few years of free locational choice were to be of much greater significance than could be foreseen at the time. The national economy and society were maturing and locational patterns in old industries were soon to prove much less easy to modify.

REFERENCES

1 *Select Committee on Railways* 1881. Minutes of Evidence, pp. 496, 501.
2 *ibid.*, p. 435.
3 S. Griffiths 1873 and *Mineral Statistics of the United Kingdom.*
4 *The Lysaght Century* p. 15.
5 *Select Committee on Railways* 1881, p. 254.
6 *Mining Journal* 10 January 1885, p. 43.

7   Recollections by H. H. Summers in the 1930s, I am grateful to Mr. P. J. Summers for the opportunity to consult a review of these.

8   J. Davies, *Galvanised Iron; Its Manufacture and Uses* 1899, pp. 26–27. *Rylands Directory* 1890, 1899.

9   For information on Burnells and on all subsequent developments at Ellesmere Port I am very heavily indebted to Mr. T. W. Roberts.

10 *Rylands Directory* 1890, 1896.

11 For much material on the early development of John Summers and Sons I am indebted to Mr. P. J. Summers, and to the talk by Mr. (now Sir) Richard F. Summers 'The Birth and Growth of the Firm of John Summers', February 1945.

12 *Mineral Statistics of the United Kingdom.*

13 *Engineer* 31 March 1893, p. 280.

14 *Mining Journal* 15 September 1849, p. 442.   E. H. Brooke, *Monograph* 1932 p. 118.

15 See F. W. Taussig, *Economic Journal* 1891, pp. 342–343, 1894, p. 581.

16 *Engineer* 8 April 1898, p. 341.

17 *Labour Gazette* March 1895, p. 78, April 1895, p. 110, July 1896.

18 *Iron and Coal Trades Review* 18 September 1896, p. 39.   *Wolverhampton Chronicle* 16 September 1896.

19 Davies, *op. cit.*, p. 7.   *Engineer* 3 November 1899, p. 459.

20 Davies p. 56.

21 *ibid.*, p. 8.

22 *Engineer* 8 February 1895, p. 126.

23 Davies, *op. cit.*, pp. 134–135.

24 *Engineer* 8 November 1895, p. 468, 22 November 1895, p. 516 and E. H. Brooke, *op. cit.*, passim.

25 E. H. Brooke. *Illustrated London News* Supplement 27 November 1909.

26 E. H. Brooke appendix.

27 *Rylands Directory* 1899.   *Engineer* 18 December 1896, p. 644.

28 *Iron* 3 March 1893, p. 192.

29 *Rylands Directory* 1890, 1910.

30 *Iron* 20 September 1889, p. 253.   *Iron and Coal Trades Review* 9 October 1908, pp. 1598, 1599.

31 J. W. Summers, *Minutes of Evidence. Royal Commission on Canals* 1906, Vol. 3, p. 25.

32 *Ministry of Labour Gazette* March 1897, p. 85.

33 J. W. Summers, *op. cit.*, p. 22.

34 *Select Committee on Railways* 1881, p. 704.   *Iron and Coal Trades Review* 11 October 1895, p. 463.

35 *Proceedings Institute of Civil Engineers* 138, 1899, p. 344.

36 A. C. Williams of the Dee Conservancy Board. *Royal Commission on Canals* 1906, p. 3 and Appendix p. 3.

37 J. W. Summers, *op. cit.*, p. 21.
38 J. W. Summers, *op. cit.*, p. 26.   Information from Mr. P. J. Summers.
39 *Times Engineering Supplement* 2 March 1910, p. 17, 26 June 1912, p. 25.
40 *Iron* 17 October 1884, p. 364, 16 October 1885, p. 354, 29 January 1886, p. 102.
41 *Engineer* 23 May 1890, p. 425, 20 November 1891, p. 428.
42 *Engineer* 6 August 1897, p. 142, 12 September 1902, p. 266.
43 *Wolverhampton Chronicle* 16 September 1896. *Borough of Wolverhampton, Corporation Minutes and Reports* 12 December 1898, *Wolverhampton Chronicle* 9 October 1895.
44 *Engineer* 17 January 1890, p. 59.
45 *Borough of Wolverhampton, Corporation Minutes and Reports*, Annual Report of the Sewerage Committee, November 1892, p. 30.
46 *ibid.*, November 1895, p. 96.   *Wolverhampton Express* 24 October 1895, p. 3.
47 *The Lysaght Century* p. 18.   Mr. E. C. Lysaght in correspondence. *Wolverhampton Chronicle* 16 September 1896 'Wolverhampton Corporation and Messrs. Lysaght', *ibid.*, 4 November 1896.
48 *Wolverhampton Journal* February 1903, p. 27, April 1903, p. 84. *Engineer* 29 January 1904, p. 122, 27 May 1904, p. 548.
49 W. R. Lysaght Presidential Address. *Journal of the Iron and Steel Institute* 1933, 1, *ibid.*, remarks of Sir Frederick Mills p. 48. Correspondence with two men working with W. R. Lysaght in the late 1920s and 1930s.
50 *Wolverhampton Chamber of Commerce* November 1857 quoted *Chronicles of the Birmingham Chamber of Commerce* 1913, p. 144.

PART II

THE GROWTH OF NEW
COASTAL DISTRICTS

CHAPTER 5

Foreign Steel, the Eclipse of the Black Country, the further Development of the Coastal Sheet Steel Districts to 1914

FOREIGN TRADE & FOREIGN STEEL

The export of British galvanised iron and steel sheet reached a new peak of 761,000 tons in 1913. There had, however, been a noticeable shift in the destination of this trade in the immediate pre-war years, dominion and colonial markets again increasing in importance while foreign sales declined. European or United States mills were cutting into this business or the countries were starting to supply their own needs. In 1900 Argentina, Brazil, Uruguay and Chile took 38,000 tons British steel, only 4000 tons less than India and Burma. By 1913 the four South American markets took 120,000 tons but India 237,000. As late as 1899 James Davies had derided the capability of an underdeveloped country like Chile to manufacture sheet iron and galvanised sheet, but the germs of growth were being planted in some, and in others tariff policies were used to induce foreigners to undertake manufacture there. In Japan, a growing market for British sheet, galvanised sheet production was begun at Osaka in 1912 with plans to obtain the supplies of black sheet from the new Imperial Steelworks at Yawata.[1]

Even colonial markets were beginning to seem less secure. In 1901 an Australian federal tariff of 15s. a ton on plain galvanised sheet iron and 30s. on galvanised corrugated iron had been proposed.[2] Soon afterwards the United States Steel Corporation was dumping galvanised sheet in Canada over the tariff. Lysaghts had selling agencies in New Zealand,

South Africa and Canada by the 1890s, but Australia remained their chief market. In 1913 the Dominion imported 110,000 tons galvanised sheet of which 104,000 came from Britain. Lysaghts in the same year sold 143,000 tons galvanised sheet, exported 127,000 tons of this, of which 85,000 tons went to Australia.[3] Naturally the first signs of a policy to build up Australian metalworking behind a tariff barrier evoked a reaction from them. In 1903 a letter from W. R. Lysaght, published by the *Economic Journal* under the heading 'Preferential Tariffs in the Sheet Iron Business' advocated almost eighteenth century mercantalist relationships for the Empire, but included some prognostications of locational change on a world scale. 'The colonies', it was stated, though the case was not proved, 'are far better fitted for the production of raw material than they are for manufacturing whereas the conditions at home are exactly the reverse. Any scheme, therefore, which tends to develop the natural resources of the colonies, as producers of raw material, and, at the same time, keeps the manufacturing in the Old Country, is economically sound'. If Canada and Australia developed their own industries with the help of preferential tariffs '. . . such firms as ours, with a good organisation, will not allow themselves to be outdone by such a condition of things, and would, as we have already done to a small extent, start themselves manufacturing in the colonies'. This further locational shift was not to become noticeable before the First World War. Of more immediate relevence was competition from foreign semi-finished steel in the British market. It brought on almost the last stage in the decline of the Black Country in sheet making, helped to change the structure of the industry in the now dominant coastal districts and led to the opening of the Jurassic ore fields of eastern England as a potentially important source of supply for sheet steel.

Some foreign steel, as billets or 'tin bars' was used by British works before the mid-nineties. Summers employed it even before they decided to build at Hawarden Bridge and so did South Wales mills. Semi-finished steel imports in 1895, however, probably totalled no more than 10,000 tons. Thereafter overextension of European and United States capacity increased dumping, and by the summer of 1897, E. P. Martin, as General Manager, was pointing out that Dowlais had almost lost its profitable tin bar trade through imports of American steel.[5] By 1899 imports were almost 80,000 tons and after that the trickle swelled to a flood.[6] In 1900 exports of galvanised sheet were at a record level and tinplate was more prosperous than at any time since 1894. The United States supplied 87 per cent. of the imports of unwrought steel, and South Wales rapidly became a major region of entry for it (Table 12). The new sheet and tinplate mills had clearly

TABLE 12

Imports of semi-finished steel into the United Kingdom and South Wales, 1899–1903 (thousands tons)

	United Kingdom[1]	Newport[2]	Swansea[2]
1899	77	8	—
1900	179	27	24
1901	182	29	12
1902	281	90	24
1903	274	122*	.

[1] Blooms, billets, bars etc.
[2] Bars
* First seven months only

been grafted onto a regional metallurgical stock of largely antiquated equipment, at any rate in blast furnaces, Bessemer plants and merchant mills, which supplied the bars. As early as February, 1901, 17 tinplate and sheet works in South Wales were working on American bars, and two years later, while Welsh works refused to sell bars at less than 85s. a ton, the Germans were delivering at 82s. 6d. and the Americans at 80s. so that 35 of the 99 openhearth furnaces in South Wales were idle.[7] In the early autumn of 1903 German billets could be had in South Wales ports for 10s. a ton below the price of locally produced material, and a few weeks later Lysaghts revealed that they had bought 50,000 tons of foreign steel.[8] Already there was agitation for import duties, the 1904 report of the Tariff Commission recommended *ad valorem* duties of 6¼ per cent. on bars, billets and rods, but no protection came for another 30 years. In that period the trade in foreign semi-finished material fluctuated wildly but remained significant

for most of the time.   The sheet trade was strongly affected
and the situation had important locational implications.

The arrival of foreign semi-finished steel was yet another
factor pulling Midland firms coastwards or, for those unable
to move, rendering them less competitive.   From the port of
entry foreign material had to be railed to the Black Country at
freight charges much less flexible than the works price or even
the sea freight.   The benefit of foreign steel was therefore less
in the Midlands than elsewhere, although, for Midland firms
which had had to rail Welsh or northern steel to their mills,
the difference was sometimes quite small, as shown in Tables
13 and 14 below.

TABLE 13

Approximate costs of delivery of Pittsburgh billets to Birmingham,
without dumping, spring, 1897

	s.	d.
Standard billet price, Pittsburgh	58	0
Price at bigger Pittsburgh works	56	0
Rail freight to New York	10	5
Transatlantic freight to Manchester	10	0
Rail freight Manchester to Birmingham	7	6
Delivered price Birmingham	83	11

TABLE 14

Approximate works and West Midland delivered prices of Welsh
and dumped American sheet bars, May 1897

	s.	d.
Welsh bars in South Wales	77	6
Welsh bars in West Midlands	87	6
American Bessemer bars at Pittsburgh	62	0
American Bessemer bars in South Wales	70	0
American Bessemer bars in West Midlands	80	0

Saving to Welsh firms using American rather than local steel	9·6 per cent.
Saving to Midland firms using American rather than Welsh steel	8·5 per cent.

Sources: Report on the Welsh Tinplate Industry and the Welsh Tinplate Export
Trade to the United States.   House of Commons Papers 88, 1897.

As early as 1897 one Midland works was said to have 9000 tons sheet bar on order from the United States.[9] Sometimes Midland prices for foreign steel compared very favourably with coastal prices, whether or not because of freight absorption by the seller is not clear. In February, 1904, German billets were 83 to 84s. a ton in Lancashire and from 84s. 9d. to 87s. 3d. a ton in the West Midlands.[10] Usually the differential was wider, from 7s. 6d. to 10s. a ton, which, however, still left foreign material cheaper than local or even northern steel (Table 15). By January, 1901, one large Midland galvaniser already had the very large stock of 30,000 tons American sheet

TABLE 15

American and Midland billet prices, June, 1900 (per ton)

	s.	d.
American billets in Liverpool	125	0
American billets in Black Country	134	6
Local billets in Black Country	140	0
	to 145	0

Source: *Engineer* 22 June, 1900, p. 656

bars; eighteen months later there were contracts for Birmingham delivery at 90 to 92s. 6d. a ton when Midland Bessemer billets were 100 to 102s. 6d. and open hearth billets 105 to 107s.[11] At the end of 1903 Wolverhampton Corrugated Iron Company was largely rolling down German steel, and much of the sheet Swan Garden continued to send to Bristol for galvanising until it closed early in 1904 was also rolled from German bars.[12] The margin between material costs and the selling price for galvanised sheet, a margin which had to cover process costs, transport to the shipping point and profit, was normally 10s. a ton less than at a well favoured coastal plant and process costs were frequently higher too. This was a significant difference when galvanised corrugated sheet prices were only of the order of £12 to £13 a ton and still more when they were as low as £10.[13]

There was no catastrophic collapse in the West Midlands, dumped foreign semi-finished steel being merely another embarrassment to an already afflicted district. Good times alternated with bad, there were periods of hope when more of the old sheet mills were again set to work, but these variations in fortune were minor oscillations of a long-term downward trend.   Growth of output in Wales and at Hawarden Bridge, expansion and limited backward integration by smaller coastal firms and the completion of Lysaghts' removal to the coast worsened the situation of those who remained.   Few had the vision and fewer still the financial resources to remove to the coast themselves.   Three which did relocated in the immediate hinterland of the Mersey estuary, showing clearly that Lysaght's choice of South Wales was an exceptional response, reflecting that firm's historical commitment in Bristol (Figure 8).

In 1896 when Lysaghts had almost completed negotiations with Newport Corporation, Wolverhampton Corrugated Iron Company extended the sheet mills at Stour Valley works, which increased their weekly capacity by 100 tons.   In less than two years it was rumoured that the company was looking for a Bristol Channel site and that the works, employing 700 men, would be moved there over a period of two years.   Such suggestions were renewed in 1902 and 1903.[14]   In June, 1903, E. Peter Jones, one of the Wolverhampton Corrugated partners, at a meeting in St. Matthews Ward about the rate question and the removal of Lysaghts, observed, 'I am sorry to say that the works with which I am connected seem likely to go the same way'.[15]   Trade revived after this, a new mill engine was installed for rolling down German material, but two weeks before W. R. Lysaght announced the final downwinding at Swan Garden it was revealed that Wolverhampton Corrugated were to put down new mills and galvanising plant on a 25 acre site at Ellesmere Port.[16]   Their new Mersey Ironworks commenced production in 1906.   Location near the Manchester Ship Canal and the London and North Western line to Birkenhead was favourable for obtaining both continental and Workington bars and exporting galvanised sheet.   Choice of a site on the Shropshire Union Canal suggests an interest in water links with the Black Country.   Correspondence with Wolverhampton solicitors about haulage and wharfage rates confirms this lingered until at least 1909.[17]   By 1910, however, the company's whole operations were at Ellesmere Port, where their capacity was 1000 tons a week, 40 per cent. that of Hawarden Bridge (Table 16).   In 1911 £200,000 was spent

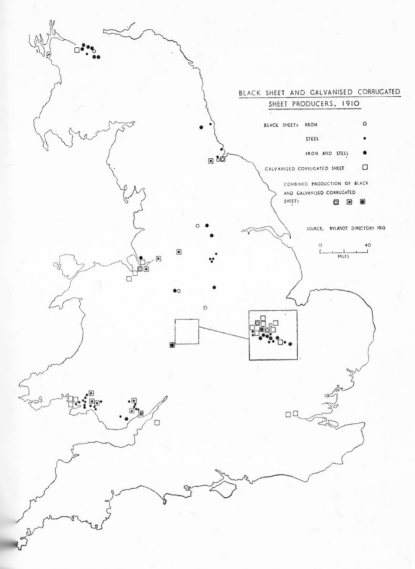

BLACK SHEET AND GALVANISED CORRUGATED
SHEET PRODUCERS, 1910

BLACK SHEET: IRON ○

STEEL •

IRON AND STEEL ⬤

GALVANISED CORRUGATED SHEET □

COMBINED PRODUCTION OF BLACK
AND GALVANISED CORRUGATED
SHEET:

SOURCE: RYLANDS DIRECTORY 1910

MILES

re 8.   The Black Country was still prominent in number of plants but
ut was growing in the Mersey–Dee area and was already greater in
South Wales.

on extensions and a large acreage of land was acquired for future growth.[18]

TABLE 16

Sheet mills of the Wolverhampton Corrugated Iron Company 1902, 1906, 1910

	1902	1906	1910
Wolverhampton	9	9	—
Ellesmere Port	—	6	13

Source: Rylands Directory and Iron and Coal Trades Review 2 September 1910, p. 380

Greenway Brothers of the Britain Works, Bradley, near Bilston, was a smaller concern, producing galvanised corrugated sheet but not black sheet.   They were said to be contemplating galvanising works at Caldicot, east of Newport in 1902, but later opened a plant at Widnes.   Sheet mills were put down there, but the Black Country works were retained.   By 1910 weekly capacity at Bradley and Widnes had reached 800 tons of bars, flats, tube strip, nail sheet and galvanised sheet.   From the early twenties the Widnes works were idle, but the Black Country works survived and were not dismantled until 1953.[19] The long established Birmingham Corrugated Iron Company had used iron sheets from the associated West Bromwich mills of Parkes and Parkes, but by 1906 the firm was galvanising about 90 per cent. steel sheet.   In 1907 90 per cent. of the company's trade was for export.   Rotten Park, Birmingham, was on both counts an unsuitable location, and in 1912 decision was taken to move to a new plant on the cheaply bought waste site of the Desota Chemical Company in Ditton Road, Widnes. Here the firm was on the main line from Garston docks through which sheet bars, chiefly Belgian, were imported, and for export had rail access to Liverpool or to Birkenhead.[20]

The acceleration of decline in the Black Country is suggested in the major removals.   Lysaghts took nine years from their first negotiations with Newport Corporation, and six years from the first mill operations there before closing Swan Garden works.   Wolverhampton Corrugated completed their transfer within four years, and Birmingham Corrugated moved at once to Widnes.   As they went, so the prospects for other Stafford shire firms darkened (Figure 9).

Attempts to organise the trade, to regulate production and to fix minimum prices continued. There were occasional price wars with coastal districts, in which, strange though it seems in retrospect, the outcome seems to have been in doubt to the participants. In 1898, for instance, the correspondent of the *Colliery Guardian* could still speculate whether the Black

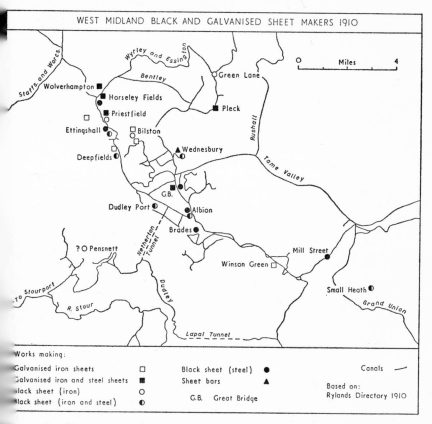

WEST MIDLAND BLACK AND GALVANISED SHEET MAKERS 1910

Works making:

Galvanised iron sheets	□	Black sheet (steel)	●	Canals	⌒
Galvanised iron and steel sheets	■	Sheet bars	▲		
Black sheet (iron)	○			Based on:
Black sheet (iron and steel)	◑	G.B. Great Bridge		Rylands Directory 1910

Figure 9. Since the mid-eighties there had been a sharp fall in the number of plants. Some localities had lost almost all their former interest in the trade.

Country or Welsh mills could stand the pace longest.[21] Soon there could be no doubt. In 1890 37 per cent. of the black sheet works in England and Wales were in the West Midlands, by 1910 only 25 per cent. Decline was indeed greater than

this suggests.   Midland works lagged in the change to steel and
were soon much smaller.   Rylands Directory in 1910 indicated
the black sheet capacity of only three Midland works, and for
them the average weekly capacity was some 265 tons.   Tupper
and Company of Bilston, a rather bigger firm, had 10 mills.
With 39 mills Summers were capable of 2500 tons sheet a week
and Lysaghts' 32 mills at Newport had equal capacity.   At
Ellesmere Port Wolverhampton Corrugated's 13 mills were
capable of 1000 tons a week (Tables 17 and 18).

TABLE 17

Works making Black Sheet, 1890 and 1910

	1890		1910	
	Iron only	Iron and steel or steel only	Iron only	Iron and steel or steel only
England and Wales	68	35	10*	40
Lancashire and Cheshire	1	3	—	4
South Wales	10	3	1	9
West Midlands	42	18	4†	13

* Includes two whose raw material is not listed
† Includes one whose raw material is not listed
Source: Rylands Directory 1890 and 1910

TABLE 18

Galvanised Corrugated Sheet Works, 1910, showing material used

	Iron only	Steel only	Iron and steel
West Midlands	5	–	6
South Wales and Monmouth	1	5	3
Lancashire and Cheshire	1	3	1

Source: Rylands Directory 1910

The black sheet mills were in an even worse position than
the galvanised sheetmakers.   As steel replaced iron their
puddling forges had to be written off, and their mills were ill
suited to roll steel in competition with the new mills of Summers
or Wolverhampton Corrugated.   Old firms and works went
down one by one.   There was some reconversion from sheet
to bar iron, as at Monmoor Ironworks, Wolverhampton, in
1893, and the Monmore Lane Ironworks in Willenhall in
1899.[22]   The variety of ends, the oscillations of trade which

periodically sparked off the old Staffordshire tendency to buy up old mills and set out hopefully with inadequate resources, all are illustrated in this period.

The Deepfields iron works of George Tinn closed in 1895, but later in the year was reopened by W. Nock, who failed within five years with liabilities of £18,000. Meanwhile, in 1898–1899, Davies Brothers closed their black sheet mills at Ettingshall which were taken over by Nock's former partner G. W. Summers of Coseley who ran them for some years.[23] The old Gospel Oak Company of Tipton and of the Mitre Galvanising works, Wolverhampton, failed, but its Tipton properties were rented and then bought by the Tipton Sheet Iron and Steel Company for £10,000, despite a valuation of £100,000 shortly before. Part was sold for £4500 and £13,000 spent to improve the rest. Dogged by breakages the company operated at a loss, and in the true Staffordshire tradition it kept no profit and loss account. Valued at £20,000 as a going concern, £10,000 even at breaking up price, it was withdrawn from sale in 1901 after bidding failed to reach a reserve price.[24] Isaac Jenks sold his Cleveland works to George Adams in 1897 and ten years later one of his Wolverhampton works was being dismantled and the other was awaiting the same end.[25] Complete dependence on iron sheets rendered Tupper and Company, one of the oldest firms in the trade, very open to the buffets of competition. Recognising its weakness, it was putting in electric mill drives in 1905 and also began cold rolling, a branch of the trade concerned with high value products which seemed less hazardous. In a brief boom in 1910 its enterprise seemed to be paying off and it was laying down two more sheet mills. By the spring of 1911, with trade depressed, it was in receiver's hands with liabilities said to be over £100,000.[26]

After the First World War Midland sheet firms were slow to convert to peacetime production and then found competition from other districts keener than ever before (Figure 10). Early in 1925 George Adams abandoned operations at the Mars and Cleveland works, Wolverhampton, and later the Tibbington works at Great Bridge was purchased for dismantling.[27] By 1928 the West Midlands had only just over 10 per cent. of British black sheet mills, and these were in

Figure 10.   Substantial further growth of the South Wales industry has occurred since 1910.

quality lines where workmanship, local markets and the smallness of many orders gave a refuge which was long to prove
tenable. The manufacture of high grade sheet had a long
tradition, some aspects of which need consideration, partly
because from the local, associated high grade sheet consumption were to grow the major sheet using trades of the
West Midlands for the twentieth century.

Deep stamping sheet, enameller's sheet, or the so-called
Russian sheet which Baldwins began producing at Wilden
Works in 1896, brought prices which rendered competition
from the coastal districts of scant concern, especially considering
the significance of the consumption in the neighbouring
industrial area (Table 19).[28]   In 1899, when 24 w.g. galvanised
sheets f.o.b. Liverpool were £11 10s. a ton, the price for high
grade tinned sheets for deep stamping was raised by £2 to
£25 10s.   In addition to the value of their products, the
situation of the quality sheet firms was eased by the fact that

TABLE 19

Midland Sheet Iron Prices, February, 1895 (shillings per ton)

Galvanising sheets (doubles)	125
Japanners' steel trunk sheets	160
Deep stamping doubles	190

Source: Engineer 8 February, 1895

by 1900 they were only three in number—E. P. and W.
Baldwin, Stephen Thompson and the Brierley Hill and Kidderminster combination of Knight and Crowther.   In 1901 the
first and last of these merged into Baldwins Limited.   Stephen
Thompson had difficulties in the nineties but modernised the
mills and improved the quality of the sheet at its Manor Works,
Ettingshall.   In 1904 it passed to Joseph Sankey and Sons,
whose development shows most clearly the evolution from
sheet to sheet using.[29]

From stamping blanks for the japanned tray makers of
Bilston, Joseph Sankey had moved into both the black sheet
business and the manufacture of holloware.   In forward
integration their greatest acquisition was the Birmingham
works of J. H. Hopkins and Sons, much of which was removed
to Bilston after 1899.[30]   In 1886 Sankeys began producing

some high grade sheet for electrical purposes. Trade grew rapidly, and in 1900 the derelict Bradley works of Hatton Sons and Company was acquired, and under the name of Bankfield works was converted to electrical stampings. To supply Bankfield with sheets Sankeys in 1904 bought the Bull's Bridge works of Thomas Jevons, intended for use until a modern sheet mill could be built at Bradley. Instead of this, Thompson's Manor Works was bought and supplied both the electrical and the stamping sheets Sankeys needed. Between 1906 and 1908 Hadfield's high silicon steel sheets replaced iron sheets for electrical purposes, and Sankeys became exclusive licensees. Sublicenses for manufacture of silicon steel were granted to the Brymbo Steel Company and for rolling electrical grade sheet to Lysaghts, who already rolled iron sheets for the electrical firms. Eventually the Midland works of Baldwins also rolled electrical sheets.[31]

Enamelling trades were still important in the West Midlands, but japanning was declining, which especially injured the high grade products of Wolverhampton.[32] Pushed into alternative lines, they entered the bicycle and motor car parts trades. By the mid-1890s the long-established holloware and japanning firm of John Marston was making Sunbeam bicycles, and a few years later cars as well.[33] In the first years of the twentieth century Sankeys' Albert Street works made the first pressed motor car wheels from steel sheets. So rapidly did this trade grow that in 1910 they purchased the Hadley Castle Works, Wellington, which Nettlefolds had first occupied over 25 years before. By 1903 a few motor car bodies were already being produced with metal rather than wooden panels on a wooden frame. In 1904, on Herbert Austin's suggestion, Sankeys began on bigger body shells, and within a few years were supplying Scottish motor firms and even exporting to the United States. Bankfield made these bodies, but along with wheels, hubs, panels, mudguards and other parts, they were soon made on a much bigger scale at Wellington, where steam drop hammers and large hydraulic presses were at work well before the First World War.[34]

The Midland motor industry now grew quickly. By 1912 Wolseley made as many as 100 vehicles a week at Adderley Park, Birmingham, and Austins turned out 1000 cars that year at Longbridge, where their own bodies were produced.[35] In 1913 the long established firm of Fisher and Ludlow, makers of tinman's furniture, began to turn out motor body work. By then, too, high quality sheet, notably from Lysaghts, was being used by the motor firms. Galvanised sheet production in 1913 reached 850,000 tons, of which 761,000 tons was exported. This justified the movement of the sheet business to the coast, and no contemporary can have realised that the insignificant tonnages of sheet steel moving to the primitive motor body shops of the West Midlands presaged a further and far more fundamental change.

REFERENCES

1 *Times Engineering Supplement* 19 June 1912, p. 26.
2 *Wolverhampton Chronicle* 20 November 1901, p. 3.
3 United Kingdom trade records. British Iron and Steel Federation statistical records and *The Lysaght Century* pp. 22, 26.
4 *Economic Journal* 13, 1903, pp. 421–423.
5 *Engineer* 2 July 1897, p. 20.
6 F. W. Gilbertson, 'Foreign Tariffs and Welsh Industries'. *Nineteenth Century* 54, 1903.
7 *Colliery Guardian* 22 February 1901, p. 414. Billy and Melius, 'The Welsh Iron and Steel Industry', *Revue de Metallurgie* quoted *Iron Age* 8 September 1904, p. 14.
8 *Colliery Guardian* 25 September 1903, p. 669, 27 November 1903, p. 1137.
9 *Engineer* 12 March 1897, p. 278, 12 August 1898, p. 166.
10 *Engineer* 12 February 1904, pp. 172, 173.
11 *Engineer* 11 January 1901, p. 50, 5 September 1902, p. 243.
12 *Engineer* 20 November 1903, p. 512. *Times* 30 November 1903, Letter from J. Brailsford of Ebbw Vale.
13 *Engineer* 23 July 1909, p. 97.
14 *Wolverhampton Chronicle* 10 June 1896, 2 March 1898, 'Wolverhampton Corrugated Ironworks—Probable Removal to the Coast'. *Engineer* 11 March 1898, p. 244. *Annual Report of the Chief Inspector of Factories and Workshops for* 1902. Part 1, 1903, p. 38.
15 *Wolverhampton Journal* June 1903.
16 *Engineer* 15 May 1903, p. 504, 11 September 1903, p. 269, 8 January 1904.
17 Information from Mr. T. W. Roberts and correspondence between E. P. Jones and H. B. Jones, solicitor of Wolverhampton, September to November 1909. Cheshire County Record Office.

18   *Times Engineering Supplement* 29 March 1911, 10 May 1911.
19   *Colliery Guardian* 25 April 1902, p. 887.   *Rylands Directory* 1910.
     Mr. J. M. Parkes in correspondence and G. K. V. Gale.
20   Correspondence with J. M. Parkes of Birmingham Corrugated
     Iron Company, 1961.
21   *Colliery Guardian* 11 March 1898, p. 437.
22   *Engineer* 4 August 1893, p. 130, 27 October 1899, p. 432.
     Engineer 9 April 1897, p. 376.
23   *Wolverhampton Chronicle* 25 December 1895, 5 June 1901, p. 5,
     22 May 1901, p. 8 and J. M. Parkes in correspondence.
24   *Wolverhampton Chronicle* 9 January 1901, p. 4, 27 March 1901.
     Wolverhampton Chronicle 19 February 1896 contains another
     extraordinary record of accounting in sheet iron.
25   *Engineer* 30 July 1897, p. 121.   *Wolverhampton and South Stafford-
     shire Illustrated Biographical and Commercial Sketches* 1898–1899,
     pp. 45–46.   *Iron and Coal Trades Review* 8 November 1907,
     p. 1776.
26   *Wolverhampton Chronicle* 20 February 1901.   *Engineer* 25 October
     1907, p. 428.   *The Times* 24 March 1911, p. 19.
27   *Engineer* 31 October 1919, p. 447.   *Iron and Coal Trades Review*
     9 January 1925, p. 78, 20 March 1925, p. 496, 10 April 1925,
     p. 604.   *Engineer* 21 August 1925, p. 189.
28   *Engineer* 18 September 1896, p. 298, 11 February 1898, p. 142.
29   *Wolverhampton Chronicle* 20 March 1895.
30   *Times, Birmingham Number* 2 October 1912.
31   *History of Joseph Sankey & Sons* 1960.   *Engineer* 2 December
     1904, p. 554, 16 December 1904, p. 606.   *Times Engineering
     Supplement* 30 November 1910.
32   W. J. Gordon, *Midland Sketches* 1896, p. 161.   Kelly's Directory
     of Birmingham 1900, 1910.
33. W. J. Gordon, *op. cit.*, p. 162.   *Wolverhampton Journal* January
     1903, p. 2.
34   *History of Joseph Sankey* p. 4.   *Times Birmingham Number* 2
     October 1912, p. 35.
35   *ibid.*, pp. 33, 34.

CHAPTER 6

Growth and Backward Integration in the new Sheet Steel Districts in the early 20th Century

The supply of foreign steel to British sheet mills was not wholly satisfactory. Initially there was much variability in weight and dimensions, which made the material difficult to manipulate in the mill, quality was poor and the range of grades available was limited. The lack of standardisation these complaints revealed merely provided a variant on a common problem of British manufacturing then coming to prominence, but given the diversity of demand the difficulty of the sheet-makers employing foreign steel was real enough. When foreign markets were depressed the supply of semi-finished steel was adequate, but when buoyancy returned it sometimes dried up and prices increased. In the late summer of 1904, for instance, with home trade conditions good, German and American material was difficult to procure, and early in 1905— much the best year to date for both German and American steel industries—German billets and bars were 8s. a ton or 10 per cent. more than a year before. Sheet prices had not advanced in proportion.[1] It had given them an important additional advantage over the West Midland firms, but the larger coastal producers began to look for closer control over their own supplies.

Although they had galvanised sheet for over 40 years, the firm of Frederick Braby did not roll any black sheet until after 1906, when six mills were installed in their Eclipse Works, Glasgow. As with many other producers at home and overseas their black sheet mills operated under a manager who had brought his skills from Staffordshire via Newport and Huyton Quarry.[2] Braby's did not produce their own steel: indeed

although seven Scottish firms rolled sheet steel in 1910 much
of their material came from overseas and not from Scottish
melting shops and bar mills.   In 1910 alone, 93,000 tons of
blooms, billets, slabs and sheet bars were brought in through
Grangemouth, Leith or Glasgow.[3]

On the Mersey Burnell's for a time galvanised steel sheets
rolled in the Black Country although probably made from
northern or Welsh billets.   By 1903 sheet mills had been put
down along with wharves to which were delivered sheet bars
from Workington and Belgium.   Having only modest capacity,
the firm proceeded no further in backward integration, though
four more Staffordshire type black sheet mills were put down
in 1911.[4]   Nearby, Wolverhampton Corrugated's acquisition
of much additional land after 1910 suggested interest in
eventual further extension, perhaps going back beyond the
sheet mill stage.   There is no substantial evidence of this
intention, but the action of the company's chief rivals make
this a likely framework of defensive forward planning.   Two
other big Mersey basin concerns went further.   John Summers'
with its large and rapidly growing make of sheet, early decided
that it was unwise to rely on American or continental semi-
finished steel, and in 1902 built a bar mill and open hearth
steel plant at Hawarden Bridge.   The melting shop was largely
supplied with pig iron from the Etruria works of the Shelton
Iron, Steel and Coal Company in North Staffordshire, a
trading link which laid the foundation for later control.
Disturbed by the unreliability of supply of foreign billets and
bars, Pearson Knowles bought 90 acres of land from the
Manchester Ship Canal Company in 1910 and built the Irlam
iron and steel works.   Irlam supplied not only the associated
companies, notably in the wire trade, but also independent
north western mills, including those making sheet steel.   Later
Pearson Knowles for a time controlled Burnells, to which they
transferred their black and galvanised sheet business.[5]   Developments in the north west were paralleled by and interacted on
the bigger changes taking place in South Wales.

DUMPING, MERGERS & EXPANSION IN SOUTH WALES

Foreign competition and the growth of giant corporations
overseas led to a gradual realisation of the need for rationalisa-

tion, or 'Americanisation' as it was then called. Big groups began to emerge at home. Dorman Long, Guest Keen and Nettlefold, and Stewarts and Lloyds were outstanding examples, while in sheet, in the months of disquiet following the formation of the United States Steel Corporation, E. P. and W. Baldwin merged with Knight and Crowther and with the Blackwall Galvanised Iron Company. Next year this group linked with Alfred Baldwin & Company and Wright Butler & Company to form Baldwins Limited. Soon this and other groups were in distress from the competition of dumped foreign steel.

In the summer of 1903 prices were low and the primary sections of the South Wales industry depressed. Nine steelworks, built to supply the tinplate mills over the previous 20 years, were idle. In 1899 7 of the 9 had been at work, even though exports of tinplate had been 14 per cent. and of galvanised sheet 47 per cent. less than in 1903.[6] By the autumn notices were also posted at Baldwin's Landore works, at Pontymister, and at the Morriston works of the Dyffryn Steel and Tinplate Companies. In October, at a time of very active dumping, Baldwins intimated that only after the gravest deliberation and hesitation had they decided to reopen their reconstructed Panteg works.[7] That they made this choice indicates the inadequacy of superficially 'cheap' foreign steel.

On the 'North Crop' of the South Wales coalfield failure or radical reconstruction had long been the unenviable alternatives. Tredegar and Rhymney in the 1890s had been the latest examples of the former, while Blaenavon, Dowlais and Ebbw Vale had widened their rolling capacity to include billets, tin bars and later sheet bars. In these trades foreign competition gave them serious trouble, though occasionally they still found substantial local outlets.[8] For nine months in 1909 the steel department at Ebbw Vale was on short time and for several weeks wholly idle. In 1910 160,000 tons semifinished material came through Newport docks into the Ebbw Vale market area, and by the end of May, 1911, 3,500 men at the steelworks and coke oven plant were laid off.[9] In the next few months, while the manager, Frederick Mills, maintained that modernisation was futile against foreign underselling by at least 5s. a ton, delegations from the Amalgamated Association of Steelworkers waited on the President of the Board of Trade and the Chancellor of the Exchequer.[10]   The unexpected out-come was a decision from the management to manufacture black and galvanised sheet at Ebbw Vale, an inward migration to one source of home semi supplies which had been fore-shadowed some years before.   Construction began in 1912, and in 1913 six of the most modern sheet mills in Britain, and galvanising plant for their whole output, were at work at Ebbw Vale.[11]

While Ebbw Vale rather unexpectedly became a sheet producer, another works, another fixed point of future develop-ment discussions, was emerging on Swansea Bay.   The Port Talbot steelworks, built by Gilbertsons of Pontardawe in 1901 and closed two years later, was reopened in 1907 as a Siemens steel plant, and by 1912 was making bars and plate.   In 1915 it passed to Baldwins who, with Ministry of Munitions financial assistance, realised earlier plans for a new, fully integrated works at Margam on an adjoining site.   Although concerned with heavy steel and especially with ship plate, Margam was eventually to play a significant role in sheet.   Links between South Wales and the West Midlands had long existed and for Baldwins survived.   Now links between South Wales and the Jurassic ore belt of eastern England became more important and this laid the foundations of further locational controversies in the sheet business.

SHEET, TINPLATE & DEVELOPMENTS IN LINCOLNSHIRE & NORTHAMPTONSHIRE

Since the 1850s large tonnages of Northampton Sand iron ore purchased from independent ore-mining concerns had been used in Welsh furnaces.   Rail transport charges were high—between 8s. and 9s. 6d. a ton in the mid-1880s from various Northamptonshire loading points, when, even with calcined material, more than 2 tons had to be shipped for every ton or iron made.   The ore supply position of South Wales works, however, was difficult, and Ebbw Vale's systematic search for new ore supplies in 1906–1907 ranged from the Forest of Dean to Spain and Norway before an extensive deposit of Northampton Sand ore near Irthlingborough, Northampton-shire, was purchased in 1913.   A drift mine was opened to provide 10,000 tons ore a week for Ebbw Vale as sinter rather than as calcined ore. Plans to ship by canal had been abandoned by the autumn of 1915, for, although nine canals or navigations were consulted, and a through rate obtained, their capacity was limited to 750 tons a week. Alternative rail movements had to be used, the sinter being mixed at Ebbw Vale with imported ore.[12] In Lincolnshire the Welsh penetration proceeded further.

Linclonshire ore was of low quality. As early as 1874 the average iron content of marketable ore from the Frodingham orefield was no more than 25 per cent. Wide variation in the iron content and in the accompanying impurities rendered the iron of uncertain quality too. On the other hand winning costs were low. Priestman cranes were used as early as 1885, but hand working predominated until the First World War.[13] Final iron costs were high, partly because the lowish quality of Yorkshire coke made it necessary to use some Durham coke as well and freight charges were therefore substantial. In 1891 the freight rate on South Yorkshire coke was 2s. to 2s. 6d. a ton and on Durham coke 7s.[14] Furnaces were small and of indifferent quality. In 1894 average furnace output was less than two-thirds that in the North Riding, and by 1906 the relative position had only slightly improved.[15] Substantial advance began when it became possible to make steel from Lincolnshire iron and when fuel economy was achieved. The Frodingham Iron Company made its first steel in 1890 and economised in fuel for the steelworks and mills by installing gas engines recently made commercially successful by B. H. Thwaites.[16] With new steel plant and, shortly after 1900, pioneering the introduction to Britain of the Talbot tilting open-hearth furnace and of 'American'-style blast furnaces to the Jurassic ore belt, Frodingham proved a successful steelmaker, able to oust north-eastern firms from the Midlands, West Yorkshire and Lancashire markets for angles, tees and girders. Commenting on this performance in 1905, Charles Maclaren, the future Lord Aberconway, saw a great prospect for the district. 'Fuel is abundant and cheap, and in another generation the Lincolnshire iron district will probably be a formidable rival to Middlesbrough.'[17] Shortly afterwards John Lysaghts decided to build an integrated works in Lincolnshire.

By the early 1900s Lysaghts had a sheet capacity of some 120,000 tons a year, but controlled no steel supplies. Baldwins, other South Wales companies and, after 1902, Summers depended less on foreign supplies, but incurred the costs of maintaining idle works when foreign material was cheap. Even before the removal of the mills from Wolverhampton was complete there were suggestions that Lysaghts would eventually concentrate operations at Newport, transferring all or most of the galvanising from Bristol. The integration, however, did not occur, and small steamships continued to shuttle across the channel and up the Avon with over 100,000 tons black sheet a year.[18]   Now that both iron and steel making were contemplated, Newport had advantages for backward integration. Its docks were a major transfer point for foreign iron ore—Spanish material could be delivered in the Usk for a freight charge of only 4s. to 5s. a ton—and the haulage cost on coking coal was only 1s. to 1s. 6d. Per ton of iron freight charges on these minerals would total no more than 12s 6d. On the other hand in Lincolnshire overall freight charges were probably even less, and the at-mine cost of both ore and coking coal was lower too. After W. R. Lysaght had surveyed various possible locations he decided to build in the Frodingham ore-field. Reduction of process costs sufficient to offset transport cost of semi-finished steel from Lincolnshire to Newport was to be achieved by full integration, with the use of hot metal. Overall costs would be less than those of Baldwins or Summers.[19]

With design and construction under the control of John Darby of Brymbo, a leading advocate of by-product coke ovens, and the full integration of ovens, blast furnaces, steel plant and mills, Lysaghts aimed to dispense with outside supplies of energy. As Darby had maintained ten years before '. . . if Semet Solvay ovens were added to an open-hearth iron and steel works plant, producing both pig iron and steel, and if 2 tons 16 cwts. of coke could be manufactured per ton of steel made, no other fuel than the waste gases would be required for the manufacture of steel, including heating and rolling.'[20] Such a heat balance for the whole works had not yet been attained in Britain, and even Lysaghts failed to achieve it for 20 years, but by planning for lowest cost operations Darby placed them in a very favourable position. He left Brymbo in the spring of 1908 to begin design work, construction started in 1910, and in 1912 the Normanby Park works came into production north of Frodingham. Besides its advanced practice in carbonisation, it incorporated American and German technical advances, and, symbolic of its 'scientific' conception, was, unlike the other north Lincolnshire works, sited just west of, rather than on top of the ore beds. Almost certainly for over twenty years it was the lowest cost producer of steel and of semi-finished material in Britain. To complete their advantages Lysaghts negotiated extremely favourable, full-train rates on the 100,000 tons of sheet bar they shipped yearly to Newport. In 1912 the new Immingham docks were opened and the alternative route checked the ability of the railway companies to raise their charges.

The Normanby Park venture was significant in at least three ways. Firstly, it proved that higher value products than forge iron or structural steel could be made from Frodingham ore. By the second half of the twenties Lysaghts were rolling the first sheet for the new motor body press shops from steel derived from the reduction of that limey ore of little more than 20 per cent. iron content by high-ash Yorkshire coking coal. Less obvious was the fact that immense care was needed to make such an operation successful. Secondly, Lysaghts' success would encourage others to follow their pattern of development, or, if unencumbered with plant elsewhere, to build up their whole operations in the Jurassic ore belt. Thirdly, although Lysaghts were rewarded for their enterprise by favourable cost conditions, their interests were now spreadeagled across the country. Later this was to be a substantial disadvantage.

One other South Wales group, although then of little significance in sheet production, developed Lincolnshire interests at the same time as Lysaghts. In 1895 Richard Thomas & Company, until then confined to the Forest of Dean, first entered South Wales with the purchase of the Abercarn Tinplate Works in the hinterland of Newport. In 1898 the company acquired the much more important South Wales Works of Morewood & Company in Llanelly, and by 1908 had acquired five other South Wales tinplate works. Meanwhile, in 1896, Frank Treherne Thomas, Richard's son, had gained control of the Cwmfelin Tinplate works, and in 1905 this and certain other properties were registered as the Cwmfelin Steel and Tinplate Company.   In 1907 Thomas bought the small Redbourn Hill Ironworks north east of the Frodingham steelworks and from there delivered basic pig iron to Cwmfelin.   By 1912, as Lysaghts completed the Normanby Park works within sight of Redbourn, Thomas was planning to build not only a steelworks and bar mills but also tinplate mills near his Lincolnshire blast furnaces.   The war cut off any such advanced integration.

REFERENCES

1   J. H. Jones, 'Dumping and the Tinplate Industry', *Economic Journal* 23, 1913, pp. 186, 187.   *Engineer* 28 April 1905, p. 433.

2   Obituary of J. H. Barnbrook *Journal of the Iron and Steel Institute* 1925, 1, p. 417.

3   *Journal of West of Scotland Iron and Steel Institute* 22, 1914–1915.

4   T. W. Roberts.

5   *Iron and Coal Trades Review* 30 September 1910, p. 375.   *Manchester Guardian Commercial* 19 March 1925, p. 324.

6   F. W. Gilbertson, *op. cit.*, p. 859.

7   *The Times* 21 October 1903.   *Colliery Guardian* 11 December 1903, p. 1241.

8   *Engineer* 9 January 1903, pp. 51–52.

9   *The Times* 22 June 1910, 23 May 1911, p. 8.

10   *The Times* 14 August 1911, p. 5.

11   *Engineer* 23 October 1903, p. 412.   *Iron and Coal Trades Review* 6 October 1911, p. 596, 29 December 1911.   *The Times* 12 February 1912, p. 17.

12   *Iron & Coal Trades Review* 22 September 1916, p. 372.

13   J. Dalglish and R. Howse, 'Some Remarks on the Beds of Ironstone occurring in Lincolnshire', *Transactions North of England Institute of Mining and Mechanical Engineers*, Vol. 24, Part 1, 1874, pp. 23–33, Part 3 pp. 157–164.   G. Dove,'On the Iron Industry of Frodingham'.   *Transactions Institute of Mechanical Engineers* 1885.

14   *Iron* 2 January 1891.

15   *Iron and Coal Trades Review* 25 January 1907, p. 293.

16   M. Mannaberg, Obituary notice, *Journal of the Iron and Steel Institute* 1930, 2, p. 395.

17   *Times Engineering Supplement* 28 June 1905, p. 143.

18   *Engineer* 9 October 1903, p. 362, 9 September 1910, p. 288.

19   J. S. Jeans, *The Iron Trade of Great Britain* 1906, pp. 113–114 and passim.

20   J. H. Darby, 'The Semet Solvay Coke Oven', *Transactions Federated Institute of Mining Engineers* 9, 1894–1895.

CHAPTER 7

Technical Change in the Sheet Industry to the First World War

Technical change has obvious significance for location. A fundamental process like the Bessemer upsets the whole material supply situation in an industry and, as the invective from the established ironmasters showed, it was recognised as likely to lead to the fall of old manufacturing districts and the emergence of new ones. Less spectacular, but cumulative modifications in technology trend in the same direction. These conditions, however, are permissive. Change is also related to the willingness of a district or company to accept technical challenges, to modify and to pioneer. Those willing to initiate change may cancel out the disadvantages of a worsening location, whereas a lack of managerial vision may vitiate a good location. A further principle, one of great significance in the development of the sheet industry, is that whereas adjustment to changing circumstances is essential, the firm which makes a series of successful adaptations may eventually fail to see the need for more revolutionary changes, which its previously less successful rivals may have to face. As in biological evolution, some apparently logical modifications prove dead ends while wholly new and more dynamic species emerge. In short, both at the industry-wide level and at that of the firms' reactions, developments in technology are significant for the spatial organisation of the trade.

The steady application of minor technological changes takes place most readily in a setting of growing demand. Changes which shake the foundations of an industry seem to be associated with either a major expansion in demand, especially when coupled with changes in the type of product required, or, apparently less radical, when an industry faces severe competition. Extreme cases of the first are the introduction of bulk steelmaking associated with railway demand or, in the sheet and tinplate business, the arrival of the wide strip mill. The related instances of the second include the attempt to introduce mechanical puddling to meet the challenge of Bessemer's process, and the various devices introduced into the sheet mills when quality sheet was first demanded in bulk in the twenties, and when the strip mill was also becoming a potential supplier. The British sheet industry through to the First World War provides an example of the other case, steadily growing demand for a slowly changing product—mainly galvanising sheet. However, this period laid the groundwork for Britain's future backwardness in innovation and for different reactions by the main concerns in the business.

On the whole there was a gradual drift of technical change in the British sheet industry. As steel replaced iron, as use of unsuitable material such as ingot or bloom ends or large plate shearings disappeared and problems of output were overcome, bending operations became much more practicable and the groundwork was laid for new uses of sheet.[1] The change to steel was accompanied by an increase in the size of the rolls from the old Staffordshire standards of 18″ to 20″ diameter to 22″ to 24″ as the common size by the First World War. The most recent mills were of 30″ diameter rolls, while the American average was 24″ to 26″. Fuel economy was a notable feature of progress. For a ton of sheet in the early 1890s up to 3 tons of fuel was used, but by 1914 fuel consumption had been cut over thirty years by three-quarters.[2] Otherwise there were no great innovations, merely an all-round advance. 'It will be seen,' observed Herbert Beard in 1914, 'that development has taken place along old lines, the chief thing being more power at the disposal of the roller.'[3] In this period, however, British practice fell behind that in other leading steel countries. One of the sheet trade members of the British Iron Trade Association delegation to Germany and Belgium in 1895, confessing they could not match the sheet rolling which had been seen, recognised 'There is a danger to the Midland district, unless we can by some means increase our output, develop our machinery and bring our sheets to greater perfection' and another, described as connected with the best sheet works in the Midlands, concluded in connection with the continental works '. . . The mode of procedure that is carried on there is so different from anything I have seen carried on in Staffordshire that it will revolutionise the whole mode of working the sheets: we shall

have to begin and learn again'.[4] Not surprisingly in the
United States, where consumption grew rapidly, both technical innovation and scale economies in operation were still
more readily adopted. Less understandably, even the new
British works failed to employ the best methods.

Over the last decade of the nineteenth century American
sheet mills, although generally very similar to those in Britain,
made various advances in technology. Plant layout was
improved and, as befitted a country with high labour costs,
cranage and haulage were more efficient. The mills were
sturdier and there had been improvements on British practice
in galvanising, corrugating, pickling, annealing and cold
rolling.[5] By the First World War various other devices,
promoting increase of output, distinguished American practice
—mill housings were made so that rolls could be removed for
dressing, thus saving the production of a shift spent in Britain
turning them in position, roughing and finishing stands were
used rather than, as in old British works, both operations being
carried out in the same mill, and American shears cut two sides
of the sheet to shape at once whereas all four sides were
separately sheared in Britain.[6] The same market growth that
encouraged these innovations permitted longer runs on each
specification than in British mills which were rolling for a
variety of markets. Isaac Jenks, a sheet-trade man, told the
Wolverhampton Chamber of Commerce of an example of this
in cotton ties, which had once been a Staffordshire staple but
had now entirely gone. On a recent visit to Pittsburgh, he had
found in one works alone three mills running constantly on
cotton ties, each turning out a single gauge and size.[7] The
growth in demand—for rail cars, hoppers, oil barrels, garbage
bins, as well as galvanised sheet—brought about a nearer
approach to standardised conditions in sheet. Gradually,
some British firms realised the need for similar organisation but
even these evidenced the lack of pluck in scrapping old plant
that Ebeneezer Parker deplored in 1903.[8] Later that year the
commission of delegates from British Trade Unions, organised
by Mr. Moseley, M.P., provided an interesting insight into
comparative efficiency and productivity of British and American
industries. Of the steel industry generally the report of James
Cox of the Associated Iron and Steelworkers of Great Britain

said, 'There is no doubt that the leading mills of American manufacture are far ahead of our own best mills in their arrangement and outputs. I have seen nothing like it in this country either in the matter of output or labour-saving devices. To the average British iron and steel workers the output of these mills will be incredible.' On the sheet industry he singled out the manufacture of their own steel, of good quality, as an important reason for success in the bigger American mills—an interesting comment at a time when imported semi-finished material was very largely employed in England. Many American mills, however, then and much later were still unintegrated with steelmaking. English mill methods were inferior—'It is so easy to blame the workman for all this and to prate upon his wastefulness and inferiority, but if the best of American workmen had to come here and work they would be as great a failure as many of our managers would be in America.' Cox singled out Lysaghts and Summers as most nearly approaching the excellence of the sheet mills at Vandergrift near Pittsburgh, with both better mills and buildings, but, 'I regret this cannot be said of all the modern mills put down within the last 5 or 6 years. . . .'[9] Unfortunately even the leaders did not follow American practice very far.

Just before the First World War when Lysaghts had 44 sheet mills in one impressive quarter-mile line at Newport 27 were still those which had been transferred from Wolverhampton. The others had been built to American design. The productivity of the old mills was much, and that of the newer mills slightly below that of United States mills. By this time the best American works, such as Vandergrift, had roller levellers throughout the plant, whereas at Newport, comparable in size, there was only one. Handling operations there were also inefficient. The building in this new works was too low to accommodate a heavy crane, and for some years every ton of sheet had to be hauled in wooden buggies along a very narrow gauge track by a gang of six men holding on to a rope and helped over rough parts by two men wielding bars. Much internal movement was involved, for about 70 per cent. of the output had to be taken to the cold rolls which were at the ends of the line of hot mills. A monorail crane was installed about 1906 but a company worker over the period 1898 to 1912 believed that enough money was lost in haulage costs to pay for demolishing the old building and erecting a structure suitable for the necessary cranage.   Further, every sheet bar and sheet was manhandled into the pickling tanks and all the loading for dispatch was done by hand.   In ordinary sheets American quality was superior, but for silicon sheet for electrical purposes Lysaghts' methods of heat treatment were still better.[10]   The Orb Works was the exemplar of the best British practice, but already in these various respects it was behind the leading American plants.   This inferiority became almost institutionalised, so that British concerns were willing to deny that superior foreign practice was applicable here, and, while the leaders slipped behind, the average producer continued almost to duplicate the old unimproved models.   The mediocrity Cox spoke of in sheet he found also in tinplate, contrasting the 'strong and well powered' United States mills with '. . . the feeble and spasmodic grind at any of our own works'.[11]   Here too, although many new mills were built in the period 1900–1914, processes remained little changed from the pre-steel era. As J. H. Mort later said, 'One of the most astonishing features of this era is that, as late as 1908–1912, mills were being built in Wales to virtually the same design as those laid down 40 years earlier, despite the fact that the strides being made by the Americans, and how they were made, were perfectly well known to most people closely interested.   These new mills were obsolete before they were placed in commission. . . .'   He also noted that '. . . mills of the 1860 design were still in commission in 1939'.[12]   In sheet, too, this poorness of plant continued, so that, even at Lysaghts' Orb Works with all its substantial postwar successes in sheet quality, the old monorail system and most of the other operating methods had not changed greatly in the years 1910 to 1930.

In this period both sheet and tinplate technology in Britain slipped well behind American or the best continental practice. When the structure of demand changed suddenly in the late twenties the old firms reacted only slowly.   Conditions were then ripe for other rapidly gowing enterprises to break in and grasp the prizes which new technologies seemed to promise for both the trades, and which now brought their fortunes closer together again.

REFERENCES

1   H. J. Skelton, *Economics of Iron and Steel* 1890 p. 220.
2   *Engineer* 13 February 1891, p. 134, and H. Beard of Gartcosh in *Journal of West of Scotland Iron and Steel Institute* XXII 1914–1915 pp. 22–24.
3   Beard, *op. cit.*, p. 23.
4   Quoted *Wolverhampton Chronicle* 18 September 1895.
5   Joseph Malborn in correspondence.
6   F. W. Harbord and J. W. Hall, *The Metallurgy of Steel*, Vol. 2. *Mechanical Treatment*, 1918, pp. 787–792.
7   *Colliery Guardian* 20 December 1895, p. 1179.
8   E. Parkes, M.P., President of British Iron Trade Association quoted S. Chapman, *Work and Wages* 1904, p. 93.
9   J. Cox in *Reports of the Moseley Industrial Commission to the United States* October–December 1903, pp. 41, 44, 45.
10 Recollections of J. Malborn.
11 Cox, *op. cit.*, p. 47.
12 J. H. Mort, 'The Welsh Tinplate Industry. Its Decline— Causes and Remedies'. *Iron and Steel* 19, 1946, pp. 225, 226. See also Sir W. Charles Wright, Presidential Address on the tinplate trade *Journal of the Iron and Steel Institute* 1931, 1.

CHAPTER 8

The Great War and the Twenties: a major Watershed in the Development of the Sheet Trade

The sixteen years separating the prosperity of 1913 from the new output highs of 1928 and the first two-thirds of 1929 were the germination period of changes in sheet manufacture more fundamental even than those of the nineties in which the hegemony of the inland districts had been lost. Products, techniques, markets, company organisation and the national framework within which individual company decisions were made were all changing at an accelerating rate. The developments in technology were so complex and so important that they are considered separately in Chapter 9. Locational change was less evident than in the earlier period, but here, too, other developments in the industry presaged an upsetting of old values.

War had always disturbed the course of the galvanised iron trade but in the Sudan campaigns or the South African war business had soon recovered and even benefited from military demands. The Great War was a much more significant interruption. Overseas markets were cut off, customers there had to obtain alternative supplies while at home mill capacity was diverted to other ends. Steel capacity was extended with government help and the competitive position of individual companies was altered as a result.

The Iron and Steel Control allocated steel capacity to munitions needs, and galvanised sheet exports from Swansea, Port Talbot and Llanelly fell to below 7,000 tons in 1916 and under 2,000 tons in 1917. British galvanised sheet exports in 1918 were only 1 per cent. those of 1913.[1] When extensions to plant were begun, the national capacity in pig iron was increased by about one million tons to twelve million tons, and in steel from eight to twelve million tons. In this substantial programme forward-looking planning was notably absent, old locations receiving new capital, a marked contrast with the Second World War when planning for a radically different post-war world was active and little capacity extension was attempted. Apart from the long-term weakness of building up old locations, construction in the Great War was achieved at inflated capital cost and much of the equipment installed was to prove inferior.

During, or immediately after the war the fifteen open-hearth steelworks in South Wales were expanded by 250,000 ingot tons, or almost one-third. In 1916 John Summers received government financial assistance for a second melting shop at Hawarden Bridge and within eleven months had tapped their first steel from it. The cost was £900,000, of which two-thirds was allowed against taxation and the rest was paid off within five years out of the large profits made when the boom of war-time merged into the good trade of 1919 and 1920, with sheets at one point reaching £54 a ton. By 1920 Summers' annual sheet capacity was about 300,000 tons, little of which was at Staly-bridge, where the sheet mills closed finally in 1929. Aided by war-time profits, and striving to find both peace-time raw material supplies and an outlet for their extended steel capacity, Summers' were now ready to expand. [2]

At Normanby Park, John Lysaght also made substantial extensions. Mechanical ore working replaced hand winning. A fourth blast furnace, two new open-hearth furnaces and new soaking pits were installed. By 1918 the make was 131,000 ton ingots, by 1920 over 4,000 tons a week, more than 60 per cent. greater than in 1912, with further increase planned. [3] Meanwhile Frank Thomas's plans for integration at Redbourn were realised, though in a fashion which completely frustrated his grand designs. Asked to go ahead to meet the demand for munitions steel, Thomas at first refused, lacking permission to make the balanced extensions he wanted, that is, including tinplate mills. When he agreed, the Ministry of Munitions was said to have promised a contribution of some £1 million to the £2¼ million estimated as needed for new blast furnace plant, coke ovens and steel plant   Construction took longer than was expected, and production did not begin until the end of the summer of 1920, when the country was facing acute depression. Unlike Hawarden Bridge, Redbourn missed the post-war boom. The investment had spiralled to about £3 million, and, despite Sir John Simon's advocacy, the government refused to make any contribution, a decision which caused Frank Thomas to characterise its word as no better than that of the Kaiser. [4]

After the war-time expansion, steel firms frequently found it impossible to operate their new plant at a satisfactory level. Inferior equipment, inflated capital costs, high wages and rail charges by the mid-twenties at least 50 per cent above the pre-war level, with steel prices only about 30 per cent higher, embarrassed them still further.[5] They were tempted to buy semi-finished steel from overseas, especially as that would help them to head off foreign finished sheet in traditional British markets. Yet, in the changing competitive circumstances, British firms met some success in re-establishing themselves in foreign markets. At the end of the twenties, however, with the combination of the Great Depression and the growth of manufacture overseas, the market for galvanised sheet almost collapsed There were growing outlets for uncoated sheet, of much higher quality in chemical composition and finish, and, closely related to this, revolutionary new techniques of sheet manufacture were reported from the United States. A final factor was the emergence of a depressed areas problem in Britain, and of a maturing social conscience which was soon to demand that company decisions took account of social as well as merely of economic values There was a great difference between Wales in the middle and late twenties and that favoured country J. H. Jones had described to the British Association in 1912 and *The Times* had portrayed in the summer of 1917. As Jones saw it . . . 'poverty due to industrial changes is practically non-existent', and *The Times* concluded that, throughout the coalfield, there had never been such a . . . 'strenuous and prosperous time . . . It may be said that there is an entire absence of hardship and poverty in South Wales'.[6] Even in 1929 the average unemployment rate in Glamorgan was 21·3 and in Monmouth 22·5 per cent. This change was to be of great importance in future locational decision taking.

MARKETS FOR SHEET STEEL IN THE TWENTIES

Galvanised sheet remained easily the chief product of the sheet trade throughout the twenties, production in 1927 and 1928 exceeding even that of 1913 and in 1929 falling little below the output of that year. Early in the period output of other sheet products decreased relatively, but after 1926 began a small but noteworthy advance.[7] (Table 20)

TABLE 20

Production of finished steel sheet 1919–1929
(thousand tons)

	Galvanised Sheet	Uncoated Sheets thinner than $\frac{1}{8}''$	Output of Uncoated Sheets as per cent. of total
1919	280	333	54·3
1920	460	359	43·7
1923	689	511	42·5
1924	759	499	39·6
1925	847	518	37·8
1926	769	416	35·1
1927	858	572	40·0
1928	889	598	40·2
1929	843	595	41·3

Source: National Federation of Iron and Steel Manufacturers Statistics.

In 1927 90 per cent. and in 1929 84·4 per cent. of the galvanised sheet was exported, but the overseas market was more competitive than before the war. In evidence to the Ministry of Reconstruction, the Sheet Makers' Conference identified Germany and the United States as its two chief competitors, but argued that, with the benefit of preferential tariffs in the colonies, their competition in independent markets like those of South America could be met, even if sales there were sometimes made at a loss.[8] In the event, competition from established producers proved very severe, some Empire markets were soon shown to be by no means secure, and several foreign consuming countries introduced measures to build up their own manufacturing capacity. Rationalising their sales in reaction, Summers and Lysaghts agreed on a broad division of the markets. Summers took South America and India, Lysaghts Australia and New Zealand. Because of its close relation with galvanised sheet, in company organisation, in technology and still more in future development, parallel experience in the tinplate trade must also be considered.

United States tinplate capacity almost doubled during the First World War, and in galvanised sheet production also competition with Britain became keener.   In 1919 W. R. Lysaght observed that the Americans were monopolising the Canadian markets at prices £2 a ton lower than could be met by British mills, and six years later Henry Bond of Richard Thomas noted that in tinplate, whereas Britain had a 5 per cent. preferential tariff in Canada, the Americans had established export prices 5 per cent. below the home trade prices.[9]

Some countries established tariff duties which favoured black sheet for finishing within the country.   The Japanese duty on galvanised sheet was twice that on uncoated material in the late twenties and total imports of galvanised sheet, which had been 34,000 tons in 1913, were well under 2,000 tons a year in the late twenties.[10]   Chile and Argentina had similar policies, and British exports of galvanised sheet to the latter fell from 77,000 tons in 1924 to 9,400 tons in 1927.   In 1925 Summers, for whom the South American trade was critical, were thereby induced to construct a galvanising plant in Argentina.   This plant worked up black sheet sent from Hawarden Bridge and turned out 60,000 to 70,000 tons of galvanised sheet a year. Notwithstanding their agreement, Lysaghts also had an Argentine corrugating and galvanising plant.   Summers additionally had a substantial investment in Chilean galvanising.[11]

In the African parts of the Empire, in the smaller colonies scattered across the globe and to a smaller extent in India there was a growth of British trade as compared with 1913, but in Canada and Australia a decline (Table 21).   With the economic maturing of the bigger Commonwealth countries it was natural that they should wish to produce their own steel products, including tinplate and galvanised sheet.   Just before the war India imported 50,000 tons of tinplate a year, and in 1916, when Welsh supplies were difficult to procure, Tata decided to build tinplate mills capable of 30,000 tons.[12]   Production of galvanised sheet began there in 1924, but by 1929 was still only 17,600 tons, or some 6 per cent. of the imports from Britain.   In the next few years, however, British supplies to India fell sharply, there was a brief influx of Belgian and Luxemburg material, and home output steadily increased. By 1934 imports of British galvanised sheet were 29 per cent. less than India's own production.[13]

TABLE 21

Exports of galvanised sheet to Empire markets
1913, 1926, 1928 (thousand tons)

	1913	1926	1928
Union of South Africa	40	41	51
African colonies	17	26	40
India and Ceylon	244	288	284
New Zealand	23	23	23
Australia	104	87	73
Canada	32	6	12
Other British possessions	19	39	40

Source: *National Federation of Iron and Steel Manufacturers Statistics*

In Australia the retreat of British mills was even more spectacular. In 1913 two-thirds of Lysaghts' exports had been sold there, but early in the war they chose a site at Newcastle, New South Wales, near the one the Broken Hill Proprietary Company had acquired for a steelworks. In February 1918 it was announced that a galvanising plant would be laid down on the site, and in 1919, in sharp contrast with the mercantalist tones of W. R. Lysaght's *Economic Journal* article of 1903, Lysaghts observed, 'We have embarked on this scheme as the rising prices of raw materials and the immense increase in wages in this country, together with greatly enhanced freights, are rapidly undermining the advantage in the manufacture of galvanised iron hitherto held here.'[14] Sheet mills were also installed, helped by an Australian government subsidy, said to be about 40s. a ton, and in 1921 Lysaghts' Newcastle works rolled its first black sheet. By 1927 over 100,000 tons of galvanised sheet had been produced there, and in 1928 the mills were duplicated. 1928 imports were still 107,000 tons, but of this only 73,000 came from Britain. In 1930 the influx of foreign material at depression prices closed the works, but the Australian government then prohibited further imports of galvanised sheet, although at the same time it withdrew the bounty, then 63s. a ton. In return Lysaghts agreed not to increase the price of their galvanised sheet without government approval. By 1933 W. R. Lysaght himself wrote a concise epitaph on the Australian trade—'Australia, once our second-largest buyer, is now making and will continue to make all her requirements.'[15] Not surprisingly, it gradually became clear to British sheet makers that their future depended upon the cultivation of the home market.

TABLE 22

Production of finished steel sheets other than for galvanising or tinplate, 1920 (thousand tons)

South Wales and Monmouth	150
West Midlands	95
Scotland	55
North East	23
Sheffield	17
Other districts	17
Total	358

Source: *National Federation of Iron and Steel Manufacturers Statistics of the Iron and Steel Industries*

The home market for galvanised sheet grew substantially, although erratically, through the 1920s—consumption in 1928, the best year, being 90 per cent. greater than in 1913. Even so, in that year home consumption amounted to only 24 per cent. of the export tonnage and no foreseeable growth could replace the markets soon to be lost overseas. In the West Midlands, which remained second only to South Wales in the higher quality sheet lines, some established sheet-consuming industries were growing or adapting their products and new fabricating trades were emerging (Table 22). True, some traditional lines were declining, as with the trunk manufacturing business or general japanned ware, but the production of enamelled hollo-ware was growing, demand for baths, for instance, going up as standards of suburban housing improved. American and French items were important in the steel furniture business, but a domestic industry was developing. Rylands Directory listed 14 firms in the trade in 1922 but 27 in 1930, and between 1924 and 1930, while the value of output of firms making iron and steel trunks, suitcases, etc., and cash and deed boxes fell from £330,000 to £169,000, the value of metallic furniture for hospital and office use went up from £160,000 to £651,000. The domestic appliance industry, although still small, was using more sheet steel and beginning its shift from cast iron, in which the cost of both material and labour was considerably greater. Heavy sheet was in demand for railway rolling stock and silicon steel sheet for the growing electrical trades.[16] In tonnage, plain sheet consumption was increasingly influenced and then dominated by the needs of the motor industry.

The pre-war contacts of the motor firms with steel manufacture had been mostly with the quality steel firms of Sheffield, 15,000 to 20,000 tons of whose products they took each year. Retooling for peace-time production of motor plants which had been expanded in the war gave them a greatly increased vehicle-producing capacity—Wolseley, for instance, had extended five- or six-fold to 20,000 vehicles a year by 1919. The motor and component firms alike were already concentrated in the country's axial belt, and, as small outlying firms which had started car manufacture after the war fell in the hard times which began in 1921, and the bigger units turned to assembly-line methods, the West Midlands became still more decisively the focus of the trade. Statistics, admittedly crude, suggest that 43 per cent. of the labour force engaged in making and repairing motor vehicles, cycles and aircraft were in seven Midland counties in 1925. The industrial region from Wolverhampton to Coventry, Cowley, Trafford Park and Luton became the chief growth centres for high-grade uncoated sheet consumption as the motor industry demand continually increased.[17]

The motor firms produced many of their own pressings but other Midland engineers also entered the trade. Sankeys were important both in fabricating and in supplying steel sheet, but in 1920 were absorbed by Lysaghts whose sheet presumably thereafter came more freely to both the Bilston and Hadley Castle press shops. Baldwins concentrated their production of motor body sheet and of electrical grades at Midland rather than South Wales works. Local sheet production, however, could no longer supply regional demand and stockholders arose to supply the small consumer and to link the district with distant producers. 'Silver finished sheet' for motor bodies became prominent in their trade advertisements. One such firm, H. F. Spencer & Company, started at Deepfields, near Bilston, and when trade outgrew this works in 1928 opened the most extensive sheet steel warehouse in the Midlands in the premises in Eagle Street, Wolverhampton, which had been occupied long before by the Mitre Works of the Gospel Oak Galvanising Company. H. F. Spencer also became a subsidiary of the Ebbw Vale Steel, Iron and Coal Company. In the last years of the period in which the galvanised sheet trade completed its removal from the West Midlands the foundations of the dominance of the area in the consumption of light-grade uncoated sheet steel were firmly laid. In the same years the sheetmakers were sorely troubled and their ranks divided by the continuing influx of foreign semi-finished steel (Table 23).

TABLE 23

United Kingdom imports of some semi-finished steel products and of plates and sheet under $\frac{1}{8}''$ (thousand tons)

	1913	1920	1924
Blooms, Billets, Slabs	514	253	708
Sheet and Tinplate bars	345	36	380
Plates and Sheets	35	16	23

Source: Minutes of Evidence, *Balfour Commission* 1925 Sir W. Larke, Table 10

FOREIGN STEEL & TARIFF PROTECTION

By July, 1919, when the ex-works price of Welsh billets was £13 10s. 0d., American billets cost £12 in Liverpool or £12 15s. 0d. in the West Midlands. American competition, however, was still irregular and in 1920 the trade was little troubled. After that the traffic mounted, with Luxemburg, France and especially Belgium the leading suppliers.[18] By early 1925 imports of sheet and tinplate bar—mainly sheet, for tinplate makers preferred home material—were running at 500,000 tons a year.[19]

The rerollers on the whole benefited from this situation. Frederick Scarf made this clear in 1925 in evidence to the

Balfour Committee on behalf of the Steel Rerollers Association. The price difference between British and continental billets was then about 30s. a ton and the cost of sheet bars rolled from such billets was roughly one-third the selling price of the galvanised sheet.   Hence he concluded '. . . any interference with the right to purchase their semi-products in the cheapest possible market would have a disastrous effect on the Rerollers' trade'.[20] The leading rerollers therefore fought the bigger steel firms over 'protection' or 'safeguarding'.   Scarf pointed out that behind a tariff the integrated firm would not only charge a higher price for its semis but would also protect its own finishing mills from the competition of the reroller.   This view was supported by other rerollers right through to the time of protection in 1932.[21] It was foreseen that a tariff would either ruin the rerollers or force them to accept absorption by the bigger concerns. Already under free trade mergers and an accompanying fervour for rationalisation were tending to bring this about.   Burnells were associated with Pearson Knowles for a number of years until 1927, when the latter disposed of their controlling interest. More important, in 1917, when cut off from their foreign supplies of semi-finished steel, Wolverhampton Corrugated had exchanged shares with Summers and thereafter were always closely associated with their larger neighbour.   Yet for many rerollers linking with a steel producer was unattractive.

In most integrated iron and steel works plant was poor, technical integration inadequate and costs were high.   By 1924 only 86 blast furnaces out of 350 owned by firms contacted by the National Federation of Iron and Steel Manufacturers were mechanically charged, and the new Fuel Economy Committee of the National Federation found that cheap fuel in the past had provided no incentive for reduction in consumption.   Of the pig iron used in steel manufacture, 55 per cent. was still charged cold.[22]   Scarf argued that use of hot metal might reduce the cost of steel by as much as 8s. a ton.   This figure was disputed by Sir William Larke, perhaps ignoring that a hot-metal shop would increase output as well as lower conversion costs per heat.[23]   A further source of extra cost was the common practice of dispatching semi-finished steel for finishing in another works of a big concern.   In 1920, 58·1 per cent. of the British output of sheet bars and 23·8 per cent. of all the blooms, billets and slabs were dispatched from the works in which they were rolled [24] In 1927 David Macmillan, Braby's assistant general manager at the Eclipse Works, Glasgow, and Secretary of the Scottish Rerollers Association, suggested that British steelworks could not meet continental semi-finished steel prices because their pig iron to ingot conversion costs were 50 per cent. greater, ingot to billet rolling costs almost twice as high and they failed to employ blast furnace and coke oven gas. [25]

These figures on cost were subject to a good deal of error but there was evidence from the bigger steelmaking sheet firms that the general conclusions were correct, for even integrated companies frequently chose to buy their billets or bars. In 1919 Colvilles acquired the Gartcosh sheet mills of Smith and McLean, eight miles away from the Dalzell steelworks by rail, yet the Dalzell billet mill was idle for years in the mid-twenties while Gartcosh bought all its sheet bars. Two-thirds of the steel needed by British sheet firms could be supplied by associated steelworks by the mid-twenties, but at least half of this capacity had been closed down by the early weeks of 1925. [26] It was said that it paid firms to make steel only in so far as they could use their own mill scrap in the furnaces, but both in the steelworks and in the primary rolling mills this level of operation implied sacrifice of scale economies. In this connection, one large company had written to Sir William Larke, on the day of his evidence to the Balfour Commission, suggesting that, if they could operate at 90 per cent capacity, they could cut the price of sheet bars by as much as 15s. a ton. [27] (Figure 11)

THE FORTUNES OF THE BIGGER SHEET FIRMS

In all this discussion, and despite the temporary successes of the rerollers, the initiative lay with the big integrated companies. With protection they would reorganise and rebuild their plants and absorb the independent rolling mills. Colvilles in Scotland, Bolckow and Vaughan, Dorman Long and South Durham Steel and Iron on the North-East Coast were big firms with interests in sheet, but their main task in rationalisation clearly lay in their traditional heavy lines. The focus of attention, and the opportunities of laying a foundation for the

K

PRODUCERS OF SHEET, SHEET BAR
AND TINPLATE BAR, 1930

BLACK SHEET PRODUCERS   ●
SHEET BAR AND TINPLATE BAR PRODUCERS   □
INTEGRATED WORKS   ▪

SOURCE: RYLANDS DIRECTORY 1930

0 ┤┼┼┼┼ 40
    MILES

Figure 11.   At this time the industry was at its most widespread.   Nearr
to local producers of semi-finished steel as well as easy access to fore
material favoured South Wales.

competitive battles which might follow protection, still lay with Lysaghts, Summers and South Wales firms.

By the 1920s John Summers were the chief sheet steel makers in Britain. Nevertheless they appear to have been less successful in that decade than their near rivals, Lysaghts. National production of galvanised sheet in 1928 was a record 888,000 tons, but even after modernisation in the mid-twenties Hawarden Bridge produced only 262,000 tons, an output well below its capacity. Attempts to produce motor body sheet at this time were hopeless failures. In 1928 the nominal sheet capacity of John Lysaght's Orb Works was 200,000 tons and in 1929 their exports were 180,000 tons, 18 per cent of the British total [28] By 1930 Lysaghts claimed that they produced up to 90 per cent of the sheet steel used in British motor press shops. [29] Yet Lysaghts' position was in some ways weaker than that of Summers. In the first place their operations were smaller and were dispersed much more widely. It was difficult to decide whether Newport or Scunthorpe was the centre of their activity and future development was to be bedevilled by this doubt. Summers controlled Wolverhampton Corrugated's Ellesmere Port mills after 1917 and in 1920 acquired the integrated works of the Shelton Iron, Steel and Coal Company in order to ensure the iron supply for their extended steel capacity, but these plants were much less widely scattered and Hawarden Bridge without question was the fulcrum of the whole enterprise. Secondly, their advantage extended to company organisation as well as to location. After acquiring Sankeys in 1919, Lysaghts themselves in 1920 were taken over by the growing empire of Guest, Keen and Nettlefolds. The G.K.N. Board seem never to have hindered progress at Lysaghts, and indeed, while W. R. Lysaght remained chairman, initiative remained firmly in family hands, but in the forward thinking of the wider group, although sheet steel manufacture was a bright section in the often dismal steel side, it was merely one of a multitude of manufacturing activities. Summers were the initiators not the objects of take-over bids or mergers and retained complete responsibility for their own destinies. Finally Lysaghts' very success in electrical sheet, and in the manufacture of deep drawing qualities for the press shops was paradoxically a factor in their undoing. In the thirties they continued to make adjustments to their technology while for others revolution proved to be essential. A few other threads in that revolutionary situation were already being spun.

RICHARD THOMAS & COMPANY, EBBW VALE AND SOUTH WALES IN THE TWENTIES

By 1928 there were 386 sheet mills in Britain of which 159 were in South Wales and Monmouthshire. Equally significant for the future of flat-rolled products, almost the whole of the tinplate trade was there too. In sheet capacity no South Wales firm could match Lysaghts, but in combined sheet and tinplate tonnage there were other big concerns. Baldwins had a sheet capacity of 100,000 tons a year at Panteg and a melting shop there to back it up, besides a considerable interest in tinplate. Gilbertsons at Pontardawe and Partridge Jones of Pontymister and Pontnewynydd combined steel, tinplate and sheet production, and in 1928 Llanelly Steel added to its new bar mill a sheet plant said to be among the most efficient in Britain.[30] All these firms were important in further development, but key roles were also played by the old tinplate firm of Richard Thomas & Company and by a traditional rail and semi-finished steel producer, the Ebbw Vale Steel, Iron and Coal Company.

Until the First World War, Richard Thomas controlled only one steelworks, at Llanelly. In 1917 their chairman, Richard Beaumont Thomas, died and, as the firm clearly needed a vigorous head to stem its losses, Frank Thomas was invited to take his place and agreed provided his own works at Cwmfelin and Redbourn were included. After 1920 Redbourn began to ship tin and sheet bars to South Wales, but quickly proved a drag on the group. Apart from a very good open-hearth plant, it had been badly equipped and was loaded with heavy standing charges. Its work force was dispirited and management indifferent, even though some of its general managers were paid at exorbitant rates in the hope that they would achieve a breakthrough. In contrast with Lysaghts' experience, rail charges to South Wales were high and Henry Bond, chairman of the group after 1926, observed that Lincolnshire steel could not be sent to South Wales at competitive prices.[31]   From 1924 to

1928 Redbourn was idle, costing Richard Thomas £30,000 a year to maintain. Shortly before the closure, there had entered the Richard Thomas organisation the restless genius of William Firth.

Firth began a tinplate merchant business in London early in the century but joined the Grovesend Steel and Tinplate Company in 1907, under the managing directorship of Henry Folland. The two men improved the tinplate and steel works at Gorseinon and in 1910–1911 added six new tinplate mills to the existing four. By 1913 acquisition was taking Grovesend into the sheet and galvanising business in addition to tinplate. Between the spring of 1919 and the summer of 1923 seven works were acquired, including two more cold-metal steelworks— Bryngwyn and Dyffryn—and the tinplate mills increased from 30 to 54. Unlike Richard Thomas, Grovesend had an important interest in sheet, with over 20 mills.[32] Redbourn was now losing money rapidly—£20,000 in the financial year 1922–1923 —and Richard Thomas was eagerly seeking an outlet for its steel. In 1919 Firth had proposed a central selling agency for tinplate, which clearly could best operate with few but larger firms. A market for Redbourn and rationalisation of the sales structure were two powerful arguments with which Firth cajoled Frank Thomas when in the spring of 1923 he and Folland joined Mr. and Mrs. Thomas in their Great Western compartment on a journey from Paddington to Swansea, apparently by chance, in fact contrived by the Grovesend directors [33] In October the merger was announced. Combined the two companies controlled 40 to 50 per cent of the mills in the tinplate trade and an annual capacity of about 445,000 tons tinplate. Their combined sheet capacity from 24 mills was about 120,000 tons a year and their steel ingot capacity some 780,000 tons.[34] William Firth now became a director of Richard Thomas and early in 1926, when Thomas was succeeded as chairman by Henry Bond, Firth became vice-chairman. Five years later he was in command of the group, and his commercial drive, ambitions and very considerable, though technically untrained, industrial vision then had full rein.

Ebbw Vale, once an important supplier of semi-finished steel to Midland and South Wales works, had rolled black sheet and galvanised since 1913. Its six sheet mills were among the first

in Britain to be electrically driven—twelve years before
Summers first converted from steam.   By 1920, on average
gauges, Ebbw Vale could roll 600 tons a week and ranked
among the smaller sheet makers.[35]   At the end of the Great
War extensions to the furnaces, steelworks and mills increased
the overall capacity of the works by about 50 per cent.[36]   Then,
like Richard Thomas, but unlike Lysaghts, Ebbw Vale ran into
trouble in bulk rail movements from eastern England.   The
company had proposed to carry 20,000 tons of Northampton
Sand ore weekly from Irthlingborough 150 miles to Ebbw Vale
in specially built 20-ton hopper wagons, but, as Frederick Mills
put it, the railway companies proposed to charge this traffic the
same rate per ton as they would a four-ton load on a general
goods train once in three months.[37]

Mills, the driving force behind these developments at Ebbw
Vale, was a man of considerable vision, who possessed strong
local loyalties combined with a certain ruthlessness.   More
obvious to the outsider, he was given to a dangerous tendency
to exaggeration.[38]   In July, 1920, at a dinner to celebrate the
completion of the blast furnace extensions, he asserted that no
firm in the country, in Europe or in the world stood in the
position of Ebbw Vale at that time.   'You are on the eve of
making the cheapest steel in the world, depend upon it.   The
firm or firms that can do that in this country will have the
world's markets in the hollow of their hands.'[39]   Substantial
profits were indeed made in 1923 and 1924, apparently from
both steel and coal operations, but no dividends were paid on
ordinary shares after 1921.   In 1925, when other firms closed
their steel plants in order to run on European semi-finished
steel, Ebbw Vale profits slipped sharply and the steel division
performed at a loss, but the works were kept in operation for
social reasons.   As Mills told the annual meeting '. . . your
directors reviewed the position with grave thought, and decided
that it was better for the company, for our work people and for
the district to work at a known loss than to close down'.[40]
However, the open-hearth plant was idle from April 1925 to
March, 1928.   In June, 1928, rejecting the Balfour Committee's
conclusions on steel as too gloomy, Mills again assured his
shareholders of a prosperous long-term outlook.   With only 'a
modest outlay' the works would be completely modern and

efficient.   'In the days before the war,' he claimed, 'Ebbw Vale made the cheapest steel in England; it will do so again, and at no distant date.'[41]   In the latter part of 1928 the plant was again fully at work and in June, 1929, it was announced that arrangements were being made for the modernisation of the iron and steel departments over the next three or four years.[42] A few weeks later continental prices dropped sharply, and Ebbw Vale faced a loss of almost 30s. per ton of steel.   At the end of September the work force of almost 4,000 was given one week's notice.   Two small blast furnaces remained at work for a while and the sheet mills continued rolling foreign bars.[43]   A few weeks later Mills left for a visit to American steel plants and, chastened, told the American Iron and Steel Institute, 'I confess to you that whilst I am taking what I call a busman's holiday I have come to the United States of America to find out how to make steel at a profit.'[44]   A month later, returning home on the *s.s. Berengaria*, Mills learned that the Ebbw Vale board of directors had replaced him as chairman by Sir John Beynon, his deputy.[45]   On his voyage Mills wrote notes on his impressions of American works and the lessons they provided for Ebbw Vale.   In the light of these he suggested four essentials in a reconstruction scheme—the completion of the ore development at Irthlingborough, reorganisation of coal carriage, alterations to the Bessemer plant and, finally, the construction of a continuous strip mill.[46]   All his other visions had faded, and no observer of the desolation of idle works at the head of the Ebbw valley in the early thirties could have believed that the last of these suggestions would be an exception.

REFERENCES

1   *Report on Wales* 1919 p. 19 by U.S. Bureau of Foreign and Domestic Commerce.   Supplement to Commercial Reports. G. H. M. Farley in *Sheet Metal Industries* June 1939, pp. 754–756.
2   R. F. Summers, *The Birth and Growth of the Firm of John Summers* 1945.
3   *Journal of the Iron and Steel Institute* 1920, 1. p. 73.
4   On these aspects of the Redbourn development I am indebted to the recollections of Hugh T. Thomas.
5   Minutes of Evidence, *Committee on Industry and Trade* (Balfour Committee) 1924–1927, Vol. 1.   Evidence of Sir William Larke, February 1925.   *Iron and Coal Trade Review* 29th May, 1925, p. 897.

6 J. H. Jones, Dumping and the Tinplate Industry. *Economic Journal* 23, 1913, p. 182. *Times Trade Supplement* September 1917, p. 126.
7 G. H. M. Farley, *op. cit.*
8 Ministry of Reconstruction, *Report of Committee on Trusts*, cd. 9236, 1919, p. 7.
9 *Balfour Committee*, Minutes of Evidence 2, p. 915.
10 National Federation of Iron and Steel Manufacturers, *Annual Statistical Report Tariff Section* 1929.
11 R. F. Summers 1945, p. 10. *The Times* 29 June 1932, p. 20.
12 *American Iron and Steel Institute, Yearbook* 1921, p. 245, 1924, p. 308 *et seq.* F. L. Estep, 'The Manufacture of Tinplate in India'.
13 National Federation of Iron and Steel Manufacturers, *Statistics.*
14 *Iron and Coal Trades Review* 15 February 1918, p. 187.
15 *Engineer* 9 January, 1920 p. 49. *Sheet Metal Industries* February 1928, p. 269, November 1930, p. 538. *Journal of the Iron and Steel Institute* 1933, 1, p. 44 Presidential Address May 1933.
16 *Sheet Metal Industries* November 1928, p. 272, February 1929, p. 404. *Rylands Directory* (various) Board of Trade. *Fourth Census of Production* Preliminary Report 16. Hardware Holloware etc.
17 *Birmingham Post* 28 February 1919. G. C. Allen 'The British Motor Industry', *London and Cambridge Economic Service. Special Memorandum* 18 June 1926, p. 4.
18 *Engineer* 27 July 1919, p. 95.
19 Sir W. Larke, *op. cit.*, p. 379.
20 F. Scarf, *op. cit.*, p. 84.
21 See A. I. Parkes (Birmingham Corrugated) *The Times* 3 December 1931, Braby's, Burnell and Melingriffith Co. (tinplate) *The Times* 13 April 1932. Evidence of Sir W. Larke.
22 *Balfour Committee*, pp. 361, 383, 397. See also W. A. Bone, *Coal and its Scientific Uses* 1919 passim. T. P. Colclough in discussions on 'Fuel Control in the Iron and Steel Industry', *Journal of the Institute of Fuel* 4, 1931.
23 *Balfour Committee*, pp. 85, 383.
24 National Federation of Iron and Steel Manufacturers, *Statistics of the Iron and Steel Industries* 1920–1921. 1922 Table 24.
25 *Times* 15 October 1927, p. 14.
26 Sir W. Larke, *op. cit.*, p. 379.
27 *ibid.*, p. 383.
28 P. J. Summers in conversation and correspondence. A. Reid, *Continuous Venture* 1948, p. 41. *The Lysaght Century* p. 29. W. R. Lysaght in *Journal of the Iron and Steel Institute* 1933, 1.
29 D. C. Lysaght in discussion of paper by R. Whitfield, *Journal of the Iron and Steel Institute* 1930, 1, p. 164.
30 *Sheet Metal Industries*, May 1928, p. 17.

31 Richard Thomas and Company General Meeting, *Times* 22 December, 1927 and conversation with those with experience of Redbourn in the twenties.

32 G. H. Brooke, *Monograph on the Tinplate Works of Great Britain* 1932, pp. 71–72.   *Iron and Coal Trades Review* 8 September 1911, p. 366.   W. J. Walters, *The Reconstruction of the iron and steel and tinplate industry in South Wales since the war.*   Unpublished M.A. thesis, University of Wales 1928, p. 40.   E. E. Watkin, *The Development of the South Wales Tinplate Industry with special reference to 1919–1939.*   Unpublished thesis 1948, pp. 156–157.

33 I am indebted to H. T. Thomas for this information about his father.

34 *Engineer* 12 October 1923, p. 407.

35 *A Souvenir of the Visit of the Iron and Steel Institute to Ebbw Vale* September 1920, p. 20.   *Ebbw Vale Works Magazine* 2, No. 6 March 1923.   *Iron and Coal Trades Review* 25 December 1925, p. 1080.

36 *Times Trade Supplement* 2nd August 1919, p. 540.

37 *Times Trade Supplement* 31 July 1920, p. vii.

38 *Iron and Coal Trades Review* 30 January 1914, p. 177.

39 *Iron and Coal Trades Review* 9 July 1920, p. 57.

40 *Economist* 4 July 1925, p. 30.

41 *Times* 26 June 1928, p. 24.

42 *Economist* 4 January 1930, pp. 30–31.

43 *Iron and Coal Trades Review* 27 September 1929, p. 494.   *Economist* 28 September 1929.   *Ebbw Vale Works Magazine* December 1929, pp. 20–21.

44 *American Iron and Steel Institute Yearbook* 1929, p. 450.

45 *Economist* 11 January 1930, p. 81, 12 July 1930, p. 86.

46 I am indebted to E. Cross of Ebbw Vale for the opportunity to see and to discuss Sir Frederick Mill's recommendations of autumn 1929.

PART III

NEW MARKETS & THE TRANSFORMATION OF THE SHEET STEEL INDUSTRY

CHAPTER 9

Product Development & Technical and Economic change, 1920-1935

Although, throughout the twenties, the output of uncoated sheet was only about one-quarter of the total sheet output, major technical changes in the manufacturing processes were begun then. While the galvanised iron trade fell very sharply from 1929 to 1930 and then trended generally downward through the thirties, demand for other types of sheet declined much less in the depths of the Great Depression and as early as 1934 had risen to new record levels. By 1935 64·5 per cent. of a smaller total sheet production consisted of uncoated sheet. New outlets helped to reshape not only the techniques but also the economic structure and location of the trade. Although Britain had pioneered in previous phases of development this role had now passed to the United States. In the changing pattern of demand and in technical adjustments Britain followed on behind.

Expansion of electricity supply, especially after the Electricity (Supply) Act of 1926, more than doubled within eight years. Increased quantities of silicon steel sheet were called for, and the Lysaght-Sankey group continued to dominate, making, at one stage in the 1930s, about 90 per cent. of the national output. Summers entered the trade then, only to leave it some years later, apparently by agreement with Lysaghts, and Baldwins, which began to make silicon sheet under the guidance of Captain Martin, previously with Sankeys, was also not a very large producer. Compared with carbon steel sheet electrical grades were unimportant in tonnage, but value was high. Steel of very high quality was required but no basic changes in the sheet industry stemmed from this, although the experience of Lysaghts with heat treatment of silicon sheet greatly helped them to play a leading role in autobody sheet manufacture. (Figure 12)

Figure 12.   The 'axial belt' was pre-eminent in electrical engineerin

The new consumer durable trades required metal possessing properties never previously demanded of material for galvanising and corrugating.   Makers of office furniture or of household appliances needed sheet which could be stamped into right angles without causing an unsightly 'orange peel' effect along the bend.   Oil drums and water-tanks also required sheet able to stand exacting shaping operations,[1] but it was the motor industry which, in Britain as in the United States, provided the chief incentive to change.

The earliest motor bodies had been made by carriage builders exactly as for horse-drawn vehicles—a wooden frame covered with wooden panels.   Later, to provide a better base for painting, metal sheets were tacked over the wooden panels, in Britain aluminium sheets being used as well as steel ones for this purpose.   Next came the 'composite' pattern, sheet-metal panels tacked directly on to the wooden frame.   It always proved difficult to maintain tight joints in this kind of construction—both between the frame and its metal cover and within the frame itself.   Sheetmakers supplied the carriage works at this stage, and, as shaping operations did not yet require any drastic deformation of the sheet, specifications were not particularly exacting.   The shaped parts were frequently prepared by hand beating, the low productivity being of little account when motor cars were customer built and the customers were a small and select group.   In the United States, however, automobile production soon began to change to a mass supply industry, sales rising from 25,000 units in 1905 to 187,000 by 1910 and to 970,000 in 1915.   Attention accordingly shifted to a less laborious method of body production, to stamped panels initially and then even to body shells pressed from a single wide sheet.   In its extreme form the single body shell proved an economically impracticable ideal, but by 1915 the E. G. Budd Corporation of Philadelphia had made the prototype all-steel body and thereafter employed much larger panels than the other American body firms, which had to weld smaller sheets together.   By 1920 mass production of all-steel bodies was under way, and as the closed-in automobile became more popular so quick-action presses demanded better performance from the steel sheet they used.[2]

American output of black sheet in 1922 was 3·2 million tons

Of this 37·7 per cent went to the motor trade, which in that year year produced 3·7 million passenger cars alone.   British output of cars, taxis and commercial vehicles in that year was only 4·5 per cent. that of private cars alone in the United States. Production, however, grew substantially from 73,000 units in 1922 to 239,000 in 1929, sufficient to justify the leaders in introducing assembly-line methods, which in turn helped to eliminate the smaller firms and, on the body supply side, justified more productive, higher capitalised operation.   A bottleneck in the new production flow lines was low productivity in the shaping of body parts and in the paintshops.   In Britain demand became prominent for high-surface quality in sheet for painting operations rather earlier than for deep-drawing properties.

Even in the United States car-body finishing until the early twenties was a most laborious process.   The body was smoothed by sandpaper and infilling—even including the use of putty— and any remaining imperfections, and the patches too, were buried beneath coats of paint and varnish, sometimes totalling as many as sixteen.   It was even said that some of the body makers used common black sheets, hiding beneath this cover both their original surface blemishes and those which reflected their inadequacy for the forming operation.   A body took up to thirty days to finish so that painting required expensive storage facilities as well as a large and skilled labour force.[3] The conditions of manufacture changed greatly in 1923 when Du Pont introduced their nitro-cellulose lacquer 'Duco', which was applied by spray by a less skilled worker, and dried quickly. The most durable finishes in fact were those in which undercoats were kept to a minimum.   In England Ford's of Manchester introduced the new painting methods, which demanded sheet steel of a new high-quality finish—the silver finishes which producers and stockholders were soon advertising.   Paradoxically, the makers of the cheapest cars bought the best sheets, for rapid throughput was essential to them, whereas the quality producers, with smaller output, could still cover the cost of their laborious painting operations by higher prices.[4]

British bodies were still made of not very severely shaped sheets so that angular lines dominated vehicle design through most of the twenties.   However, by 1923–1924, as firms adopted flow-line assembly methods, body supply became a potential bottleneck, and in 1925 William Morris went to the United States to investigate the all-steel body.   In 1926 the Pressed Steel Company of Great Britain was established at Cowley with sponsorship and, until 1930, some financial interest from Morris but controlled by the Budd Corporation.[5]   Vauxhall, Austin, Singer, as well as Ford at Trafford Park, had their own important body shops, but the introduction of the quick-action power press at Cowley, involving both a very large capital outlay and productive capacity, heralded the emergence of other specialised body makers.   In 1929–1930 the Birmingham works of Fisher and Ludlow were thoroughly reconstructed and new heavy presses for panels and complete bodies were installed, and when the Dagenham works was building Briggs Bodies Ltd., another offshoot from an American enterprise, installed similar equipment beside the motor works on the Dagenham Industrial Estate.[6]   Each of these new works was market oriented, near the motor manufacturers, the source of their large tonnages of sheet steel exercising no noticeable influence over their location (Figure 13),   Some press shops, especially those of Pressed Steel, supplied other motor producing areas besides those in which they were located.   Before the Second World War both Pressed Steel and Fisher and Ludlow had also entered the domestic appliance trade with refrigerators and washing machines respectively.

By requiring new physical properties, notably of surface finish and of deep-drawing qualities, the new lines of consumption modified and then revolutionised the technology of the steel sheet industry.   One must consider some aspects of this technical change in a little detail for the requirements were complex and exacting and not all the firms proved equally able to stand the pace.   As one participant in South Wales put it '. . . it was a gradual process, alterations being made in the various plants within the limits which the various firms could afford.   This meant that there were quite substantial differences in methods . . . every plant differed in its method to make as good a sheet as the equipment available would permit.'[7]

L

THE STEEL SHEET INDUSTRY 1930
IN RELATION TO THE AUTOMOBILE INDUSTRY

PLANTS PRODUCING COLD-ROLLED   O
CLOSE-ANNEALLED SHEET
PRESSED STEEL BODY SHOPS   △
PRIVATE CAR MAKERS   ●

SOURCE: RYLANDS DIRECTORY 1930

Figure 13. The West Midlands and South East contained the m
consumers of sheet for the expanding motor business.   Output of the h
qualities of sheet which this required was concentrated in South Wale

TECHNICAL ADVANCE
IN SHEET STEEL PRODUCTION

Care was essential in rolling and heat treatment, but a necessary prerequisite was good steel, which from the start biased the struggle in favour of sheet firms which had their own melting shop. For black sheet for galvanising, and even in tinplate production, a certain stiffness in the sheet was an advantage, and moderate phosphorus and nitrogen levels were not troublesome. For deep-drawing sheet it was necessary to reduce these elements and the silicon content considerably, and have carbon at approximately 0·15 per cent. Slag had to be carefully excluded in tapping the open-hearth furnace. The most suitable steel was of 'rimming' quality, that is where the gases which segregate during the cooling of the ingot are confined to the centre, leaving an outer rim of pure metal, so that when the ingot is rolled down the interior blow holes weld satisfactorily.[8] This requirement demanded a plant capable of casting and handling large ingots for with small ones the gas blow holes are too near the surface and therefore open in the soaking pit and scar the slab or sheet bar with surface defects. Steel users sometimes criticised the quality of steel British sheet-makers employed. J. C. Arrowsmith of Pressed Steel commented on the lack of homogeneity and on the need for more research into steel quality.[9] Some firms, however, went to extreme lengths to ensure good-quality steel. Care was necessary also in the rolling and selection of sheet bars. 'Autobody quality' bars were rolled from selected casts and pickled to remove as much as possible of the scale that had been rolled into their surface layers in the bar mills. Rolling each sheet from a separate bar, it was difficult to ensure uniformity of quality. The most critical stages of production involved the sheet-mill operations and heat treatment.

In the sheet mill the most serious problem in improving quality was that of reconciling a range of new requirements—high-quality surface finish, drawability, close and regular tolerances in gauge and weight. Demands for each of these could be satisfied but to meet them all was much more difficult. Attainment of a quality finish might alter the physical structure of the sheet so that the press shops were faced with a high scrap rate. The rolling of extra-wide sheets for larger body parts risked excessive variation in gauge and grain structure from one part to another so that again the material would not behave uniformly in the press. To this puzzle of conflicting properties the firms reacted in various ways, modifying and replacing their mills, introducing new practices, changing methods of heat treatment, and in all this limited by their equipment, their capital resources, technical expertise and enterprise. In this period, especially, these different reactions are significant to the student of industrial location, helping to determine which firms survived as important producers and, of the survivors, which became so fully committed to one method that their initiative was severely restricted when a better way was found. On the other hand it must be remembered that there was no mechanistic prescription for success or cause of failure attributable simply to technology. Timing was also important, and the critical decisions were taken throughout not by plant engineers or as advised by consultants but in boardrooms and in the office of the chairman, and then not always for strictly commercial reasons. This decision-taking process will be further analysed later. The practical problems of the sheet firms can be examined under the heads of gauge, surface finish and physical properties and the associated heat treatment.

Rapid cooling made it impossible to roll sheets thinner than about 1/10th inch, or 12g, singly on a 2-high mill, the standard plant in the early twentieth century. It was therefore universal practice to roll thin sheets in packs, several being piled one above the other. Even so, with the inevitable spring of the rolls, gauge often varied substantially over the surface of the sheet, which caused the press shops considerable trouble. The new mechanised mills, using a 3-high roughing stand and 2-high finishing stands, which were installed by a few more enterprising firms in the early thirties, were less subject to this variation than the old handmills, but even with them the required precision in gauge was difficult to attain. When cold rolling in 4-high mills became more common, gauge was kept more uniform, for the rolls retained their shape better at lower temperatures and the back-up rolls reduced spring.

Responses to the demand for better surface finish varied. In pack rolling, a thin layer of oxide was left on the surface of each sheet after the pack had been opened leaf by leaf by the mill worker before rolling to final gauge, and this enabled the sheets to be separated. Even so, some welding together did occur, leaving the interior sheets rough-surfaced. The smoother outer surfaces of the pack could be spoiled by scale adhering to the rolls. The remedies reduced mill output and profit margins and still did not completely solve the problem. Efforts to keep the rolls in good condition often involved rubbing them down every hour or so and even polishing them. Some works had collars turned on their rolls so that the surfaces could be kept apart but it was then difficult to roll certain specifications. After pickling to remove sheet bar scale the packs also were pickled after the first rolling—'mould pickling' —and later, before heat treatment and cold rolling, the sheet was pickled again. One method to improve surface quality was 'loose pack' rolling: if the rolls were not fully screwed down deformation of the packs was less, and roll surfaces were cooler and less liable to damage. The American technique of loose pack rolling involved dipping the sheets into a bath of hot water containing charcoal in suspension, a film of which, deposited on their surface, lessened sticking between sheets in the final rolling and gave a superior finish. Lysaght's found that they could never be sure of an even cover of charcoal and that blobs of material from the bath could spoil the finish. They discovered that sheets at barely a dull red heat when taken from the mill furnaces were below the temperature for sticking and a very smoky atmosphere in the furnace provided an alternative film to that of the charcoal dip. Eventually new cold rolling mills with lower temperatures and absence of oxide and scale produced the desired silver finishes, but raised new problems in the physical properties of the material.

Annealing—heating to a high temperature followed by slow cooling to air temperature—had long been standard practice to remove rolling strains and improve sheet ductility, but the treatment became gradually more elaborate. The earliest practice had been simply cooling on the mill floor but, as small grain size became recognised as necessary to good surface finish, so close or box annealing, the furnace treatment of sheets stacked on a bogie under a steel cover, was introduced. Still sheets frequently 'pulled coarse' in the press and quality differed from

one sheet to another.   The normalising furnace introduced at
Vandergrift, Pennsylvania, in the First World War, seemed a
solution.   A fair quality sheet resulted but grain size was at
first too small, and the very high temperatures employed spoiled
surface finish, until long tunnel-like furnaces were built for continuous normalising.   Lysaghts installed normalising furnaces
early in the thirties for their deep drawing grades, but retained
older methods of heat treatment for other grades for these still
gave a superior finish.   By the end of 1931 half the motor body
sheet made in Britain was normalised.   These sheets still
proved 'stiff' in working, which was overcome by box annealing
hot rolled sheets after normalising.   The increased employment
of cold reduction in the thirties brought new problems of hard-
ness and stiffness and for these sheets box annealing became
commoner than normalising.   Cold rolling and box annealing
gave a much smaller grain size and a better surface finish than
normalising a hot rolled sheet, in short, a smooth, 'tight'
surfaced, ductile sheet, suitable for deep pressing.[10]

All these changes involved enterprise and capital expenditure.
The bigger firms kept abreast of recent American advances—
for instance, to the relatively small sheet plant of the Sharon
Steel Hoop Company in Youngstown, Ohio, two visits were
made in the twenties by representatives of Lysaghts, Smith and
McLean, and South Durham Steel and Iron Company and at
least one from Dorman Long, Samuel Fox, Briton Ferry,
G.K.N. and Braby.[11]   The smaller firms inevitably fell behind,
for even if they were aware of the progress in the United States
they could not finance such changes in their own plants.

THE REACTIONS OF BRITISH SHEETMAKERS
TO THE NEW DEMANDS

Certain basic desirables for successful operation under the
new, more exacting sheet trading conditions began to weed out
some concerns as unsuitable.   For instance, minimum employment of bought scrap with its possible 'dirtiness' from 'tramp'
elements which reduced ductility was very important.   This
placed cold metal melting shops at a disadvantage.   Lysaghts
used little or no bought scrap at Normanby Park and concentrated attention on improved steel quality.   To make bars

suitable for deep drawing sheet from high phosphorous Frodingham ore they introduced a complex system of grading of steel casts, selecting only the best for the more exacting specifications. The heavy core of the ingot was used and the top and bottom rolled only for lower-grade jobs. This made the best of an inferior but cheap iron. Lysaghts used practically no foreign ore at this time for, although this would have given better results, the product would have been much more expensive.[12]

Lacking hot metal and technical staff on the scale of Lysaghts, the independent South Wales works were substantially handicapped. The steel they bought from local works, though suitable for tinplate or galvanised sheet, was too poor for sheet of extra deep drawing quality. The ingots produced at the Siemens steel works were too small for rimming steel, and their cranage was inadequate for bigger ingots without a wholesale reconstruction of the buildings. This their small output did not justify, and consequently, although some of them advertised motor body sheet, many Welsh mills could supply only intermediate grades Brymbo experiments with rimming steel, some of which was rolled down at Newport, were similarly disappointing for their ingots were only about one-fifth the size of those at Normanby Park.[13] Hawarden Bridge could produce large ingots but lacked hot metal, used bought scrap, and found both pig iron and steel from Shelton too poor for high-grade sheet manufacture.

A further necessity for quality sheet was care in rolling, and here Lysaghts' established wider interests, including the rolling of electrical grades, served them well. Baldwins by the early 1930s had some 3-high German mechanised mills and a rather indifferent cluster mill for cold rolling at their Midland works. From these they supplied their share of the motor body sheet market. Reluctantly, Henry Summers was persuaded in the late twenties of the necessity to break into new markets even though galvanised sheet sales was still quite buoyant Experiments with motor body sheet were first made in the Top Yard mill at Hawarden Bridge. The results were hopeless and remained so for some time. In 1928, by agreement with the American Rolling Mill Company, a party of American millmen, led by Mr Hoover, came over to try to produce high-

grade sheet in the newer Marsh mills.   The Hawarden Bridge
melting shops could not meet the steel specifications, and
American know-how proved unable to overcome the deficiency
in the raw material, so that there was little success until 1933–
1934.   Then, however, Summers began to roll their 'special
grade' sheet, and thereafter kept close contact through personal
visits with the needs of the body press shops.[14]   At Ebbw Vale,
under the direction of A. Huxley, the sheet mills turned out
sheet of acceptable surface finish though probably less good in
physical properties.[15]

Additionally to their care in ingot production and selection,
Lysaghts were extraordinarily careful in rolling and processing,
which, as they still employed many millmen they had brought
from Wolverhampton, may to some extent be regarded as a
latter-day Staffordshire triumph.   They overcame the disadvantage of lack of a direct contact between the steelworks
and bar mills on the one hand and the sheet mills on the other
by a very complete system of exchange of data.   Contact was
close at the other end of the line also, E. C. Lysaght visiting
Cowley once or twice every month and often spending days in
the presses observing the performance of Lysaght sheet or of
sample batches.[16]   In 1926, when Charles Hook of the
American Rolling Mill Company made scathing remarks
about European sheet, A. T. Enlow of the Dominion Sheet
Metal Corporation of Hamilton, Ontario, defended Lysaghts'
practice at Newport.   'I have never seen a mill anywhere
which approximates this in cleanliness, orderliness and the
extreme care which is used to keep the products up to the
highest possible mark.'[17]   Some found, however, that the mill
equipment had certainly not kept pace with American practice,
and for all their success Lysaghts seem to have neglected basic
research.   Until 1929, for instance, no microscopic work was
done at Newport.   Improvisation, often brilliant, was the key
to their success: eventually it contributed to their failure.

Both for those who reacted vigorously to the challenge and
opportunities of the late 1920s and early 1930s and for those
who held back there was a much more testing time to come.
News of completely new American processes of sheet manufacture filtered across the Atlantic and shook the confidence of
even the biggest and most successful sheetmakers.   For most of

the others the scale of thinking the new developments demanded was far beyond their horizons and they never grappled constructively with the possibilities they opened up.

THE STRIP MILL

The idea of continuous rolling, where several stands are placed in line and the piece being rolled is in at least two stands at one time, had long fascinated rolling mill engineers.[18]   For billets, with standardisation possible, and for bars and rods where, additionally, rapid processing was desirable, continuous rolling had been achieved by 1900.   In Britain, with consumption growing relatively slowly, progress was slower than in the United States.   In sheet manufacture formidable technical problems had to be solved before the labour intensive, to-and-fro rolling and passing operations of the pull-over hand mill could be replaced by the progressive reduction to gauge in a continuous forward movement through successive mill stands. The shaping of roll contours and the co-ordination of roll speeds in the stands of the mill train as the piece became thinner and moved at increasing speed were the two chief difficulties.   They existed for other products, but for the precision rolling of such a damageable product as thin steel sheet were especially serious.[19]

The approach to the continuous strip/sheet mill was through the semi-continuous mill in which, although there was a steady movement and high output, the piece was not in two stands at once.[20]   A semi-continuous unit was put down at Teplitz in Bohemia in 1892 but inadequacies in contemporary technology ensured its failure and it was abandoned fifteen years later.   At this time American conditions were becoming favourable for new attempts.   As James Cox reported after participating in the Moseley Industrial Commission, 'Throughout the States there are universal evidences of having entered upon a new era in the demand for iron and steel for purposes hitherto undreamed of,'[21] and in this expanding market there developed still further the already distinctive American attitude to plant and to pioneering.   There was more readiness to scrap existing plant when better became available.   This in turn made business for the plant engineering firms and stimulated further improvements.   The first American attempt to improve sheet rolling, however, came from within the steel industry and started with attempts to link and improve existing 2-high sheet mills.

Using ordinary sheet bars and eight stands in tandem, C. W. Bray began experiments at the Monongahela Works of the American Sheet and Tinplate Company in 1902, and from 1905 to 1910 with nine stands at the company's works at Mercer in north-western Pennsylvania. The two attempts differed in detail, but in both labour savings over old methods were more than offset by higher costs for rolls and losses in seconds and in scrap. The central problem of co-ordinating successive mill speeds was not tackled for the mill was not continuous.[22]   By the First World War John B. Tytus of the American Rolling Mill Company was experimenting, and after the brief post-war boom Tytus' experiments were resumed and pushed on with remarkable tenacity in the newly acquired works at Ashland, Kentucky. By January, 1924, a tandem mill there was rolling single sheets by a continuous process. Costs of production were considerably lower even than in the improved hand mills of the 1920s, and it was here that the problem of designing roll contours to deal with the changing shape of the piece was solved. Ashland's undoubted success and its valuable technical contributions notwithstanding, the main line of ancestry of the wide strip mill ran through convergent developments in a formerly distinct line of production, that of strip steel.

For many years continuous mills had rolled long lengths of narrow strip, between which and the product of the sheet mills there had been little or no competition. Gradually, strip widths were widened from 7″ in American mills in the early nineties to 16″ by 1905 and for heavier strip to 24″ by 1922.[23] In the mid-1920s two engineers, A. J. Townsend and H. M. Naugle, building on contributions from the steel plate industry and the equipment firm, United Engineering and Foundry, Pittsburgh, produced strip up to 42″ wide in semi-continuous operations at the Butler Works of the Columbia Steel Company. They also independently worked out the principles of roll shaping and, equally important, solved the very serious problem of co-ordinating roll speeds in successive mill stands.

Strip mills began to cut into the market of the conventional sheet mills, and their initiative increased as practicable rolling widths were increased—by 1934 to as much as 69″.   Equally important, strip/sheet soon proved superior in quality.   The operators of quick-action presses found with satisfaction that the finish, gauge and physical properties generally of the strip mill product were better, and that sheets were more uniform.   As one operator in sheet production in Ohio recalled, 'When a big user of sheet for stamping or any fabricating that demands an excellent surface finish, a safe drawing and stamping quality and a very close and regular gauge and weight tolerance uses strip mill sheet he will never go back to the old hand-produced sheet.'[24]   To the steel companies the strip mill, although costly in initial capital layout, gave lower scrap yields, a smaller output of seconds, and lower running costs per ton of product than the hand mills.   In 1928 Wheeling Steel Corporation took the revolution a step further when the introduction of the cold reduction tandem mill proved that suitable material could be produced for tinning from hot strip mill coil.   This new association of the sheet and the tinplate industries acquired great significance in Britain in the thirties.   Meanwhile the United States experienced most of the conflicts between the old hand mill operators and the strip mills which were to occur or at any rate to be feared in Britain over the next dozen years or so.

The economic boom of America's 'Golden Twenties' seemed to offer a place for both the strip mills and the old type sheet mills, and total production of sheet, strip and black plate rose by $1\frac{1}{2}$ million net tons from 1925 to 1929.   The hand mills introduced more improvements in efficiency and in quality— mechanised roller and catcher tables, improved bar furnaces, better heat treatment for the sheet and the development of cold rolling.   Yet, by the end of 1927, three new continuous mills had joined Ashland and Butler, and although for a time the old style mills with their improvements prospered on gauges and widths outside the competence of the strip mills, the steady improvement of the latter soon rendered this position untenable. The Great Depression emphasised the hopeless task of the old style mills.   In 1932 United States output of sheet, strip and blackplate was only 41·4 per cent. the 1929 level, but the strip mills had increased their output by 13·9 per cent.[25]   By the end of 1935 there were seventeen strip mills in the United States. The competitiveness of the new technology had been conclusively proved, and by the mid-1930s firms which had attempted to meet the challenge by improvement of older methods were installing wide continuous strip mills instead.

British firms had closely studied American attempts to improve hand-mill sheet quality, and now both mill engineers and directors made pilgrimages to Ashland to Butler and to the other new American mills. Company boards had to make the decisions but the technical experts were the first to consider the applicability of the strip-mill technique to conditions here and to expose some of the problems involved. Technically the mills were an undoubted success, but a doubt persisted as to their suitability for Britain.

Some of the issues had been anticipated in Bedson's paper on continuous rolling in 1924 and in the discussion which followed.[26] Bedson quoted, although without identifying, an 'American authority' on the preconditions for, and effects of, continuous rolling—'Those who are most closely identified with continuous mill development know that its possibilities have scarcely begun to be realised. They do not hesitate to predict that, whenever a speciality in hot steel reaches the required point of standardisation and demand, a continuous mill for that speciality will be forthcoming, and that its appearance will mark a substantial reduction in the cost of that speciality.' Since Bedson's paper those preconditions had given rise to the continuous wide strip mill in the United States; but was Britain at the right stage? L. D. Whitehead discussed this point in 1924. Since 1907 he had operated a semi-continuous mill for rods, bar and strip up to 3″ wide at Tredegar which had '. . . proved to be an economic success every hour of its existence', and since 1921 a continuous hoop and strip mill had been working at his new works at Newport, rolling skelp up to 8″ wide. Despite these successes, he believed economic conditions in Britain rendered it impossible to operate an American type speciality continuous mill and essential to equip for some sort of combined product range. As a large user of foreign steel he also held strong opinions about location, although these were not so obviously applicable under protection or with fully integrated operations. 'He did not think that any continuous mill in Great Britain would ever pay if it were placed inland. It would need to be placed on the coast where it could have the backing of foreign as well as home business. It would always have to be fed with home and foreign material; it was no good relying on English material alone.'[27]   Ten years later, with the strip mill a confirmed success in the United States, discussion of its suitability for Britain was vigorous.

In 1934 a strong plea for British strip mills, although of much smaller size than in America, was made by E. R. Mort of Griffithstown, Monmouthshire. Claiming that '. . . worthwhile cost reductions which might in part be passed on to the motor industry could only come through the strip mill', he suggested that American 20-gauge autobody sheet which cost £12 10s. 0d. to make in old type mills could be rolled for £4 0s. 0d. a ton less in strip mills.   This figure probably underestimated the high standing charges of the strip mill, especially serious when operating rates were low, as they had been even in the United States over the previous four years.[28]

In 1935 G. A. V. Russell considered the reshaping of the tinplate trade with a 4-high cold reduction mill turning out strip for tinning as the central unit of plant backed by reconstructed or new facilities at the existing steelworks and bar mills. He claimed substantial savings could be achieved in material and labour costs.[29]   In 1936, discussing the applicability of the strip mill in the sheet and strip trades, Russell voiced the conviction of many that giant mills of 600,000 tons nominal capacity, like those installed in the Unites States, were unsuitable here. Depreciation, interest and other standing charges on such a plant would amount to over 9s. a ton with an operating rate about 83 per cent. of this capacity, but at a 46 per cent. rate about 17s. a ton.[30]   Although fear of a financial millstone deterred many from considering the strip mill right through the 1930s, all technical experts agreed that running costs were low. Russell put labour rates in typical American strip mills as low as 2s. 6d. to 4s. 0d. a ton and power costs at about 1s. 6d., while, in the discussion of his paper, A. W. Kieft provided estimates of the savings of a variety of new mill types over the costs of conventional 2-high sheet mills, but excluded the straight strip mill costs (Table 24).   Kieft was mapping out the various routes along which the better rather than the best solution might be sought.   Even so, in the conditions of the 1930s, the waywardness of those who followed them was understandable.   The doubts of this period also concerned the size, ownership and location of new plant.

TABLE 24

Estimated Production Cost advantages of modified or new-style Mills over 2-high hand Mills in the manufacture of 20 gauge motor body Sheet, 1936

	Reduction below hand mill costs per ton	
	s.	d.
Mechanised mills rolling sheet bar	17	6
Mechanised mills rolling strip breakdowns	18	6
Strip mill product finished on three high mills	23	0
Universal plate mill breakdowns finished on hot and cold mills	37	6 to
	39	0

Source: A. W. Kieff, *Journal of the Iron and Steel Institute*, 1936, 1.

E. R. Mort argued that American size plants could have no place in Britain but suggested that for £600,000 a mill with a wide product range capable of making 100,000 tons a year at well below current costs could be installed.[31]   In his 1935 paper G. A. V. Russell recognised the need to economise in new capital outlay and to avoid destruction of unamortised old-style plant, and supported the grafting of the new technique on to old plant.   In 1936, agreeing with Mort that while in prosperous times one or more American sized mills could find full employment in Britain their long-term return on investment would be disappointing, he suggested the installation of strip mills of about 200,000 tons annual capacity.   These could prevent the harmful social results of excessive localisation of production, and, as growth justified, the units could be duplicated in the various old-established sheetmaking or tinplate centres.   Kieft, as a director of Grovesend Steel and Tinplate Company an interesting contributor to the discussion, disputed Russell's conclusions on size and location.   He argued for a mill of American scale, to be built by an association of the firms already making tinplate and sheet and in a location chosen for operating efficiency.   Russell replied that this would necessitate taking account of the cost of carriage of hot rolled strip to the finishing mills or to scattered consumers.   This was true, but possibly less important than the opportunity to minimise raw material assembly and process costs in a single, large well located mill.   Kieft suggested that the members of the co-operative venture should reduce the output of their old-type mills in proportion to their capacity to enable the strip mill to work to capacity and to spread the effect of labour displacement, but clearly there was the implication that some of the business of the new plant would be taken from non-member firms.   Russell added a decisive point in suggesting the danger of clash of interest among the various projectors and owners of the new hot strip mill.[32]

The reconstruction of the British steel and tinplate industry was to reflect a rough compromise between the views put forward in these various papers and discussions.   The first two mills were of American size but were built by individual companies not by groups.   Each project encountered serious financial trouble and so, of necessity, required differing degrees of co-operative action with other members of the trade.   This experience led to fuller recognition of the advantages of common action and so to wider, though still regional, groupings of interests.   Mort, Russell and other plant engineers were looking at the sheet and strip industry rationally, aiming for as near an approach as possible to an ideal pattern of development.   They took financial considerations into account but oversimplified the issues.   To those in the boardrooms, in trade association offices or in Steel House the matter seemed more complex, the figures of output, of production costs and of labour displacement were lit by the glow of clashing personality and prejudice.   Yet inevitably, it was within this framework of the actual that the new pattern of strip/sheet production gradually emerged.

REFERENCES

1 R. W. Shannon, *Sheet Steel and Tinplate* 1930. Also correspondence with J. Malborn.
2 J. C. Arrowsmith, 'Pressings for Automobiles', *Proceedings of the Institute of Automobile Engineers*, 25, 1930–1931.

3   E. S. Lawrence, *The Manufacture of Steel Sheets* 1930, p. 3.   J.
    Malborn in correspondence.   W. T. Hogan, *The Development
    of American Heavy Industry in the Twentieth Century* 1954, p. 78.
    G. C. Allen, *British Industries and their Organisation* 1951 Edition
    p. 173.
4   E. C. Lysaght in correspondence and conversation.
5   P. W. S. Andrews and E. Brunner, *The Life of Lord Nuffield*
    1955, pp. 131–133.
6   *Sheet Metal Industries* December 1929, p. 437, April 1930, p. 691,
    December 1947, p. 2447.
7   W. S. Lewis in correspondence.
8   Shannon, *op. cit.*, pp. 23–24, Lawrence, *op. cit.*, pp. 8–19.
    H. H. Stanley and G. F. Gillott in conversation and cor-
    respondence.
9   J. C. Arrowsmith in discussion of C. H. Desch, 'Cold Pressing
    and Drawing—the metallurgical aspect', *Proceedings Institute
    of Automobile Engineers* 29, 1934–1935, p. 607 and of E. R. Mort,
    'The Manufacture of Full-Finished Steel Sheets', *Journal of the
    Iron and Steel Institute* 1934, 1, p. 234.
10 Shannon, Lawrence, Mort and Desch, *op. cit.*   R. Whitfield in
    Journal of the Iron and Steel Institute 1930, 1.   J. B. Hoblyn in
    Proceedings Institute of Automobile Engineers 24, 1929–1930, p. 141.
    G. L. Kelly, 'Modern Steel Motor Car Body Building', *ibid.* 29
    1934–1935, pp. 480–482.   E. S. Lawrence, 'Great Britain
    versus American Sheet Steel', *Sheet Metal Industries* December
    1931, p. 541 and correspondence or conversation with E. C.
    Lysaght, A. R. Gray, G. A. V. Russell, H. H. Stanley, J.
    Malborn and G. F. Gillott.
11 J. Malborn in correspondence.
12 E. C. Lysaght.
13 W. S. Lewis and H. H. Stanley in correspondence.
14 A. R. Gray, P. J. Summers and G. F. Gillott.
15 As recalled thirty years later by former trade rivals.
16 G. F. Gillott in recollection.
17 *Iron Age* 20 May 1926, p. 1415.   3 June 1926, pp. 1598–1599.
18 J. P. Bedson, 'Continuous Rolling mills and their growth and
    development', *Journal of the Iron and Steel Institute* 1924, 1, pp.
    43–66.
19 On the earlier general problem of continuous mills see F. W.
    Harbord and J. W. Hall, *The Metallurgy of Steel Vol. II Mechanical
    Treatment* 1918, pp. 598–599.
20 The development is fully analysed in *The Modern Strip Mill*
    published by the Association of Iron and Steel Engineers in 1941,
    or extracted from there, developed further and put in a British
    context in S. E. Graeff, 'The Development of Continuous Hot
    and Cold Rolling of Flat Rolled Iron and Steel Products',
    Proceedings of the South Wales Institute of Engineers 1948.

21 James Cox, *Reports of the Moseley Industrial Commission* 1903, p. 39.
22 Shannon, *op. cit.*, pp. 76–77. J. Malborn, 'Hot Strip Rolling Mills. The Evolution of the Modern Four High Mill', *Sheet Metal Industries* July 1950, p. 581 and J. Malborn in correspondence.
23 Shannon, *op. cit.*, pp. 74–75.
24 J. Malborn in correspondence.
25 D. Eppelsheimer 'The Development of Continuous Strip Mills' *Journal of the Iron and Steel Institute* 1938, 2, p. 195.
26 J. P. Bedson, *op. cit.*
27 *ibid.*, pp. 61–62.
28 E. R. Mort 'The Manufacture of Full-Finished Sheets' *Journal of the Iron and Steel Institute* 1934, 1.
29 G. A. V. Russell 'The Manufacture of Tinplate' *Iron and Coal Trades Review* 11 January 1935, pp. 86–87.
30 G. A. V. Russell 'Some considerations influencing plant facilities for strip sheet production under British conditions' *Journal of the Iron and Steel Institute* 1936, 1.
31 Mort, *op. cit.*, p. 345.
32 G. A. V. Russell 1936 *ibid.*, pp. 53, 76, 83, 89 and passim.

M

CHAPTER 10

British Strip Mill Plans to 1935

Late in 1928, in the Free Trade Hall(!), Manchester, Lord Melchett, chairman of Imperial Chemical Industries, addressed a meeting on behalf of the newly formed Empire Industries Association's campaign for safeguarding of British industry. Iron and steel firms, he remarked, had fallen in arrears. 'Works were situated in the wrong centres, plants were obsolescent; there was great duplication and a want of central control.'[1]   Many others were diagnosing and prescribing for the industry's ills at the same time.   Charles Schwab, who had built up in turn Carnegie Steel and Bethlehem Steel, speaking as the visiting president of the American Iron and Steel Institute, urged protection, the creation of three or four great concerns and the need to reap the technical and managerial economies of scale.   In 1929 the Labour government brought in another American expert to advise on reorganisation, and next year the Sankey Report on the steel industry and a study commissioned by Montague Norman of the Bank of England and undertaken by Charles Bruce-Gardner were completed. By the summer of 1931 the economist H. S. Jevons was suggesting a £150 million complete overhaul and extension of the industry.[2]   Yet even after protection was provided by the 33⅓ per cent. *ad valorem* duty in April, 1932, reconstruction made only a slow start and was never nearly as comprehensive as these outsiders had suggested.   The reasons are important for they also account for the diffidence with which British firms approached the construction of a wide hot strip mill.   For capital cost 1931–1935 was an ideal period to embark on such a project, whereas, as a sympathetic American visitor of the time recalls, even men who had seen American strip mills and studied their operating record maintained that similar plants were not for Britain and entertained fantastic alternative notions of reorganisation.[3] Between the extremes of a clean sweep of existing plant, followed by rebuilding, and the mere patching of old fabric, it was essential to make way for the new, mass production technologies in thin flat rolled products, but, still plagued by the Staffordshire disease of extreme individualism and lacking vision or willingness to disturb settled ways, most older established firms held back. This vitally important climate of thinking was summed up by one in intimate contact with the sheet firms as a member of a major consumer's staff. 'It is hard for anyone who was not personally involved during those times, fully to appreciate the conditions and the state of mind of the people concerned after more than ten years of depression. Morale in the steel industry was very low, few had any confidence in the future and large amounts of capital were generally not forthcoming. Those companies which were still able to operate at some profit became ultra-cautious and extremely conservative and quite unwilling to embark on any scheme involving a complete change of process and heavy capital outlay.'[4]

Any proposal for strip mill development had to provide for a costly new installation and ancillary plant—whose need and therefore expense was frequently not fully recognised—and the writing off of much existing but frequently only partially amortised equipment. In the United States depreciation schedules had been established on the basis of an investment of about $132 million for the 1,320 hand-mill stands existing in 1926. By 1940 much of this plant had been abandoned and 28 strip mills had been built at a cost of $500 million.[5] Few British firms were of a size to operate an American size strip mill and fewer still could raise the £4½ million these figures suggested as the cost. Mort spoke of British mills of 100,000 tons capacity, Russell of 200,000 tons, but at the end of the twenties the average British hand-mill could roll about 5,000 tons a year and only four works had more than 20 mills. John Summers made 262,000 tons sheet in 1928, John Lysaght's output was smaller than that, although they, too, could match Russell's capacity figure. In some cases ownership of more than one plant gave a sheet firm substantial extra capacity and black plate was also important at some South Wales works, vitally as it transpired. Yet dispersal in small capacity plants was dominant whereas the new technology emphasised the desirability of centralisation.

Only four groups were big enough to consider even a small unit practicable—John Summers, the Lysaght-Sankey-Guest Keen Nettlefold group, Baldwins and the Richard Thomas-Grovesend combination.   On the fringe were firms whose main interests were in other lines of steel but which had sheet mills and to which shadowy ambitions to build a strip mill were occasionally attributed.   Colvilles, controlling Smith and McLean, the new Tees-side amalgamation of Dorman Long and Bolckow Vaughan with sheet and light plate mills at Bowesfield, Ayrton and Eston works, and the South Durham Steel and Iron Company were the chief members of this class. In the regional concentration of sheet capacity only the North West and South Wales could accommodate even such a moderate-sized installation as Russell had described.   In South Wales existing sheet capacity and tinplate tonnage together suggested the possibility of two mills of an effective annual output of as much as 500,000 tons each (Table 25).

TABLE 25

Annual Capacity and Production
of black and galvanised Sheet, 1936 (thousand tons)

	Effective Capacity	Annual make based on October, 1936, figures
South Wales and Monmouth	670	530
North Wales and Cheshire	392	341
Midlands	142	110
North East Coast	160	112
Scotland	160	139
TOTAL	1526	1233

Source: British Iron and Steel Federation. Report on the Black and Galvanised Sheet Industry 1937

Trends in demand could not be clearly discerned.   Contemporary American experience suggested that the availability of high-quality sheet seemed to call into being new lines of fabrication, supply creating new demand, but this might not happen in Britain.   On the other hand the motor industry had proved remarkably buoyant in the depression; in 1931, its worst year, private car output was only 14 per cent. below the 1929 level, and thereafter revival was rapidly followed by expansion. Pressed Steel made 100 bodies a day in 1930 but 700 by 1939.[6] Not surprisingly, some of the early moves in strip mill planning came from the motor firms, although it now seems clear that suggestions of installing their own units were largely designed to cajole the steel industry to take the step itself.

Even in the United States, Fords were the only automobile makers to build a strip mill. Their loss of leadership in vehicle production to General Motors in the late twenties was partly attributable to over-extension in their effort to control supplies. The Rouge strip mill of 1935 was a late example of this. Although the quality of sheet steel supplied to British motor firms had improved, complaints continued.[7] Lord Nuffield was the most outspoken critic of the steelmakers—'all big cigars and nothing to do' summed up his impression of the Federation's Steel House. Nuffield argued that the firms chose to shelter behind the new protective tariff rather than increase production and lower prices. Some of the steelmakers conceded there was substance in this accusation, but it was unfair to assume that the mass production techniques which worked so well in Nuffield's own durable consumer goods trade and which the strip mill also involved could be applied simply to an old industrial structure. Moreover, the market for sheet steel was a demand derived from that for finished metal products, and to Nuffield's accusation that British steel prices were one-third higher than those which foreign automobile makers had to pay, the sheet producers pointed out that whereas the average British light car contained less than 3 cwt. of sheet, worth about £3, the price of the car was £40 to £60 more than that of American models of similar quality. The steel firms were thus exhibiting a strange ignorance of the economics of the assembly line. Nuffield threatened to buy abroad over the tariff, or even to set up a steel plant himself if the industry continued to defy him.[8] The idea of a Nuffield strip mill was hazy, and there is no published evidence to suggest the scheme had reached serious consideration about the type, size or location of the plant. In the First World War Brymbo and Baldwins made a thorough analysis of the possibility of steelworks near Deddington south of Banbury, and subsequent thinking about Oxfordshire ironstone had visualised locations to the north west on the Avon, but it is not clear whether Nuffield had planned along these lines.[9] In any case these high phosphorus and siliceous ores were unsuitable for the production of autobody sheet.   The existence in Cowley of both Morris and Pressed Steel raises interesting questions concerning use of scrap but these too cannot be answered.   It is probably fair to see no more in the rumours of Nuffield's plans than an effort to induce the steel firms to act themselves.   The Austin Motor Company proceeded further.

At the beginning of 1935, perhaps even earlier, the Commissioner for Special Areas was exploring the possibility of Austin's taking over Ebbw Vale to make their own autobody sheet, and as late as October 1935, Sir Herbert Austin was still having to deny that his company had made that purchase.   In fact Ebbw Vale was too big for their requirements and they were thinking of developments nearer to their Longbridge works.[10]   In 1935 through the establishment of the Tunstall Steel Company Ltd. Austins planned a works to produce 100,000 tons finished steel a year in forgings, plates and sheet to supply their own needs and those of other Midland motor firms, partly from a stamping plant on the same site.   An order was placed with an American firm for a single 4-high reversing mill to produce light plate of around 3/16″ thickness to be further cold reduced to autobody gauges on a single stand mill. The cost was estimated at about £500,000 and a 50- to 60-acre site bounded by railway and canal was acquired at Aldersley, two miles north of the centre of Wolverhampton.[11]   Apart from the fine sense of sheet trade history it displayed, the choice of this location is puzzling.   As the plant was designed to reroll bought slabs, nearness to the scrap supplies from Midland metal fabrication was of no importance, and Aldersley is 23 miles from the body shops of Longbridge, and most of the other big Midland car works and component makers were also on the other side of the conurbation or beyond, in the Coventry area. As an important railway junction Wolverhampton had certain advantages as a centre for rerolling although these cannot be reckoned to have been great.   Brymbo works, which made rimming steel, not of the best quality, was reopened in 1934, largely through the exertions of Sir Henry Robertson, who, as a director of the Great Western Railway, secured the company freight-rate concessions. Brymbo was still seeking new outlets for its steel, and an Aldersley mill could have been a very important addition. All this, however, is speculation and members of the established sheet firms recall that they were not greatly disturbed by the obviously ill thought out Austin proposals. By December, 1935, Sir Herbert Austin visited the Ebbw Vale sheet mills in company with Sir William Firth, and in 1936 the Austin General Meeting was told that the mill project had been abandoned in view of the larger schemes the steel industry had itself now produced.[12] Both Nuffield and Austin were fully preoccupied with the very rapid expansion of their own activities and both realised that an economic output from even a small strip mill could scarcely be absorbed by the motor industry alone.

The thinking of the heavy steel firms concerning strip mills was probably much less hazy than that of the motor companies, but it too was exaggerated by press reports and the fears of the established sheet makers. In 1876 the Bowesfield works at Stockton were the first in the North- East to roll light steel sheet. In 1898 Dorman Long acquired the Ayrton sheet mills and in 1912 a large interest in Bowesfield, while in 1916 their neighbours, Bolckow and Vaughan, acquired the Eston Sheet and Galvanising Company at South Bank. Ayrton works was reconstructed in the early twenties. In 1923 Lord Furness told shareholders of the South Durham Steel and Iron Company that there was so much over capacity in heavy products that the company was thinking of developing lighter lines, 'I refer in particular,' he added, 'to the galvanised sheet and tinplate trades.' In the following year a plant designed for 700 tons a week of galvanised sheet was constructed at the company's Malleable Works, Stockton.[13] These developments provided the foundation for the mid-1930s rumours of an intended entry to the quality sheet trade. In July, 1935, the Dorman Long board decided to install a cold mill to roll sheet and strip up to 72" wide at the Cleveland works, but built neither this plant nor the strip mill which rumour added to their plans.[14] In the same summer South Durham announced plans for a continuous billet and sheet bar mill at Cargo Fleet and for mills to cold roll sheet and strip wider than ever before achieved in England, and in the autumn the Annual Meeting was told that the new methods of producing tinplate and sheet were being investigated.[15]   The north eastern firms had one advantage to ease their entry to wide quality strip production—their large outlets for plate.   In all British firms fears of an inadequate load for a strip mill were endemic.   For narrower strip the possession of tinplate capacity provided an outlet additional to sheet, but for wider strip this was not practicable and it was common to combine strip/sheet with the production of lighter gauges of plate.   An authority, who visited a large number of the American strip mills a few years later, recalls that mills over 60″ wide not equipped with a plate line were rare.[16]   In his 1936 paper G. A. V. Russell outlined a possible strip mill for British conditions, with universal plates up to $\frac{3}{4}$″ thick as well as strip/sheet among its products.   In the discussion of this paper at the Iron and Steel Institute, Benjamin Talbot of South Durham showed what might well have seemed to the sheet firms an unhealthily keen interest.[17]   In fact South Durham installed a combination billet, section and bar plate mill, in which provision was made for four 4-high stands to finish 60″ wide hot rolled strip.   The project was not a success.[18]

United Steel Companies, the largest British steel firm, had sent some of its leading officers and the manager of the Appleby rolling mills, Scunthorpe, to examine American wide strip mills as early as 1928–1929.   In 1932 H. T. Hildage of United Steel was in a party of Europeans which visited the Steckel mill of the Youngstown Cold Metal Process Company and the Middletown strip mill of the American Rolling Mill Company.[19]   It was shown, however, that the ingot capacity at the Appleby and Frodingham works and the slabbing mill at Appleby were inadequate to supply both a strip mill and the existing plate and structural mills, and, when thoughts of entering the strip/ sheet business were revived after the depression, their steel proved unsuitable for high-quality sheet.[20]   The problem admittedly originated in the low-grade Frodingham ore, but at the nearby Normanby Park works Lysaght had proved that much of this disability could be overcome.   The crux of the problem was to be found in the equipment.   For quality control, especially with poor ore, relatively small fixed open-hearth furnaces were necessary, whereas, to supply its lower-grade operations, Appleby-Frodingham had installed large tilting furnaces By strip standards the steel was 'cold' and 'dirty'.[21] Rather than reconstruct their Scunthorpe works to enter these new fields, United Steel Companies decided to acquire interests in existing sheet making firms. Some of these lacked the vision, courage or financial resources to instal new plant, and in the end all the old-established concerns were forestalled by a comparative newcomer.

Baldwins had improved their sheet quality, and at the end of the twenties, before John Summer's made their own painful breakthrough, were probably second only to Lysaghts in supplying deep drawing sheet to the body shops. Their lower grades of sheet came from South Wales, most of their quality black, tinned, railway panel, electrical and autobody sheet from their Midland mills, where they had put in mechanised bar and sheet furnaces, improved the hot mills and had a cold reduction mill before Lysaghts. Some of this plant may have been indifferent in quality, but the firm had an established reputation and operated at a high level through most of the depression. As a result the need for a wholly new framework of thinking was disguised. In 1931, Baldwin's chairman, Sir Charles Wright, had made a wild claim when he assured his shareholders that their sheet was '. . . in quality and finish equal to any in the world'. In 1937, the chief metallurgist of Baldwin's Midland works still maintained that the great variety of sizes and small overall tonnage consumed would make strip mills too inflexible for British conditions.[22] In that year, however, British vehicle production was well over double the level of any year before 1933 and mass production was bringing an emphasis on standardised material. At the same time the associated heavy steel company Guest Keen Baldwins studied the quality, width and thickness of sheet consumed as indicated by the invoices of G.K.B.-Baldwins-Lysaght-Sankey and showed conclusively that in this wider group there was sufficient demand to justify a full-scale strip mill.[23] Personality clashes were one important factor contributing to frustrate attempts at co-ordinated action from this group. Meanwhile John Lysaghts shared these doubts and were much more justifiably diverted by their past successes.

Lysaghts examined American methods of motor body sheet production in the mid-twenties, in 1927 made the first British extra-deep drawing sheet for the Pressed Steel body works and by 1930 claimed that they made upwards of 90 per cent. of the sheet used in the country's press shops.[24] Although they suffered severely in the depression—Newport operated at less than 50 per cent. of capacity in 1931—they continued to improve the plant. Normalising furnaces were installed in 1933, the firm was the first in Britain to use mechanised hot mills for autobody sheet, and two years later for the small investment of £180,000 they put in a three-stand tandem 80″ cold reduction mill able to turn out high quality strip up to 72″ in width. Customers confirmed the high reputation of their sheet and even Vauxhall's, American controlled and in the early thirties obtaining almost all its press shop supplies from the American Rolling Mill operations at Hawarden Bridge, was soon buying about half from the Orb works. In 1934 claims for faulty material covered less than 100 tons of the 50,000 tons deep drawing sheet Lysaghts rolled.[25] Yet Lysaght had only taken a step in the right direction.[26] The Lysaght management realised that hand mill 'breakdowns' could be only a second-best means of supplying the cold reduction mill and that a semi-continuous hot strip mill was essential. Given the nature of their product, this had to be an 80″ mill, but this need placed the firm in a quandary. Adequate employment for such a plant was doubtful, for, unlike Richard Thomas and Company, Lysaghts had no tinplate tonnage and their overall sheet output was little more than half that of John Summers. So the further logical steps, to which Mort invited Lysaghts and which the firm recognised as clearly as its critics, could not be justified commercially.[27] These conclusions were reinforced by the particular set-up in the Lysaght management team.

In general, while failing to pursue any fundamental research, Lysaght had a high-quality team, D. C. Lysaght, who managed the mills, being outstanding. In this critical period of the early and mid-thirties, W. R. Lysaght, as chairman, was still effectively the arbiter of policy. He had entered the sheet trade in

1874, and in sixty years his mind had become rather less open
to new ideas. In his 1933 presidential address to the Iron and
Steel Institute he spoke revealingly, 'Again during the last three
or four years,' he said, 'we have been much concerned at the
instalment and development of *monstrous* continuous strip mills
in the United States of America.'[28] British sheet consumption
was under one-third that of the United States and consisted of
numerous gauges, so that, 'with our present knowledge, it would
be impossible in this country to run one of these giant mills
profitably'. He added '. . . whether they will eventually
supersede the older type (of sheet mill) remains to be seen'.[29]
Later this scepticism about the economic viability of British
strip mills was echoed by E. Lysaght, by J. B. R. Brooke, who
was in charge of the company's Normanby Park works, and by
G. C. Richer of Orb works.[30] Richer had left the Patent Office
to become W. R. Lysaght's secretary at the Spelter Control in
the First World War, afterwards became his technical adviser
and now seems to have played a key role. He combined
brilliance with strong prejudices and an inability to see faults in
the arguments with which he backed these, and he helped to
swing Lysaghts still more conclusively against the strip mill.
In the autumn of 1935 he received a report from the company's
representatives who had visited some twenty steel plants and
mills and in addition press shops and mill equipment builders
in the United States. They suggested that in a hot strip mill
rolling costs from the ingot would be more than 25s. a ton below
those in the mechanised Orb hot mills. But he advised the
Lysaght board, that high capital cost and a restricted market
'. . . convince me that there is no possible justification for the
reproduction in England, for the manufacture of autobody
sheet steel, of continuous hot and cold strip mills of the type
now commonly employed in the United States.'[31] Five months
earlier Richard Thomas & Company had decided to build a
hot strip mill. Shortly before Richer's report, at a memorable
Annual Dinner of the Newport and District Metallurgical
Society, before D. C. Lysaght could reveal his company's plans
for a cold reduction mill at Newport, Sir William Firth had
stolen his thunder by announcing that the strip mill would be
at Ebbw Vale.

RICHARD THOMAS & COMPANY

In combined sheet and tinplate tonnage Richard Thomas was the largest producer of thin flat-rolled steel in Britain by the early 1930s. Its ingot capacity was only about three-quarters of a million tons a year and was shared by four West Wales cold metal melting shops and the integrated works at Redbourn. Similarly the wide scatter of its mills and steelworks hindered rationalisation. As a result big new developments, such as the new Morgan continuous bar mill of 300,000 tons capacity planned in 1927 to produce material which the sheet mills could roll to new standards of quality, involved much more extra carriage to finishing works than did the operations of Lysaghts or Summers. It was difficult to find a centre at which reconstruction and expansion could be concentrated. Meanwhile in the late twenties, like others with American technical advice, Richard Thomas tried to improve the quality of their small motor body sheet output. They might have spent many years reshaping their South Wales mills but for two circumstances, one managerial, the other the problem of their Scunthorpe works.

Redbourn throughout most of the twenties was a costly producer and a burden on the rest of the group. From 1924 to 1928 the works was idle, yet costing £30,000 a year to maintain, and by the late twenties much of the equipment was already outdated. Following an American technical report in May, 1928, it was decided to remodel the ironworks and bar mill. By the end of 1929 the reorganised works was making sheet bars at an annual rate of 150,000 tons, half of which was railed to the the company's South Wales works, and the rest sold to other sheet makers. Between September, 1929, and November, 1930, imported sheet bars fell from 103s. to 73s. a ton, and Redbourn was again closed at the end of 1930.[32] A year later it was said that, with dumped foreign bar, tinplate could be made for 5s. to 10s. a ton less than the cost of home material. In these circumstances Richard Thomas used foreign material for a time, but the Import Duties Act revived hopes that Redbourn's low iron costs might be fully exploited by the revival of Frank Thomas's vision of Lincolnshire finishing operations.[33]

A month after dumping closed Redbourn, Henry Bond described its advantages most explicitly to the Annual Meeting.[34] 'But even under existing conditions, we probably should not have had to close our Redbourn plant if we had had a finishing end to use a substantial part of its production on the spot, and so save a railway carriage of over 12s. a ton. We have, for reasons which I have explained, had to temporarily abandon these plans for want of money. Should conditions alter, should we be able to obtain the necessary funds, we have established a cost of steel at Redbourn which will place us in a very favourable position.' He added, 'We are in constant and intimate touch with the latest American and continental practice.' Although this may not refer to a strip mill scheme frustrated by the Great Depression, already the germ of this type of thinking had been planted in Richard Thomas & Company.

In old-type operations the cost of steel was about 40 per cent. that of finished tinplate, so that the attraction of full integration with low-cost steelmaking at Redbourn was considerable. After 1928 American success with cold rolled strip mill coil for tinning introduced the prospect of a much larger, more concentrated operation than with the old-type pack mills. Tinplate strip was of lower quality and narrower than that used as strip/sheet so that a large tinplate tonnage permitted a cheaper installation than where the emphasis was on high-grade sheet. For this reason and with its large capacity and variety of qualities, Richard Thomas became a more suitable host for a strip mill than any other British sheet or tinplate company. Henry Bond, even after a long career in the industry, still had an open mind, but lacked the drive and imagination of his Vice-chairman, William Firth. Firth had entered the business from tinplate marketing, but although he had no thorough technical grounding he had an intuitive grasp of the trend of the forces of change. In 1928 leading members of the company, reporting on a visit to the new strip mills at Trumbull and Weirton, were already arguing that eventually all the Welsh mills would be rendered useless. Bond at this stage was still willing to dismiss such a suggestion as ridiculous, but Firth separately probed the idea and had another independent report made. This second judgement, however, was less radical than

the first, and the depression pushed thoughts of major reconstruction into the background until after the tariff.[35]

In the financial year 1931–1932 Richard Thomas & Company operated at less than 50 per cent. capacity in the steel
works, and at only about 50 and 60 per cent. in the sheet and
tinplate mills respectively, but Firth, becoming chairman in
1931, was still considering the prospect of a strip mill, as he
revealed in the following year to others thinking independently
along the same lines.[36]   A few months after protection was
granted, Firth queried whether world demand was capable of
absorbing the output of existing plants, '. . . increased as it has
been by the introduction of labour-saving machinery and other
devices, marvels of efficiency from a scientific and cost of production point of view', and pleaded for co-operative reorganisation, suggesting that '. . . the days of individualism in staple
industries have gone'.[37]   Joint action with other Welsh firms,
however, was never possible.   For this there were two reasons,
the old individualism and exclusiveness of the tinplate and
sheet makers and, judging by subsequent developments, Firth's
own indiplomacy.   Convinced his plans were right, he pushed
them through against all the sensibilities of those who had been
much longer in the trade.   Yet he had initiated earlier co-
operative arrangements and in the history of these some of the
roots of subsequent trouble may be traced.   In March, 1919,
as a tinplate merchant and a director of the Grovesend Steel
and Tinplate Company, Firth had proposed a central selling
agency for tinplate, and by 1924 this had appeared as the
South Wales Tinplate Corporation which periodically restricted
output to maintain prices.   Numerous producers with wide
variations in efficiency—in 1919 production costs per basis box
were said to differ by as much as 2s., almost 6 per cent. of the
selling price—made it difficult to administer the scheme, and
the bulk of the Corporation's capacity was controlled by
Richard Thomas & Co. especially after 1932.   Significant for
the future, Baldwins never joined.[38]   Firth eventually became
disillusioned by this approach, and early in 1934, in two letters
to *The Times* and one to the *Engineer*, he laid down a framework
for advance.   In the process he took open issue with his trade
rivals.[39]

Almost half the British export of iron and steel was either

tinplate or sheet, Firth pointed out. Two years after protection was granted little radical reorganisation was evident, and, while the cost of raw materials was rising behind the tariff barrier, the two trades were still only operating at about 55 per cent. of capacity. Previously the problems of the industry had been tackled in various ways—by keen competition, which had reduced selling prices to 10s. to 15s. below production costs, by vain attempts to eliminate cross hauling and operate the most efficient plant by amalgamation, and finally by a price and quota system, which, although avoiding the concentration of unemployment in one area, had forced up costs and reduced international competitiveness by giving 'temporary profits to inefficient manufacturers'. There was no incentive to modernise when the rest of the trade would not grant an enterprising firm an increased quota, and when therefore investment in reconstruction would mean laying-off large numbers of workers from the other works of the same concern. If his firm installed modern tinplate equipment beside blast furnaces—'which would probably reduce our costs by 30s. a ton'—without an increased quota, and the new plant was capable of satisfying 25 per cent. of total demand, it would be necessary either to undercut all their competitors, or to close 75 per cent. of their existing plant to absorb the increased output. Centralised operations were essential for low costs, and to ensure them he advocated government help 'to enforce amalgamations on an equitable basis'. In his letter to the *Engineer*, Firth criticised the trade and gave interesting insight into his own ambitions. 'In the present state of world unrest and poor demand, if my company was interested only in the home trade, I should probably be content to refrain from criticism rather than invoke government intervention that might deprive me of the "glory" of individualism, taking the line that so long as my company secured a reasonable return on their capital and the livelihood of the work people was not jeopardised, my business life would be happier agreeing with my friends in the trade; but feeling strongly that what they are doing is shortsighted and likely to endanger the livelihood of our work people, because our loaded prices will make us vulnerable to foreign competition, I cannot remain silent.'

Having failed to secure co-operative reconstruction with other major firms, including Baldwins, Lysaghts and United Steels, to enable Richard Thomas to secure a large enough quota to permit a high operating rate for the strip mill it was now planning, Firth resorted to the piecemeal acquisition of other smaller companies.   Between 1933 and 1936 Richard Thomas bought 61 tinplate and 19 sheet mills.   Included in these were Gilbertsons acquired in 1933, but the shareholders of Briton Ferry rejected the overtures by a large majority.   By 1937 224 of the 518 tinplate mills in Wales were in Richard Thomas control and between 1933 and 1938 its share of tinplate capacity went up from 34·1 to 49·4 per cent.[40]

Circumventing the opposition of the firms in the tinplate and sheet trade, at the cost of an alienation which brought retribution later, Richard Thomas encountered the opposition of organised labour.   In 1933 the Whitehead Iron and Steel Company had transferred its semi-continuous bar mill from Tredegar to Redbourn and early in 1934 Ernest Bevin heard of a proposal for a strip mill in Scunthorpe.   He attacked it vehemently at the 1934 Annual Tinplate Conference.[41]   The strength of the opposition was understandable for the disturbance involved in a major new technique was combined with a wholesale shift in location.   As the Transport Workers put it at the 1934 Trades Union Conference, 'an industry can be moved without any obligation at all and the community that is left derelict has to pay the cost'.[42]   There was no doubt that the strip mill would change the conditions of labour even more than of management, and for both American experience was a useful guide.   In the spring of 1934 a Conference of the American Amalgamated Association of Iron, Steel and Tinplate Workers had considered this issue, and its views were reported in Britain just when the matter was becoming a practical problem there too.   On an American strip mill 400–600 tons material could be rolled in a day by a no bigger work force than that needed to turn out 25 tons on a handmill.   On the 12 existing strip mills 1,600 men produced as much tonnage as 32,000 on 636 hand operated sheet mills.   The conference even suggested that the American government should spend $150 million to buy and scrap all the continuous mills.   Two years later Inland Steel of Chicago employed only 228 men in a strip mill for an output which by British methods would

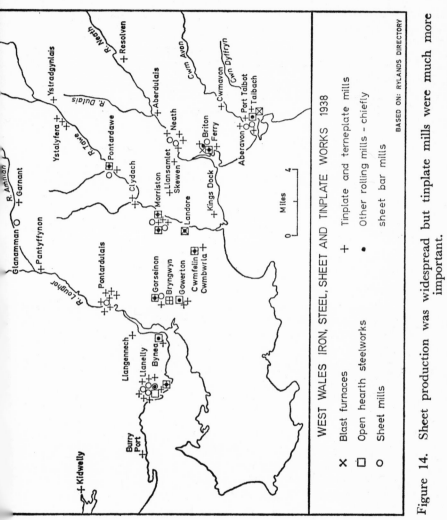

WEST WALES IRON, STEEL, SHEET AND TINPLATE WORKS 1938

+ Tinplate and terneplate mills

• Other rolling mills – chiefly
    sheet bar mills

× Blast furnaces

□ Open hearth steelworks

○ Sheet mills

BASED ON: RYLANDS DIRECTORY

Figure 14. Sheet production was widespread but tinplate mills were much more important.

provide work for about 2,000.[43]   Against such figures the
argument that the better product widened the demand for
sheet steel and so encouraged growth in its production was
unconvincing.   In the spring of 1936, speaking at Llanelly,
Firth tried this approach.   'What does it matter', he asked,
'if strip plants do employ a less number of men per ton of
output if, by increasing demand, we can employ the same
number of men under better conditions, at better average
wages and for much less arduous work?'[44]   He had not proved
that as many would be employed or, even if market growth did
eventually bring this about, what would happen to them
meantime.   In Britain, creeping uncertainly from the slough
of unemployment, the social factor was now for the first time
becoming a locational influence to reckon with (Figure 14 and
15).

In July, 1935, Richard Thomas, announced plans for a £1·1
million Redbourn strip mill to make 150,000 tons sheet and
tinplate a year.   The estimated saving over costs of production
with existing methods, involving carriage of semi-finished steel
from Lincolnshire to South Wales, was £200,000.   At 12s. a
ton for carriage of semi-finished steel from Redbourn to South
Wales, this leaves a saving of approximately 14s. a ton attributable to the new strip mill or to improved practice in iron and
steel making.   Not only would the plant be a low cost producer
but it was fairly well located to supply Midland outlets for
sheet.   Although there was a direct threat to Summers's and
Lysaght's sheet trade, it was the effect on employment in South
Wales that first aroused most attention.   To the Richard
Thomas Annual Meeting on 16th July, Firth had observed 'We
fear the prospect of our company manufacturing tinplate in a
district other than Wales will not at first blush be welcomed by
our Welsh work people, or our Welsh competitors,' the
concluding phrase being especially revealing, which Firth
followed up by observing 'It is indeed a matter of regret to
your directors that the same low production costs cannot be
attained in Wales . . .'[45]

Delegates of the tinplate workers had met in Swansea on the
previous Saturday and demanded an immediate government
enquiry into the proposal to shift tinplate capacity to Redbourn.

The workers expected Richard Thomas to close a considerable share of their South Wales plant, believing that the company had not requested an increased quota.[46] On the day of the Richard Thomas meeting, the Mayor of Swansea urged the

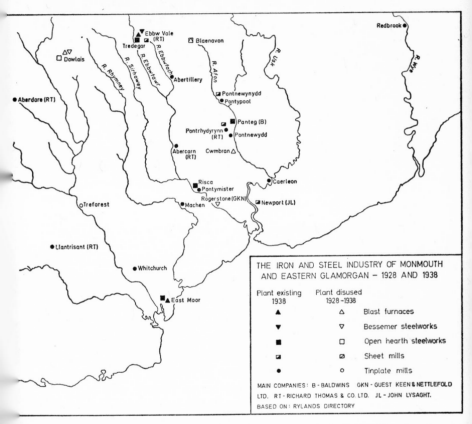

ure 15. The 'relic' nature of the Ebbw Vale location is indicated by the changes of this period.

government to avoid the creation of another area of chronic unemployment. Shortly after Sir William Firth discreetly left for a holiday, but almost immediately rumour ran that his company was willing to reconsider the movement to Lincolnshire, a belief encouraged by extensions at their Llanelly and Pontardawe plants.[47] Negotiations soon became entangled

with the attempts to reduce unemployment in the vicinity of
the Ebbw Vale works, which had been idle for six years.

After the enforced retirement of Sir Frederick Mills there is
no evidence that the Ebbw Vale company ever contemplated
a strip mill. Late in 1930, speaking at Ebbw Vale, Aneurin
Bevan noted that he had asked Sir John Beynon if the works
would be restarted if a tariff was granted to the steel industry,
and had received the reply, 'No; new money would be
necessary'. Bevan concluded what other sources confirm, that
the chairman was not interested in the steel trade.[48] There
were periodic investigations of the prospects for restarting the
works, but early in 1935 investment of £½ million was reckoned
essential for any chance of success.[49] In Ebbw Vale society,
however, if not within the company, the idea of the strip mill
was already germinating, and private individuals attempted
to interest Lysaghts, Baldwins and others in the Ebbw Vale
works. Understandably their attempts were unsuccessful. As
early as 1932 this action group had had a discussion with Firth on
the idea of a strip mill, but certainly there was then no thought
of Richard Thomas taking over Ebbw Vale.[50]

In the early autumn of 1935 the pressure groups concerned
to reopen Ebbw Vale and to stop the Lincolnshire development
were gradually brought together. A conference convened in
mid-October by Newport Chamber of Commerce was attended
by representatives of a wide range of South Wales society.
Claiming that the Ebbw Vale works cost the country £150,000
to £175,000 annually in unemployment allowances, that the
economic costs of an idle works as revealed in the accounts of
the Ebbw Vale Company ignored the additional substantial
social costs, it was decided to petition the government to help
in getting the plant restarted. On October 23rd a delegation
led by the Mayor of Swansea visited the President of the Board
of Trade, Mr. Runciman, to explain Welsh objections to the
Lincolnshire development. In less than a week negotiations
for the purchase of Ebbw Vale by Richard Thomas & Company
had already proceeded very far, and on 9th November it was
announced that the strip mill would be built there, not in
Lincolnshire. Five days later the American technical press
revealed that G. Arthur White of the Rotary Electric Steel
Company of Detroit would be in charge of the construction of

the new works. It appears not to have been a matter for concern that his company had no strip mill.[51]

Early in 1935 Sir John Beynon had discussed the possibility of reopening Ebbw Vale with the Commissioner for Special Areas, whose encouragement fostered the belief that government pressure brought about the modification of Richard Thomas plans. At the end of July Firth himself complicated matters by appealing to the government to prevent strip mill development by others, the proposed Dorman Long 72″ mill being his chief concern. On 12th November, two days before the General Election, Stanley Baldwin, speaking in Newcastle, clearly claimed a part in the change of Richard Thomas plans '. . . here', he said, 'I am touching on something that I have taken a great personal interest in, and that I have helped quietly and out of the limelight to do my bit in pushing along.'[52] Publicly, Firth added to this impression. With others, including Aneurin Bevan, Firth had agreed not to make political capital out of restoring activity at Ebbw Vale, but Lady Firth was deeply involved in the Primrose League and a telegram was sent to the Ebbw Vale Urban District Council announcing the purchase of the works and the plan for the new mill. The government, it indicated, had helped in this development. Challenged on this point by his business associates, but political opponents, Firth assured them that he was referring only to the general help given to the steel industry by the protective tariff of 1932, and that, in spite of Sir Malcolm Stewart's efforts to reopen Ebbw Vale, Baldwin's remarks or his own telegram to the Council, there had been no government pressure to build at Ebbw Vale and no financial assistance. There may, however, have been some government agreement to try to dissuade others from building strip mills.[53]

Later, Firth claimed that the Ebbw Vale decision had been taken after carefully comparing costs there and at Redbourn. Ebbw Vale had good blast furnaces so that the necessary plant could be built up at lower capital cost. A detailed cost analysis showed that with coal nearby, sintered ore from Northamptonshire, and an ample labour force in the area, Ebbw Vale would also be cheaper to run. These claims, however, conflict with what he had said earlier about Lincolnshire costs, what he was subsequently to reveal about Ebbw

Vale, and what would be expected from the situation of the two areas. Ten years later one technical journal recalled the old Ebbw Vale works as one of the most efficient in the country, with record blast furnace outputs. But in autumn, 1929 when, admittedly, output was being cut down, production costs for hematite pig iron at Ebbw Vale were 71s. 10d. a ton.[54] At this time Cleveland No. 3 iron and Lincolnshire basic iron, both certainly inferior irons, were produced for 60s. and 50–55s. a ton respectively, and in May, 1929, a detailed survey of the Scottish steel industry had suggested that, with gas credits, a Clyde estuary blast furnace could produce hematite iron for 60s. 3d. a ton.[55] Then in the spring of 1936, in an apparently sudden apostasy, Firth announced that the strip mill would be built near the Irthlingborough orefields of the Ebbw Vale Company and 12 miles from the new Corby works of Stewarts and Lloyds, whose ironmaking costs were the lowest in the country. High phosphorous ore, very suitable for tube production, was not an attractive material for quality flat-rolled steel, but Firth was appalled by site conditions at Ebbw Vale and accompanied the Irthlingborough proposal with harsh comment about production conditions in South Wales, which could not easily be reconciled with his attempt to rationalise the choice of Ebbw Vale. He said 'it would be absurd and against national interests to build modern works in South Wales. Northamptonshire and Lincolnshire were undoubtedly the natural centres for the economic production of British steel, and the recent Welsh protests about the introduction of modern machinery to those counties showed that Welshmen were too apt to take a local view'.[56] Already a Swansea conference had issued a protest against this, and in mid-July James Griffith, M.P. for Llanelly, asked the President of the Board of Trade 'to urge on Messrs. Richard Thomas & Co. a recognition of their social obligations'. At Llanelly, which, however, was not directly involved at all, there was a population of 40,000 completely dependent on one industry, whereas the population of the Northamptonshire village to which the company's attention was apparently moving was less than 5,000.[57] Yet all the time work was going ahead at Ebbw Vale, and Ernest Bevin was probably right when in June he advised the Swansea Conference of tinplate workers not to be unduly worried by a threat merely intended to keep the government to its commitment to dissuade new entrants to the sheet and tinplate trade.[58]

Although there is much conflicting evidence and much still not revealed, Firth could hardly have been convinced that Ebbw Vale would be a lower-cost location than Redbourn. The question of the amount of government pressure remains unresolved. Probably it was not entirely absent. Socially there is little doubt that the decision for Ebbw Vale was right, though only in short-term values; for long-term operating efficiency equally certainly it was wrong. In spite of high costs of site preparation, Ebbw Vale would cut the costs of sheet and strip production substantially—the *Economist* later put the reduction at 30 per cent.—and would establish new quality standards.[59] Equally predictably it upset the rest of the trade. In 1935 the project had been announced with a capacity of 150,000 tons sheet and tinplate a year, concentrating on tinplate, but by the end of the year Firth was estimating 300,000 tons as necessary to make the works pay, much of the increase to be in sheet.[60] The strip mill was to be limited to sheets of 48″ width, but some material up to 60″ wide was to be rolled on a cross mill. Lysaghts, rolling motor sheet up to 72″ wide on their new cold reduction mill, and with other trade interests, were certainly affected by the new project but not critically. Baldwins were similarly widely based. Even so, Firth later recalled that both companies opposed him bitterly from the day the Ebbw Vale mill was announced, although the survivors of those he accused deny this. The conviction in part reflects his own rather messianic character.[61] The motor sheet business and the proposed galvanising plant for Ebbw Vale hit most directly at John Summers. The impact of the scheme was intensified by Firth's outstanding indiplomacy.

At the extraordinary general meeting held in January, 1937, to gain approval for raising more capital for Ebbw Vale, Firth read extracts from a memorandum, sent by the Society of Motor Manufacturers and Traders to the Federation and almost certainly not intended for public ears. British sheets, the Society claimed, were still so poorly tempered that fracture was frequent, the press shop routine was upset and scrap losses were high. American material was cheaper and better, and

over freight and tariff could be delivered in Britain for only a
few shillings more a ton. Some firms were consequently
thinking of importing it again, as they had done before 1932.
But the motor firms welcomed the Ebbw Vale strip mill—'Its
introduction in this country will be regarded with the greatest
interest, and it is earnestly hoped that when brought into
operation it will be used to produce the type of material
required for the production of motor bodies'.[62] Although a
large firm of sheet makers provided data showing that its hot
rolled material was used on large runs of motor body components with a negligible rejection rate, there was an obvious
threat of consumer preference for strip sheet.[63]   The other
indiscretion in Firth's address was in production policy.   Until
December, 1936, when it adopted a resolution that 'all proposals
in regard to the expansion of plant should be submitted to a
Committee of the Federation . . .' the British Iron and Steel
Federation had no formal agreement for central oversight of
reconstruction.   Even so, launching the Ebbw Vale project
without consultation with the Federation was imprudent.
With new and old plant, Richard Thomas would have half the
British capacity of two million tons tinplate and sheet a year—
though their share in sheet was much smaller than in tinplate,
and they had not acquired formerly independent mills on the
same scale.[64]   To accommodate a hot strip mill would be
difficult, especially as, at the beginning of 1937, the old-type
mills were working at only 67 per cent. of capacity.   Firth was
quite unwilling to accommodate the whole of the strip mill
capacity at the expense of his company's existing mills, understandably, for this would have meant closing over 80 per cent.
of the mill power still at work.   Instead Richard Thomas had
informed the other members of the trade that Ebbw Vale would
be worked at full capacity, but, 'so as to maintain . . . orderly
competition' they were willing to restrict production at their
old-type plant on a *pro rata* basis with that at their rivals' works.
In other works Ebbw Vale would cut into the trade, while the
loss of business to the hand or mechanised mills would be
allocated to Richard Thomas and their rivals only on the basis
of their old plant capacity.   Such conditions were clearly
unacceptable, and provoked an early reaction.

REFERENCES

1 Lord Melchett reported *The Times* 6 December 1928, p. 13.
2 C. Schwab, *Journal of the Iron and Steel Institute* 1928, 1, p. 702. H. S. Jevons, *The British Steel Industry* (published as a booklet 1932).
3 J. Malborn in correspondence recalling extended visits and discussions of 1931 and 1934.
4 G. F. Gillott, then of Pressed Steel, in correspondence.
5 F. Purnell in *American Iron and Steel Institute Yearbook* 1940, p. 47.
6 *The Lysaght Century* p. 32.
7 J. B. Hoblyn in *Proceedings Institute Automobile Engineers* 24 1929–1930, p. 141. J. C. Arrowsmith *ibid.* 25 1930–1931, pp. 377–383, 29 1934–1935, p. 607. G. L. Kelly *ibid.* 92 1934–1935, p. 480.
8 *Engineer* 22 November 1935, p. 531. *Economist* 24 August 1935, p. 367.
9 W. F. Cartwright in correspondence.
10 *The Times* 24 October 1935.
11 *Engineer* 22 November 1935, p. 531, *Sheet Metal Industries* December 1935, p. 746. *Blast Furnace and Steel Plant* March 1936, p. 253 and J. Malborn.
12 *Iron and Coal Trades Review* 6 December 1935, p. 967.
13 *Economist* 1 December 1923, p. 981. *Manchester Guardian Commercial* 29 January 1925, p. 124.
14 *Engineer* 2 August 1935, p. 117.
15 *Times Trade and Engineering* July 1935, September 1935. *The Times* 19 December 1935 quoted D. L. Burn. *The Economic History of Steelmaking* 1867–1939 1940, p. 459 note 6.
16 W. F. Cartwright in correspondence.
17 G. A. V. Russell, *op. cit.*
18 G. A. V. Russell in correspondence.
19 *Iron Age* 23 June 1932, p. 1363.
20 P. W. S. Andrews and E. Brunner, *Capital Development in Steel* 1951, p. 170.
21 G. A. V. Russell and G. F. Gillott in correspondence.
22 *The Times* 11 April 1931, p. 17. E. Marks, 'Body Panel Sheets', *The Automobile Engineer* July 1937.
23 W. F. Cartwright and D. J. Young in conversation and correspondence.
24 D. C. Lysaght in discussion, *Journal of the Iron and Steel Institute* 1930, 1, p. 164.
25 *The Lysaght Century* pp. 31–32. *Proceedings Institute of Automobile Engineers* 29, 1934–1935, p. 604. Correspondence with Pressed Steel Company and conversation with E. C. Lysaght.
26 E. R. Mort 1934, *op. cit.*, pp. 246–247.
27 E. C. Lysaght in conversation.

28 *Journal of the Iron and Steel Institute* 1933, 1, pp. 44–45, my italics.
29 *ibid.*
30 Discussion of E. R. Mort 1934, *op. cit.*, pp. 228–232.
31 G. C. Richer 2 December 1935.
32 *Times* 22 December 1927, 21 December 1928, p. 24. *Iron and Coal Trades Review* 27 December 1929, p. 1004. *Times* 19 December 1930, p. 23.
33 See also *Sheet Metal Industries* August 1931, p. 249.
34 *Times* 19 December 1930, p. 23.
35 Conversation with H. T. Thomas, a member of the first group.
36 E. Cross in conversation.
37 *Times* 29 November 1932, p. 21.
38 E. E. Watkin, *The Development of the South Wales Tinplate Industry with special reference to* 1919–1939. Unpublished dissertation 1948, pp. 98–108. *Iron and Coal Trades Review* 21 March 1919. J. C. Carr and W. Taplin, *A History of the British Steel Industry* 1962, pp. 390, 438.
39 *Times* 22 February 1934, p. 10 *Engineer* 2 March 1934, p. 225. *Times* 16 April 1934, p. 7.
40 W. E. Minchinton, *The Tinplate Industry*, p. 200. E. E. Watkin, *op. cit.*, p. 44.
41 A Bullock, *The Life and Times of Ernest Bevin*, 1 1880–1940, p. 540.
42 *ibib.* quoting T.U.C. Report 1934, pp. 374–376.
43 *Engineer* 30 March 1934, p. 329. J. A. Smeeton in discussion of G. A. V. Russell 1936, p. 85.
44 *Sheet Metal Industries* April 1936, p. 287.
45 *The Times* 16 July 1935, p. 24.
46 *The Times* 15 July 1935, p. 16.
47 *Engineering* 16 August 1935, p. 169.
48 *Western Mail* and *South Wales News* 24 November 1930, p. 8.
49 *Times Trade and Engineering* January 1935, p. 29.
50 E. Cross in conversation.
51 *Engineering* 18 October 1935, p. 419, 1 November 1935, p. 474. *Iron Age* 14 November 1935, quoted *Sheet Metal Industries* December 1935, p. 747.
52 *Engineer* 4 January 1935, p. 27. *Iron and Coal Trades Review* 26 July 1935, p. 142. *Economist* 30 July 1938, p. 252. H. A. Marquand, *South Wales needs a plan* 1936, p. 55. *Times* 13 November 1935, p. 6.
53 E. Cross in conversation. Mr. Cross was closely associated with Sir William Firth at this time.
54 'Ebbw Vale Reawakes', *Iron and Steel Industry* 12, 1938–1939, p. 413. Notes by Sir Frederick Mills, November 1929.
55 P. E. P. *Report on the British Iron and Steel Industry* 1933, pp. 41–42. H. A. Brassert, *Report to Lord Weir of Eastwood on the Manufacture of Iron and Steel* (by a group of Scottish companies). Unpublished, May 1929, pp. 51, 142.

56 *The Times* 2 March 1936, 27 May 1936, p. 13. Reports of speeches at Newport and Swansea respectively.
57 *The Times* 6 April 1936, p. 9, 16 July 1936, p. 8.
58 *Sheet Metal Industries* July 1936, p. 510. *Economist* 21 November 1936, p. 368.
59 *Economist* 6 July 1938, p. 71.
60 *Engineer* 22 November 1935, p. 544.
61 Sir W. Firth unpublished papers.
62 *Iron and Coal Trades Review* 29 January 1937, p. 246. *Sheet Metal Industries* February 1937, p. 177. *Economist* 30 January 1937, p. 272.
63 *Sheet Metal Industries* March 1937, p. 259.
64 *Iron and Coal Trades Review* 29 January 1937, p. 246.

CHAPTER 11

Reaction and Experience: Some Consequences of the Ebbw Vale Development, 1935-40

By 1931 John Summers were making motor body sheet successfully, and within three years the firm was rolling considerable tonnages of 'special grade sheet'. Henry Summers had vigorously advocated protection and was now highly critical of the slow progress of the modernisation the steel industry had promised would follow.[1] In March, 1934, he wrote to *The Times:* 'For nearly two years the steel trade, at the urge of the government, has been drawing up schemes which, if adopted, can only prove futile and abortive. The main objects which the authors seem to have had in view were to bolster up redundant and obsolete plant, and by rings and quotas to put up the cost to the consumer. Anything which could help us to make our industry more efficient and more capable of competing in the markets of the world is lacking.'[2] Understandably, therefore, Firth had claimed Henry Summers as an ally in his struggle to rationalise sheet manufacture. Firth pointed out that, as Chairman of the Sheet Trade, Summers '. . . has for many years made strenuous and unwearying efforts to induce the trade to agree to amalgamations, to put an end to the uneconomic methods of spreading production by quota arrangements, and I believe is in entire agreement with me that some form of statutory control will be necessary before economic amalgamations on a sound financial basis can be achieved'.[3]

But although senior members of other sheet-making firms appear to have enjoyed harmonious personal relations in spite of their business rivalry, Firth was never happily accepted, and the announcement of the strip mill, followed by his new indiplomacies, incensed the management of Summers. There was even a rumour that they planned tinning pots at Hawarden

Bridge in retaliation for the proposed Richard Thomas incursion into sheet, although this threat was probably no more serious than Firth's talk of development at Irthlingborough; it was probably intended only to provoke a reaction from others. Even so, Richard Thomas sent a director to Summers's London flat to persuade him to abandon the idea. Although Henry Summers, now 70, was reluctant to break into wholly new technologies, it became clear to the Summers Board that the firm must build a strip mill. In 1936 a Sendzimir mill was installed to cold roll strip up to 40″ wide, but the hot mills remained inadequate. Despite their sheet output of about 8,000 tons a week, however, doubt remained whether Summers would be able to operate near enough to capacity to make the development pay, especially on the expanded scale of the Ebbw Vale mill. There had been many visits to the U.S. strip mills since the mid-1920s, before N. Rollason, the Summers managing director, and R. F. Summers early in 1937 visited a number of plants and the major steelworks equipment firm, the Mesta Machine Company of Pittsburgh, then reckoned technically somewhat ahead of United Engineering and Foundry which had done much pioneering work on strip mills ten years before. Returning, Rollason and Summers recommended construction, the Board took the decision by March, by May the first concrete plans had been discussed in London with L. Iversen, Mesta's President, by midsummer approval from the Federation's development committee and the Import Duties Advisory Committee had been obtained, and site work began in September.[4]

Firth, challenging the I.D.A.C. comment that the John Summers mill would only replace their hand mill output, asked for an undertaking not to turn their old sheet mills to producing black plate for tinning.[5] Presumably some such guarantee was given, for in August Henry Summers observed that some of their workers would inevitably lose their jobs as old-type mills at Hawarden Bridge and Ellesmere Port were closed, although some hot mill coil was to be further rolled at the company's outlying plants. At the same time he observed that his company had to build a strip mill to maintain its position in the trade—a compliment to Firth' pioneering role.[6]

Other major tinplate and sheet firms were making far more hesitant moves in the same direction.

BALDWINS AND LYSAGHTS

By the late 1930s the operating cost advantage of strip mills was universally recognised although no simple comparison applied to all plants—the American example shown below is merely a broad guide. (Table 26.)   Some managements long continued to doubt their overall advantages in British market conditions.   Early in 1937, before Summers's plans had been made public, Sir Charles Wright observed that Guest, Keen

TABLE 26

Manufacturing Costs of tinplate by various types of Mill.
Experience of one Ohio valley plant, Spring, 1938

(dollars per net ton)

	Hand mills	Mechanised mills	4-high reversing mill	Strip mill
Ingot cost	21·45	21·45	21·45	21·45
Process costs	67·90	56·92	52·05	47·99
TOTAL COST	89·35	78·37	73·50	69·44

Source: Correspondence with a U.S. authority

and Baldwins had designed the wholly rebuilt Cardiff works so '. . . as to be able to put down a strip mill for supplying hot strip in coils for the manufacture of tinplates and sheets should this be required by their parent companies or their associated concerns'.[7]   The associated firms to which he referred were presumably Baldwins, G.K.N. and its subsidiaries, including Lysaghts and Sankeys.   The main members of this group differed widely on the type and location of mill needed, and the situation was further complicated by a degree of personal animosity between the chairmen of G.K.N. and Baldwins. The idea of a central, large producer of hot rolled material for finishing in scattered small works, which Sir Charles seemed to indicate, had been anticipated in the reorganisation plans of a tinplate committee convened by Frank Gilbertson in 1928[8] and was a persistent theme in reorganisation plans for another 10 years. Superficially it was attractive, for it would enable the existing pattern of South Wales industry to be largely preserved; this was at the same time its grave practical deficiency.

The Cardiff site was in fact already badly cramped and lacked space sufficient to accommodate a strip mill. Once it was written off the only other integrated works suitable for development on that scale was the G.K.B. works at Port Talbot. Already active planning by the Port Talbot management had begun, and by early 1938 their thinking had produced a scheme for a combined plate and sheet operation. In March, 1938, tentative plans were drawn by American engineers for a four-high reversing plate mill, with room at the end of the plate line for a four stand four-high hot strip mill to be built later. By 1938 an old Port Talbot blast furnace had been rebuilt, a new one was being erected and half the coke oven battery was renewed. This plate/strip mill scheme was not by any means an ideal project and the approach of war fortunately cut out all thought if its implementation. Planning, however, went on, the various schemes, some of them of great elaboration, already running through the alphabet from A to J before the autumn of 1939.[9] While a decisive basis was in fact being laid at Port Talbot, it seemed through the 1930s that Lysaghts were more likely to build a strip mill.

Three weaknesses dogged Lysaghts throughout the decade— their possession of two major works, their continued success with mechanised mill sheet finished on the cold reduction mill, and, not unrelated to that, the failure to see the inevitability of the strip mill. As late as 1937 an American guest, at a joint banquet of the Sheet Makers and the Sheet and Tinplate Confederation, was upbraided by W. R. Lysaght for the view that in ten to fifteen years most of the sheet mills would have gone. Lysaght still believed that strip mills would never roll thin sheets—24 to 29G—as cheaply as mechanised mills. As the firm's opposition weakened the problem of location arose— was a strip mill to be built at Normanby Park or Newport? After an extensive reconstruction in 1930–1932 Normanby Park was probably still the lowest-cost steel producer in Britain, a model of fuel economy and heat balance, employing scrap only from its own mills. By the mid-thirties its costs were higher than those of Corby, but Redbourn was still inefficient in fuel consumption, as Firth admitted, and until 1939, when its first coke ovens were built, costs at the much bigger Appleby-Frodingham works were also higher.[10] This plant was therefore an extremely attractive location for further development, and indeed early in the 1930s Lysaghts had considered installing mechanised sheet mills there before opting instead for Newport. Early in 1936 they were reported to be planning a Normanby Park strip mill, but this was almost certainly unfounded rumour, for only six weeks before G. C. Richer had concluded that a strip mill was not justified in Lysaghts' trading conditions.[11] Instead the development again went to Newport in the form of the cold reduction mill. Further developments although reducing overall costs perpetuated the separation of steelmaking and finishing—a new coke oven plant for Scunthorpe and new cold reduction developments for Newport.[12] Between the two an improved bulk transport system was introduced. The long-established rail haul had cost as little as 10s. 6d. a ton of sheet bars, but now three special coastal vessels were purchased to carry up to 4,000 tons bar a week from the wharf at Flixborough on the Trent, some four miles from Normanby Park, to Newport. Costs were minimised by arranging that the vessels should then carry Welsh coal to Normandy and return to Flixborough laden with Caen ore, considerably richer but no less phosphoric than Frodingham ore, for mixing with that stone in the Normanby Park furnaces. The cost of delivering sheet bar to Newport was thereby reduced to 6s. a ton.[13] By the end of 1938 there were new reports of a project for a Normanby Park strip mill, enquiries about equipment were said to have been made but no proposal was made public, and the existence of a highly efficient operating structure, the fear that the Lysaght ore reserves in North Lincolnshire were insufficient to support operations on a strip mill scale, and the claims of development at Newport ended thinking along this line.[14] The emphasis was now on development planning at Newport.

Although the cold reduction mill at the Orb works was successful, its sheet was inferior to that from the strip mills, and from the start it was realised that strip mill coil was a much better material for the cold mill than the mechanised mill 'breakdowns' which were employed. Attempts were now made to find a hot strip mill of a suitable type for Lysaght's operations. The problem had been much less serious for Richard Thomas & Company because of the greater importance of tinplate stock and therefore of narrower and rather poorer strip in their operations. For their substantial motor sheet trade Lysaghts wanted an 80" mill rather than the 56" mill of Richard Thomas or the 60" mill of Summers. A mill of this size would have a large capacity and it was difficult to see an assured outlet. By 1938 it was believed that at last E. W. Plumley, the Development Engineer at Newport, had designed a suitable mill. Two stages were envisaged. In the first a reversing roughing mill and then a three or four stand finishing mill were to be installed. The roughing mill would produce plate and also material for hot and cold rolling on the same finishing train and would be supplied by slabs brought by water from Scunthorpe, and from other works. In stage two, when trade conditions justified, a steel plant and eventually blast furnaces would be built at Newport, west of the Usk, with a frontage suitable for ore dock development. There was considerable scepticism as to whether a single unit could perform both hot and cold rolling operations, especially to meet the high standards of cleanliness recognised as essential in cold mills. The project is recalled by one director as 'half-baked', in the sense of literally unfinished.[15] Some would have used this term in its other, colloquial sense. One recalls 'It was the most ridiculous suggestion that I have ever seen'. Any attempt to realise the first stage of the Lysaght strip mill scheme was frustrated by events. The firm had the encouragement of S. R. Beale, chairman of G.K.N., but G.K.B. were actively planning at Port Talbot. Early in 1939 Sir Charles Wright, as chairman of G.K.B., called the associated concerns together and a committee was appointed to examine the strip mill issue. This postponed the possibility of building work on the Lysaght mill for some six months and the committee, while recognising the desirability of a strip mill, did not decide whether Port Talbot or Newport should be its location. The outbreak of war stopped development thinking for a while,

o

and when it was revived the Lysaght case for the hot strip mill was not urged very strongly.[16]

Two other strip mill schemes were of a size and form which suggested that while the advantages of the new technique had been appreciated the scale of the associated problems had not. Both stemmed from the tinplate trade, though undoubtedly they would have involved sheet capacity as well, and both reflected fear of competition from Ebbw Vale, for again in March and September, 1938, Firth had declared his company unwilling that Ebbw Vale should be brought into the tinplate pooling arrangements without an increased allocation for Richard Thomas. In the sheet trade Summers had agreed to do this with their strip mill.[17]

Immediately after Richard Thomas had revealed their first strip mill plans in 1935, the Briton Ferry Steel Company, third-largest of the tinplate concerns, although much smaller than either Richard Thomas or Baldwins, had announced that they were putting in a mill at their Albion Works, which could be converted into a strip mill if the Redbourn mill was built. In mid-1938 J. M. Bevan, chairman of Briton Ferry, acknowledging the superiority of tinplate made from strip mill coil, suggested there was room in South Wales for a second mill, and in the following spring another member of the same company gave a further hint of a new strip mill when speaking at the banquet of the Port Talbot Chamber of Trade. Later Bevan revealed that no decision had been taken, 'as they had been asked to hold up their plans temporarily, pending a review of the steel and tinplate trade in South Wales'.[18] The company had a billet and sheet bar mill on to which they proposed to build plant to roll strip up to 36″ wide, for tinning and also for many classes of sheet. The plant, however, was said to be so poor that, as put by a disinterested plant engineer outsider, one wondered how it rolled anything.

By early 1938 five tinplate companies of Llanelly and Pontardulais with 46 mills and a combined capital of about £1 million were entertaining preliminary thoughts of amalgamating to build a strip mill at Llanelly.[19] In November they wrote to their shareholders concerning the competition from Ebbw Vale, which had been working for four months and which '. . . in the view of the Boards of all the companies is likely to render it difficult, if not impossible, for the companies as at present organised to continue operating'. Very optimistically they considered their pooled resources such that '. . . the amalgamated concern should be in a position itself to erect a strip mill, should this be found essential'.[20] Reorganised as the Llanelly Associated Tinplate Companies, the group enquired in the United States for a plant suited to their needs. In February, 1938, before the link between them was formalised, a Steckel mill was suggested. This mill, the invention of Abraham Steckel of the Youngstown Cold Process Company, rolled down slabs into strip on one mill stand, and, for an investment small compared with that in a continuous or semi-continuous strip mill, and with a much smaller capacity, could nevertheless turn out higher-quality strip than could the hand mills. Welsh companies had long wondered whether a wide strip mill could roll different sizes and tonnages and still remain economic, and the Steckel mill was claimed to have quite low operating costs even in these conditions. Further the installation of a few of these smaller plants rather than a single strip mill could eliminate some inter-mill freight charges and, by preserving old finishing centres, avoid many of the problems of a radical change in the technique and scale of industry.[21] Steckel mills had, however, some disadvantages. Rolling from the slab to the finished hot rolled strip on the same mill stand frequently caused temperature control difficulties, and scale from the early stages of rolling was sometimes a nuisance during finishing. Consequently it was often reckoned that high-grade autobody sheet could not be rolled successfully on a Steckel mill, and this troubled the planners of Llanelly Associated. The Dominion Iron and Steel Company of Canada had installed a Steckel mill but their concern was chiefly with tinplate, and they eventually built a hot mill for the primary rolling, to reduce the problems of quality control in the Steckel mill. In Detroit, however, the McLouth Steel Corporation had since 1934 successfully rolled autobody sheet on a Steckel mill—an operation continued with success until 1954.[22] The other major disadvantages of a one stand installation were higher operating costs and rather low yields, offsetting its lower capital costs. In one American case of 1937–1938, working on slabs at $21·33 a ton, a con-

tinuous strip mill had conversion costs to coil ranging from
$3·69 to $4·79 a ton against $9·39 a ton on a Steckel mill.
Yields on the Steckel mill were 90–93 per cent. of the slab
weight, on the hot strip 96–97 per cent.[23] Whatever the
merits of the Steckel process, Llanelly Associated was deterred
from further explorations at this time.   In the summer of 1939
the Independent Chairman of the British Iron and Steel
Federation, Sir Andrew Duncan, asked the group to wait until
a redundancy scheme could be worked out for the whole
tinplate trade and until their development plans could be fitted
into a wholesale reorganisation.   Without this, he suggested,
the necessary capital could not be found.[24]   Llanelly Associated
was, however, to play a significant role in influencing the
pattern of post-war developments.   Meanwhile even the bigger
companies had run into difficulties over finance.

CRISIS AND REORGANISATION
IN STRIP MILL CONSTRUCTION

In 1935 the whole redevelopment programme at Ebbw Vale
was costed at £4½ million, but site conditions and national
recovery from depression raised construction costs.   In January,
1937, Rothschilds had offered £7 million of Richard Thomas
stock to finance the slabbing, hot and cold strip and cross mills
at Ebbw Vale and the new coke ovens at Redbourn, but
within twelve months it was clear that even previous high
estimates, up to £8½ million, were too low.   By March, 1938,
there were press rumours that Richard Thomas was in financial
distress, but these were denied by Firth.   Meanwhile the slump
of 1938 reduced the basis price for tinplate and motor car
production, which had increased annually since 1931, declined.
1938 output of uncoated sheet, therefore, was only 61·3 per
cent. the record level of 1937, (Table 27.)   At the end of April,
white-faced, Firth disclosed to his fellow directors, to whom the
difficulties appear not to have been fully revealed before, that
the cash reserves were almost exhausted and that he had just
been engaged in discussion with Montague Norman, the
Governor of the Bank of England.[25]   Another £6 million was
needed to complete the plant.   The Bank of England at once
made £1 million available.   On 17th June the Ebbw Vale

case was brought before the B.I.S.F. expansion committee. Seven other company chairmen attended this meeting. Later S. R. Beale of G.K.N. and Sir Charles Wright of Baldwin's informed Duncan that they were willing to join the Richard Thomas Board. Meanwhile a financial and technical examination of the Ebbw Vale project was made for the Bank of

TABLE 27

Production of Tinplate, Galvanised Sheet and Uncoated Sheet, 1928–1938 (thousand tons)

	Tinplate Terneplate and Blackplate	Galvanised Sheet	Uncoated Sheet
1928	—	888	598
1929	880	843	595
1930	814	579	444
1931	717	446	406
1932	745	358	436
1933	767	336	489
1934	—	350	617
1935	708	389	707
1936	—	361	801
1937	957	345	926
1938	610	247	568

England by an independent expert, highly regarded in the trade, John E. James of Lancashire Steel.[26] Wright, Beale, James and the accountant, J. Adamson, were appointed to the Richard Thomas Board, and Norman, with a consortium of banks, agreed to find the necessary £6 million provided a control committee with power to appoint or remove directors was set up. Norman, Firth, Viscount Greenwood, the Chairman of Dorman Long, and E. H. Lever of the Prudential Assurance Company were appointed to this committee. Firth seemed appreciative and anxious to co-operate, but there is evidence that he was dissatisfied from the start. Privately he intimated that Baldwins and other South Wales firms had somehow contrived to increase the construction costs, which, because of the difficulties of the Ebbw Vale site, were considerable enough anyway.[27]   Two years later he recalled that 'in very dirty weather some pirates pushed us on the rocks and boarded us'; they were, as he put it, 'disguised as national interests'.[28]

In the summer of 1939, when his relations with Beale and Wright were terribly strained, Firth asked for a change, Norman agreed, and the two resigned.   With Firth's approval they were replaced by three more distinguished steel company chairmen, but from trades other than tinplate and sheet—the Earl of Dudley, A. C. Macdiarmid of Stewarts and Lloyds and Sir James Lithgow, who had acquired Beardmores and the Steel Company of Scotland and was now on the Colvilles board. John E. James became Managing Director, relieving Firth of the strain of combining this post with that of Chairman. Illness soon made it necessary to replace James, and G. H. Latham, Chairman and Managing Director of Whitehead Iron and Steel, was appointed, possibly at Firth's own suggestion. Firth, however, soon disagreed violently with Latham, who, while Firth was away on a government mission in France, dismissed some key American personnel at Ebbw Vale and pointed out to visiting journalists what he regarded as inadequacies in the planning of the works, including the suggestion that the Bessemer plant could not make satisfactory steel for sheet. In April, 1940, the Control Committee removed Firth from the Board.   After a short interim period E. H. Lever became Chairman on 1st August, 1940, Latham Managing Director and James remained associated.   Firth now became an implacable opponent of the management of the company whose leadership in sheet and tinplate production his enterprise had undoubtedly secured.[29]

Compared with the troubles of Richard Thomas those of John Summers were small.   The scheme had been more modest—as R. F. Summers later recalled, it involved 'the minimum amount of plant necessary to make a practicable unit, with the idea of using much of our old finishing equipment which we hoped could be replaced over a number of years. . . .'[30] The site needed much piling and the full range of ancillary plant necessary to make the mill efficient was not appreciated. Also, apart from the disadvantages of cold metal operations, Summers tried to heat and roll slabs with equipment which had been used to produce sheet bars and which was quite unsuitable to serve a strip mill. It had been thought that the Appleby works of United Steels could supply surplus slabs to the Summers strip mill, but, as shown above, the steel soon proved of unsuitable quality. In 1939 a scheme was proposed for the delivery of 2,000 to 3,000 tons a week of slabs from United Steels' Workington plant by coastal vessel. The transfer of a slabbing mill of good quality from a works at Douai in the northern industrial region of France was stopped by the outbreak of war.[31] The strip mill came into production in November, 1939, when its roughing stands were still steam-driven. In 1938 the firm was already in financial difficulty, and like Richard Thomas asked the Bank of England for assistance. In 1939 G. H. Latham was invited to report on the project for the Bank and for the Ministry of Supply. Representation on the company directorate by nominees of the Bank was again a condition of help, but, as the financial problems of Summers were less than those of Richard Thomas and the threat to other company interests from the strip mill much smaller than from Ebbw Vale, no trade rivals were imposed on the board. Some agreement seems to have been made with Richard Thomas for a degree of co-operative running of the two mills.[32] £2 million was raised by public issue, United Steel Companies provided another £1 million and exchanged directors with Summers, and the Bank of England secured the final £1 million needed to complete the plant, in exchange for which it insisted on the right of veto at the shareholders' meeting. In November, 1938, a year before the strip mill began rolling, Henry Summers was succeeded as chairman of the company by R. F. Summers. Within two years Firth was forced to resign from the board of Richard Thomas and W. R. Lysaght retired after 66 years in the sheet trade. The further progress of reorganisation of sheet and tinplate production was to be under new guiding hands.

By the end of 1939, as the Hawarden Bridge mill was run in, British strip mill capacity was about 1·1 million tons, Ebbw Vale having slightly the larger part. Approaching two-thirds of the national sheet or tinplate capacity was still in hand mills or in mills mechanised or improved in varying degrees. In spite of competition from the new plants, there was still a good enough market prospect to justify the further improvement of the old ones. Lysaghts, Baldwins and others still retained a large share of the trade in motor body sheet, and if war had not intervened there might well have been two new strip mills, a Guest, Keen, Baldwin plant at Port Talbot and a Lysaght mill at Newport. Llanelly Associated and Briton Ferry still nursed their ambitions. Furthermore, in 1938 Firth had spoken to his close associates of the need for a second Richard Thomas strip mill on the coast of South Wales, and had looked to a time when South Wales would be the largest centre of tinplate and strip sheet production in the world. The re-organisation and relocation of the British sheet steel industry clearly was far from completed, it was obviously an almost wholly Welsh problem and, as events were to prove, there was abundant material for protracted controversies over the size, type and location of new developments.

REFERENCES

1   Letters from H. Summers and W. Firth appeared on the same day in opposition to the Free Trade views of A. I. Parkes of Birmingham Corrugated Iron.   *The Times* 3 December 1931. 4 December 1931.
2   *The Times* 17 March 1934.
3   *Engineer* 2 March 1934, p. 225.
4   A. Reid *Continuous Venture* pp. 23–25.   Import Duties Advisory Committee Report, *The Present Position and Future Development of the Iron and Steel Industry* July 1937, p. 40, and P. J. Summers.
5   *Iron and Coal Trades Review* 9 July 1937, p. 76.
6   Import Duties Advisory Committee Report July 1937, p. 40. *Iron and Coal Trades Review* 13 August 1937, p. 269.
7   *Sheet Metal Industries* May 1937, p. 456.
8   H. T. Thomas in conversation.
9   W. F. Cartwright and D. J. Young in conversation and correspondence.
10 W. J. Brooke, 'Co-ordinated heat conservation at the Normanby Park Steelworks, Lincolnshire'. *Journal of the Iron and Steel Institute* 1933, 2.
11 *Iron and Coal Trades Review* 24 January 1936, p. 211.
12 *The Times* 29 June 1938.
13 E. C. Lysaght. *Iron and Coal Trades Review* 1 January 1937, p. 25. *Sheet Metal Industries* September 1938, p. 1013.
14 E. C. Lysaght in conversation and correspondence.

15 E. C. Lysaght and H. H. Stanley in conversation and correspondence.
16 E. C. Lysaght.
17 Letter of H. C. Thomas to H. Leighton Davies (of Baldwins) 23 March 1938, referring especially to fears expressed by J. Paton of Partridge Jones and John Paton Ltd. Letter of Sir W. Firth to H. Leighton Davies 22 September 1938.
18 *Sheet Metal Industries* July 1938, April 1939, July 1939.
19 *Sheet Metal Industries* September 1938, p. 1012.
20 Letter of 21 November 1938, to shareholders of all five companies.
21 Review of Steckel mills in correspondence between W. E. Phillips of Llanelly Associated and W. E. Lockwood of the Cold Metal Process Company of Youngstown, Ohio. June to August 1946.
22 Letter to Chairman of Llanelly Associated 30 March 1939.
23 J. Malborn in correspondence.
24 Minutes of Llanelly Associated Tinplate Companies 3 June 1939, 4 August 1939.
25 Recalled by a fellow director.
26 *Engineer* 1 July 1938, p. 30.
27 *Engineer* 2 October 1936, p. 333. Unpublished papers of Sir W. Firth and Sir E. Lever.
28 *The Times* 31 July 1940, quoted by D. L. Burn. *The Steel Industry* 1939–1959, p. 56.
29 While drawing on published material by Burn and by Carr and Taplin I have also consulted Sir E. Lever and E. Cross with whom Firth corresponded on these matters.
30 R. F. Summers, *The Birth and Growth of the Firm of John Summers and Sons*, Lecture 27 February 1945.
31 G. A. V. Russell in conversation.
32 Sir H. Clay, *Lord Norman* 1957, p. 349.

PART IV

WORLD WAR II &
POST-WAR DEVELOPMENT

CHAPTER 12

The Sheet Trade in the Second World War and under the first post-war Development Plan

I. THE NEW WELSH HOT MILL

The development of the British sheet steel industry was in its most significant and controversial phase between 1943 and 1947. At that time decisions were taken leading to the construction of the biggest sheet and tinplate complex in Britain. The process of decision taking which led to the formation of the Steel Company of Wales and the new works at Port Talbot, Velindre and Trostre was protracted and extremely complicated. As one who was engaged in the process comments, the issue can be 'obscured by a flood of evidence', but one must nevertheless probe into the development reports of the time and try to make one's way through a labyrinth of frequently conflicting personal recollections. There are one or two themes which keep recurring. The question of concentration or dispersal of new plant arose on various occasions. Secondly, there was a steady increase in the size of development contemplated, and an equally persistent underestimate of the capital investment involved. The scale necessitated a grouping of companies as opposed to the single-firm projects of Ebbw Vale and Hawarden Bridge. To the obvious possibilities of conflict this involved was added a more open and aggressive government intervention than in the pre-war period. In the process of reconciling the various forces it emerged that locational choice was now much more restricted than ever before.[1]

After the commissioning of the hot mill at Hawarden Bridge in November, 1939, it was almost twelve years before another British strip mill began rolling. Except perhaps in the earliest, darkest period of the war, however, discussions and development planning continued among at least some of the interested parties. About equal tonnages of tinplate and sheet capacity remained to be modernised but whereas the tinplate mills were localised in South Wales about half of the sheet tonnage still in hand or mechanised mills was outside Wales. (Table 28.) This was mostly in smallish, scattered units and, apart from the Midland works, generally involved lower grades of sheet. One must stress that the modernisation of the sheet steel industry remained inextricably bound up with, and usually dominated by the reorganisation of tinplate production. Given the location of concentrations of activity in quality sheet

TABLE 28

Projected Sheet and Tinplate Production mid-1940s
(thousand tons per week)

	Tinplate	Sheet
By modern plant*	5	11
To be modernised	10 ⎫	14
To be left to-old type mills	5 ⎭	
	——	——
TOTAL	20	25

* Ebbw Vale and Hawarden Bridge
Source: Technical Committee of Tinplate Processes Ltd. August 1944

and the structure of the main existing firms, this ensured that new developments were almost inevitably a South Wales matter. (Figure 16.) Locations elsewhere were rumoured. For these much could be said in theoretical terms, and they were occasionally used to build up political pressure, but they were never seriously considered.

Both in tinplate and in sheet prospective demand seemed to justify rationalisation, and for export the superior product of the strip mill was essential if markets were to be held. Although overheads mounted alarmingly, operating costs in new-style plant were much lower than in the old mills, and apparently considerably more so for tinplate than with sheet. (Table 29.) Reconstruction would clearly further concentrate production, requiring the demolition of mills or their conversion to other

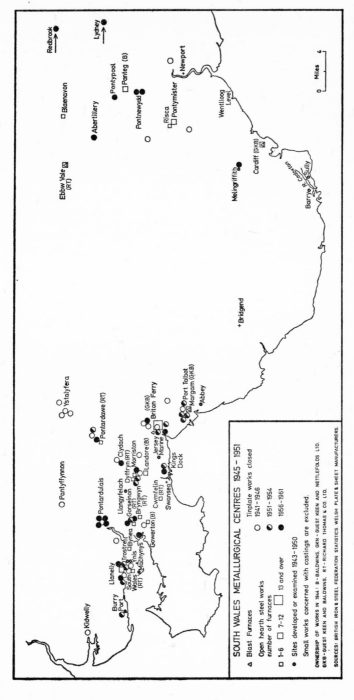

Figure 16. Plant was heavily concentrated in West Wales, a decisive factor in the locational choices of this period.

TABLE 29

Comparative Production Costs in old- and new-style Sheet and
Tinplate Plants, 1945 (shillings per ton)

| | NEW PLANT | | | OLD TYPE PLANT | |
	Prime Costs	Capital Charges	Total	20 per cent. plants with highest costs	Next 20 per cent. plants
Sheet	345	75	420	470	444
Tinplate	500	105	605	725	675

Source: British Iron and Steel Federation. *Report to the Ministry of Supply on the Iron and Steel Industry* 1945, p. 20

products, and producing social disturbance. Strong company
and political reactions to any proposals were therefore
inevitable. Early in this period there was continuing antipathy
to change, or an unwillingness to co-operate wholeheartedly to
bring it about by many of the established interests. This had
defeated Firth in his headlong, often intolerant progress, and
now the whole round of negotiations had to be taken further.
Even Firth's much more diplomatic successor, Ernest Lever,
was moved to point out to the members of the Tinplate
Conference that if they were unwilling to close and rationalise
plant by collective arrangements those in the strongest position
would have to take individual action. For those concerned with
planning rather than with negotiations, experience at home
and in the United States laid down certain guide lines, and the
many projects and the third strip mill that eventually emerged
from them may partly be judged against these standards. In
summary, the new mill should be fully continuous, larger and
wider than either Ebbw Vale or Hawarden Bridge, completely
integrated and therefore located at a port able to handle at
least medium-size ore boats for the essential large proportion
of foreign ore.

Much thinking until the end of the war involved mills no
bigger than the two existing installations. Subsequent technical
progress ensured that the plant was to have a much greater
output than could be envisaged even in 1947 or 1948. This
was important, for whereas in 1944 or 1945 there would seem

to be scope soon for yet another mill, the long-term expansion of Port Talbot meant that the choice of 1945 was decisive and that the opportunity to develop other locations later was very considerably reduced. The type of mill was connected with the question of capacity and therefore also with the size of the group of companies involved in co-operative reorganisation. If the output they were to replace was only about half a million tons then a semi-continuous mill was perhaps the most suitable unit. Capital costs could be reduced, though running costs would be higher than in a fully continuous mill. Even in a semi-continuous mill output could be increased and operating costs cut by installing more finishing stands. One American analysis at this time suggested that for tinplate stock the saving in a fully continuous mill could be over $4 a ton, at existing exchange rates more than £1, yet only a big group could provide a continuous mill with a loading which would enable its low running costs to compensate fully for the extra capital investment.[2] As G. A. V. Russell had foreseen in the mid-1930s, creation of such a group needed the reconciliation of opposed and strongly entrenched interests.

The question of width brought some of these inter-company conflicts to the surface. In the late thirties American firms were already building second strip mills. Those with narrow mills—less than about 48″—built wide mills, those with wide mills a new unit for narrower strip. Some firms in the first category burdened themselves with mills almost 100″ wide which were for a time seriously underemployed. Ebbw Vale had a 56″ mill, able to roll coil up to 48″ wide. The Hawarden Bridge mill was 60″ wide, so neither could roll the wider sheets increasingly demanded by the press shops. Ebbw Vale rolled sheets up to 100″ wide by cutting coils which were then rolled further on a cross mill, but only Lysaghts' 80″ cold reduction mill could supply directly material as wide as 72″. Some adventurous spirits advocated a British mill 96″ to 100″ wide, but one of the negotiators recalls that this scheme failed when the motor firms indicated that annual demand for sheet of this size could be produced from a wide mill in one day.[3] The executive side of the industry, more cautious, money conscious and less concerned with sheet than with tinplate, advocated another 56″ or 60″ mill, but in the winter of 1943 an

P

Iron and Steel Control technical study confirmed the need for an 80" mill.[4] This conclusion was not accepted by all concerned, but, given the greater expansion of demand for sheet rather than tinplate, it would surely have been a mistake to put up a third medium-width mill.

By 1945 the project already visualised an ingot capacity of about 1 million tons. In a new location a large traffic in imported ore could be expected. Two circumstances, however, lessened the impact of this fact—home ore as an important admixture and considerable supplies of steel from West Wales Siemens works. These helped to disguise the need for a deep-water location, a need which the Severn estuary was not well provided to satisfy. But all agreed that the new mills would turn out both a superior and a cheaper product, and, as D. L. Burn neatly put it afterwards, when overall costs might be cut by £2 or more a ton why bother if the location chosen was perhaps 5s. a ton less favoured than the best.[5] Cost minimisation was, of course, rational and 'economic', but there were existing plants and communities to take into account, and many other interests and considerations were involved as well as the merely commercial. It is perhaps significant that one person intimately associated with the reorganisation of the sheet and tinplate trades at this time wrote, 'We never paid very much attention to Mr. D. L. Burn's statements at Steel House when I was there.' Against a background of the 'ideal' pattern, the pieces of the locational game were still moved by many hands and with widely varying motives; though more capable than ever before of rational evaluation, development decision-taking was still the art of the possible.

REORGANISATION PLANNING BY COMPANIES & COMMITTEES TO 1943

By continuing during the war the modernisation programme they began in 1938, Guest, Keen, Baldwins eventually ensured that the existing Port Talbot-Margam Works became the location of the new hot strip mill and the nucleus of the reorganisation. A new blast furnace was completed at Margam in 1941 and another in 1943. Meanwhile the list of G.K.B. strip-mill development schemes lengthened. Although it is now clear that the persistency of G.K.B. planning was decisive, others were also busy along different lines. G.K.N. had a controlling interest in G.K.B. and a continuing concern for the future of Newport, but at Orb Works the Lysaght management was so wholly preoccupied with war work—rolling duralium and brass rather than steel—that long-term planning lapsed. At the end of the war they were confronted with an already elaborate project for Port Talbot. Richard Thomas, with E. Lever as the new chairman and G. H. Latham and J. E. James as chief production officers, were pursuing their own studies for further modernisation, but now, in marked contrast to the situation when Sir William Firth was chairman, in close co-operation with the Tinplate Conference.

On 29th October, 1941, after a five months' enquiry, the Essendon Committee reported its findings on concentration and rationalisation in the tinplate industry. Up to 30 per cent. of existing tinplate capacity should be sterilised, but it was suggested that Ebbw Vale would be able to deal with only one-fifth of post-war demand and that plans for more hot strip mill capacity should be prepared immediately. The tinplate firms reacted vigorously but variously to these proposals. Baldwins with 65 hand mills, over one-eighth of the total British capacity, provided the most powerful opposition. Their continuing intransigence was an important factor contributing to their merger with Richard Thomas three years later.

In November, 1942, T. O. Lewis, C. F. Gilbertson and F. S. Padbury produced a report on various reconstruction possibilities for Richard Thomas. In particular they considered three schemes designed to produce as little disturbance as possible and to use existing plants. They first reviewed and rejected the idea of a new slabbing mill at Llanelly to feed expanding output at the Ebbw Vale strip mill and to replace slab from Redbourn, even though such an installation would have preserved employment by drawing approximately 260,000 tons ingots a year from three existing steelworks, Cwmfelin, Bryngwyn and the nearby South Wales works. Secondly, they considered the possibility of building slabbing, hot and cold strip mills at Llanelly to be supplied with a slightly larger tonnage of ingots from existing works, Grovesend this time being substituted for Bryngwyn. Cold reduced black plate from Llanelly would be finished at six to eight existing tinplate works, extending from Burry in the west to Pontardawe in the Swansea valley and even inland to Glanrhyd east of Ystalyfera. Capital costs would be high, operations would still involve cold metal and long hauls on ingots, strip and tinplate. These haulage costs would average 5s. 2d. per ton for ingots and 13s. 9d. for tinplate, or over £190,000 more per year for transport than in a coastal works making its own ingots and tinning its own strip. Finally they considered dispersal of both hot and cold mills in smaller units nearer older steel and tinplate works, to use existing buildings, modify rather than replace existing bar mills and economise in capital expenditure. This scheme would also reduce transport costs and lessen redundancy in existing centres of production. Commenting that this scheme seemed to fit better than the others their company's dispersed operations Lewis, Gilbertson and Padbury recommended a full investigation. In fact developments along these lines would have produced a makeshift reorganisation employing indifferent plant and sacrificing economies of scale.

Although nothing significant proceeded from this study, the three schemes are illuminating on the turmoil of conflicting ideas, their general immaturity and the predicament of Richard Thomas & Company. Development thinking at this stage involved only tinplate and even the biggest schemes were still of smaller scale than Ebbw Vale. Planning was dominated by the ideas of seven or eight years before, involving dispersed operations and an unwillingness to scrap existing plant wholesale, but with no blast furnaces and no good tidewater location Richard Thomas & Company could never make a very satisfactory job of reorganising their West Wales works. They were to think of Llanelly developments again, but inadequacies there were another influence driving them to contemplate association with Baldwins and so with Guest, Keen, Baldwins. The next step, explicitly recognising this, came only two months later in a memorandum which, though concerned with South Wales as a whole, was prepared by G. H. Latham and John E. James of Richard Thomas & Company.

The Latham-James memorandum, 'The Future of the Tinplate Trade', was itself unbalanced, for by its terms of reference it did not consider the prospect of combining big new develop-

ments in sheet with rationalisation in tinplate. It broke important new ground, however. The scale was bigger, involving
ingot consumption over 200,000 tons more than at Ebbw Vale
and tinplate output 40 per cent. greater. West Wales steel was
now recognised as undesirable even for tinplate manufacture.
The Siemens works were classed as costly producers, high scrap
charges introducing substantial harmful tramp elements, their
small slow-running furnaces unsuitable for the low carbon,
rimming steels or the bigger ingots that were needed. Nevertheless, Latham and James envisaged some ingots being drawn
from these works, presumably for lower-grade products.
Llanelly Steel Company, in which the Llanelly Associated
Tinplate Companies had a financial interest, and the independent Briton Ferry Works, both rather bigger than the general
run of West Wales works, were more promising sources of steel,
but even they were cold-metal plants and their expansion was
doubtfully economic in the long run. Attention therefore
switched to the two big, integrated coastal works, use of either
of which as a focus for development would require regrouping
of companies. The G.K.B. Cardiff works was on all counts a
better proposition than any of the cold-metal plants, but
G.K.N., and to some extent the Baldwins Midland Works,
could use all its output, it was well away from the main centres
of tinplate production and inevitable future redundancy, and
the site was too small to accommodate a hot strip mill. Latham
and James, perhaps understandably, now gave explicit form to
a 'better-rather-than-best' argument which was to become
common, '. . . it would seem undesirable to place yet another
hot mill in East Wales unless, for technical reasons, West Wales
is found to be *entirely* unsuitable.'* They concluded that a
new melting shop, slabbing mill and hot strip mill should be
built at the G.K.B. Port Talbot works.

At this point Latham and James attempted to reconcile
efficient centralised production of hot rolled coil at an integrated
coastal works with division of ownership and dispersal of finishing. This was the first essay in a sometimes extremely bitter
controversy which dragged on for almost five years. The hot
mill should be jointly owned by existing tinplate firms, sharing
the investment and allotment of its output in proportion to their

* *My italics*

tinplate production in some recent year, 1940 being suggested. The smallest practicable cold reduction unit was said to have a capacity of about 50,000 tons tinplate a year, but the report recommended five mills with an average output of 70,000 tons, each about 28 per cent. the size of the Ebbw Vale unit.   The motive for dispersal was partly to economise capital expenditure but mainly social, for, as the report put it, '. . . owing to the comparatively low cost of transporting hot strip, and having regard to the social considerations which have to be taken into account, there seems to be no reason why the complementary cold reduction plant or plants need to be placed in the same works as the hot mill'.   The transport costs suggested by Lewis, Gilbertson and Padbury had indicated that the cost of dispersal was not 'comparatively low', and within three years one of the authors of the new memorandum had reversed his opinion and was urging concentration of cold reduction.   Latham and James recommended that each of the five cold mills should be near an existing concentration of works, so minimising labour displacement.   The Iron and Steel Trades Confederation had at one stage suggested Llanelly, Swansea, Neath or Port Talbot, Gorseinon and a site in East Wales as suitable locations.[6]   The memorandum now proposed that hot rolled coil should be delivered to each cold mill at a uniform price, so that, as each was owned by a separate group of tinplate companies, competition could still be maintained.   Almost unbelievably in the light of subsequent experience the whole reconstruction scheme was estimated as likely to cost only about £7 million. (Table 30.).

   Like its predecessors, this plan aroused controversy when submitted to the tinplate trade in the spring of 1943.   Although all admitted that a new hot mill and more cold reduction capacity were necessary, they disagreed on the amount of modernisation to be aimed at.   The Llanelly Associated Tinplate Companies appear to have originated the contention that, as an important centre of both steel and tinplate making, Llanelly had a good case for the hot mill too.   They criticised the report's failure to assess the cost of bringing in supplementary supplies of steel to Port Talbot, the complete neglect of prospects for sheet, and the recommendation of a reversing rather than a continuous mill.   Finally, diverging completely

TABLE 30

Estimated Cost of the Latham-James Reorganisation Scheme,
1943

	£ million
New melting shop and strip mill capable of working up 516,000 tons ingots a year	3·5
Five cold reduction mills capable of 7,000,000 basis boxes (c. 390,000 tons) a year	1·4
Electrolytic tinning lines	c. 1·25
Annealing plant	0·35
Working capital and starting expenses	0·50
TOTAL	7·00

Source: Latham and James, *The Future of the Tinplate Industry*, 1943

from Latham and James, they advocated two complete plants, with both hot and cold mills, the latter each to be capable of about 225,000 tons tinplate a year, plus a large tonnage of sheet. One of the units should be in Llanelly, the other either between Swansea and Morriston or in the Neath-Port Talbot area.[7]

Baldwins, who had been investigating strip mill possibilities in their own interest, indicated in May, 1943, that they might co-operate—clearly a vital step if Port Talbot was to be made available. Soon a rift appeared when, in a British Iron and Steel Federation Council discussion of post-war planning, both E. Lever and Captain Leighton Davies of Baldwins claimed to speak for the majority of the tinplate trade, and from different standpoints, the latter wishing to delay reorganisation until government policy on exports was known. Davies was also urging smaller hot strip mills instead of one large mill, and even seems to have contemplated a Baldwin's mill in addition to a G.K.B. mill at Port Talbot, though it can scarcely be credited that the latter was not preferred. At this time Baldwins and the rest of the tinplate trade seemed very likely to act separately. Meanwhile by August, 1943, Richard Thomas engineers had drawn up plans for a hot strip mill layout in the Llanelly area, and a few weeks later trial bores were sunk on the Machynis site on the coastal flats south east of the town and on the Ynys site just to the north.   At Ynys the terrain was proved unsuitable and was abandoned.   Meanwhile each party agreed to keep the other informed of plans and the obvious danger of the overbuilding of very costly new plant helped to prevent a wider split.   Soon the Iron and Steel Federation and the government were also exerting pressure for orderly development.

On 5th May, 1943, the Ministry of Supply invited the British Iron and Steel Federation to investigate the question of post-war reconstruction.   In July the Post-War Reconstruction Committee held its first meeting under the chairmanship of Sir Alexander Dunbar.   Before the end of July the Committee had asked to meet leading representatives of the tinplate trade, and soon development planning meetings of tinplate companies were taking place in London, the work being subsequently incorporated as Tinplate Processes Ltd.   By the autumn a technical committee of this group was at work to find the most suitable unit and location for the production of about 10,000 tons a week of hot strip—again a considerable increase over the levels of Latham and James only nine months earlier—and for the necessary cold reduction plant or plants.   Gradually the conflicting interests were brought together.   In December, 1943, four East Wales tinplate firms, Abertillery Works, Avondale Tinplate, Redbrook Tinplate and Partridge Jones and John Paton of Pontypool and Pontymister formed the Monmouthshire Group of Tinplate Manufacturers to examine prospects for a cold reduction mill in that area to retain their share of the tinplate trade.   In June, 1944, they took shares in Tinplate Processes Ltd., and two of their representatives joined the eleven existing members of its board.   Re-organisation in sheet was scarcely mentioned, tinplate companies dominated the meetings, and John Lysaghts seem not to have been represented.

THE INCOMING OF BALDWINS, 1944

In August, 1944, the technical committee of Tinplate Processes Ltd. recommended a hot mill with an annual throughput of 700,000 tons ingots, at least 60 per cent. to be made on the same site, and two cold reduction mills, one for narrower, lighter tinplate and sheet and the other for wider, heavier grades (Table 31). The committee seems to have exceeded its terms of reference in thinking of 12,000 tons a week production of cold rolled strip and a capital expenditure of £15,000,000. There were three other significant new departures. Space was to be provided at the site for blast furnaces should these later prove desirable, the committee specifically considered sheet as well as tinplate, but in spite of this, and the earlier report to the Iron and Steel Control, it saw no justification for a hot mill wider than 56″ (Table 32). The 25,000 or perhaps eventually 50,000 tons wide sheet needed

TABLE 31

South Wales Production of Tinplate & Sheet, according to 1944 plans (annual output, thousand tons)

	Tinplate	Sheet
By new methods	250	275
By old methods	750	350
(of which to be modernised)	500	?

Source: Report of Technical Committee of Tinplate Processes Ltd, 1944

TABLE 32

Analysis of Demand for Tinplate & Sheet by Width, 1944

	Tinplate	Sheet
Under 30″	almost all	c. 50%
30″–40″	little	c. 50%
Over 40″	—	very little

Source: Report of Technical Committee of Tinplate Processes Ltd, 1944

annually should be bought in the United States on long-term contracts. Four locations, none very good, were suggested for the plant. Ynys, Llanelly, which Richard Thomas engineers had ruled out eleven months earlier, was again on the list. Machynis, nearby, was coastal, but was not a suitable site for a possible blast furnace plant. Jersey Marine, on the coast between Swansea and Briton Ferry, had flat land and good access to nearby King's Dock and Swansea harbour, but the site was limited on the north by hilly ground, on the west by Crumlyn Bog and southwards by the dunes of Crumlyn Burrows. Later developments showed that dunes could be flattened to provide a suitable site for heavy plant, but the area was probably not big enough to accommodate large future growth. Melingriffith, four miles north of Cardiff, was perhaps a possible location for a small cold metal steelworks but quite unsuitable for a large operation with prospects of integration back to pig iron and much future growth, unless it was linked with the existing Cardiff works—a link which the location of the latter across the other side of Cardiff suggests could never have been by hot metal. This list of possible sites illustrates the difficulty of realistic planning without the co-operation of G.K.B.

In January, 1944, Baldwins informed the other South Wales companies that they had decided against a hot mill to supply only their own needs of about 170,000 tons tinplate stock a year, and in favour of a bigger project involving a 72″ mill. Almost half its output, about 150,000 tons strip a year, would be available to independent West Wales tinplate firms. The Tinplate Conference pointed out that this would leave the independents inadequately supplied, yet be so large as to render any other hot mill project marginal. Even with a market for 300,000 tons strip a year, Baldwins could scarcely have operated a mill of this size with profit. The need for a closer link between the various interests to secure outlets was becoming clearer than ever. Sir Charles Wright of Baldwins, to whom a copy of the technical committee's report was sent, wrote in September to stress the Baldwin view that an 80″ mill was essential to meet the future needs of the motor trade, which the tinplate orientation of previous thinking had neglected, and also to ensure government backing for an installation equal to American plant. Now, with a much greater investment involved, whatever the mill's width, informal discussions continued between Baldwins and the Richard Thomas group, helped by G.K.N.'s hesitancy to commit themselves to big developments in G.K.B. After secret negotiations for some months, and a careful evaluation of the two group's physical assets, a merger was announced on December 31st, 1944, and Richard Thomas and Baldwins was formed.

Sir William Firth attended the Extraordinary General Meeting held by Richard Thomas and Company on 29th December, 1944, to oppose the amalgamation, claiming that much obsolete plant was being taken over.   There was apparently substance in his argument.   Baldwin's plate trade from Port Talbot had shrivelled in the depression, Ebbw Vale had cut into their sheet and tinplate business, and they had suffered from wartime concentration in these trades, so that their 1940–1944 ingot output was only 72·5 per cent. the 1937 figure as compared with 97·7 per cent. for Britain as a whole.   Sheet and plate output was down 24·5 per cent. from the 1937 level, tinplate production 26·5 per cent.[8]   Their tinplate mills were in poor shape, although, except for Ebbw Vale, those of Richard Thomas were probably worse.   They had, however, compensating assets, especially their share in Port Talbot's integrated and fairly modern plant, coastal location and potentially very big site. Llanelly, the only Richard Thomas works with any claims to tidewater status, was very inferior to this.   Similarly they were associated with a good, forceful G.K.B. production team, as shown by their planning in immediate pre-war years and their substantial achievement in installing new plant.   The next decade confirmed their quality though it also revealed strong leanings to independence that eventually broke some of the links made with Richard Thomas in December, 1944.

Given the deficiencies of Port Talbot, which later became more obvious, other possible South Wales locations for the new strip mill need examination.   Yet it is vital to reaffirm that the decisions had to be taken within very constricting circumstances.   The problem continued to be seen as a tinplate re-organisation problem, sheet was important but secondary, and the great post-war boom in consumer durables which gave sheet demand such impetus could not be foreseen.   Partly because of this but partly because of the existing Port Talbot nucleus, the problem was above all looked upon as a West Wales affair—the existing commitment in plant and workers prejudiced any locational debate strongly against East Wales just as it prejudiced the issue in favour of South Wales rather than anywhere else.   Much could be said for considering wholly new locations but this was ruled out by the reluctance to write off whole plants and with them communities.   Eventually this had to happen but by then a new nucleus of employment within commuting distance had been created : without the employment, of over 20,000, built up in Port Talbot and its West Wales subsidiaries the hinterland of Swansea Bay must eventually have been desolated.

There was, however, the alternative advocated in the Llanelly Associated comments on the Latham-James memorandum— the construction of two strip mills.   One, concerned with tin-plate, could be in the west, grafted on to Port Talbot, the other possibly in the east where Lysaghts at Newport and Baldwins at Panteg had already a substantial part of that trade well placed for road access to the English market and where also a hot strip mill could provide the coil for a new cold reduction unit to serve the Monmouthshire tinplate concerns.

One new site halfway between east and west was strongly urged, according to Burn.[9]   Barry was able to dock much larger ships—up to 20,000 tons—than Port Talbot, had very good rail facilities and flat, unoccupied land along the north-eastern extension of the harbour and along the Cadoxton River and Sully Brook.   The sites, however, were not large and there was no existing steel plant to arm a case which appears never to have been pursued very far.   There were two other possible East Wales locations, Cardiff and Newport.   As at Port Talbot both involved the co-operation of G.K.N.   Guest, Keen and Nettlefold controlled a little over 54 per cent. of the ordinary shares of Guest, Keen, Baldwins, the English Steel Corporation 5·4 per cent. and Baldwins the remaining 40·5 per cent. G.K.N. had much wider interests than any of the other parties to the negotiations and the re-organisation was therefore to them less vital.   Sir Samuel Beale as chairman seemed person-ally rather lukewarm to the whole business, and the revelation of the secretly conducted negotiation between Baldwins and Richard Thomas cooled still more the already strained relations with Sir Charles Wright, Baldwins chairman.   J. H. Jolly, as managing director, was keen to maintain the G.K.N. majority interest in G.K.B. but was sceptical of optimistic forecasts of future tinplate exports and therefore was reluctant to endorse the rapidly growing size of the project.   Even if prepared to co-operate in the hot mill project G.K.N. would not for months commit itself to any development involving acquisition of antiquated tinplate capacity. The question '. . . do you want to take over 25 to 30 antiquated tinplate works?' seems at one stage to have been a barb with which members of the Board prodded one another.[10]

Guest, Keen and Nettlefold showed, however, considerable concern for the future of its John Lysaght subsidiary. During 1944 the possibility of purchasing an 80" hot strip mill from an American aluminium company was explored, although how vigorously is unknown. At the end of that year there were passing discussions with John Summers about co-operation, a prospect attractive to Summers as well as Lysaghts, for although Hawarden Bridge had a hot strip mill it had no comparable cold reduction unit. The wide separation of the two works made any significant development difficult. In January, 1945, a proposal from within G.K.N. suggested instead two new hot mills, a wide one primarily for sheet production, located at Newport, and a narrower one for tinplate at Port Talbot. Lysaghts urged priority for the sheet mill although later they accepted that perhaps the tinplate mill should go ahead first— provided it was understood that the Newport mill should be built later. Replying to early approaches from E. Lever in January, 1945, Sir Samuel Beale reflected this feeling among some members of his board although he moderated its impact. G.K.N., he observed, did not consider the Port Talbot scheme completely satisfactory, it did not serve either sheet or tinplate interests fully, and installing a wide mill there, as Baldwins advocated, would make the product directly competitive with John Lysaght's wide sheet and raise the cost of the tinplate stock. These conditions would make more difficult '. . . the subsequent installation of a fourth mill which we believe is essential in the national interest. . . .'[11]

A Newport location for a hot strip mill had many attractions. The west bank of the Usk estuary gave scope for the develop-ment of ore docks with water of moderate depth by the standards of the time. Immediately to the west stretched the Severnside pasturelands of Wentlloog Level, providing site con-ditions quite as suitable as the dunelands and wastes south of Port Talbot. The Orb Works was across the Usk but eventually the whole operation could be concentrated on the better new site. Coking coal collieries were as near as those which would supply Port Talbot, and Newport was nearer to Oxford-shire ore, at this time forecast to provide substantial tonnage. Furthermore dock development at Newport could also reduce the cost of supplying ore to Ebbw Vale, although the need to cut costs there was probably not appreciated in 1945. With all these advantages, however, Newport could not claim to be the location of a single strip mill project for South Wales, for the balance of existing capacity was heavily concentrated in the west. Emphasis on tinplate and the posture of the various companies made almost certain that Port Talbot would be chosen, and all doubt was removed when, troubled by the prospect of the consequences of closing a number of old-type steel and tinplate works, the Government issued a directive for the development to be west of Bridgend. With one location practically decided by this instruction Newport's case was lost; to build two mills would increase the capital investment per ton of product and would make demands the equipment makers could not satisfy. Small mills were still considered practicable —early in 1945 one expert estimated the likely weekly through-put of the Port Talbot hot mill at only about 15,000 tons as compared with 12,000 for Ebbw Vale—but the development of more powerful, larger units was soon pushing the desirable minimum size upwards, an additional argument against build-ing two mills. In January, 1945, the Iron and Steel Federation was encouraged to give its blessing to Port Talbot in a study made by T. P. Colclough and S. L. Bengston.[12] Although the plant proposed by the technical committee of Tinplate Pro-cesses Ltd. would accomplish only about half the total modernisation of the tinplate and sheet industry and therefore a demand sufficient to justify two mills was likely, 'considering the heavy programme for rolling mill manufacture, the country cannot, for another six to seven years at least, consider building more than one such mill, and the 80″ mill proposed should therefore be recommended for adoption and given the highest possible priority'. On 26th January, 1945, E. H. Lever as chairman of Richard Thomas and Baldwins informed the President of the Board of Trade that it had been decided to build the hot strip mill at Port Talbot. Many problems still remained but in each case the solution was to be heavily biased by this decision.

There had been a persistent fear among Welsh M.P.s that the reorganisation of the tinplate and sheet trades would involve their removal to eastern England. These fears were wholly unfounded as far as the planning and negotiations of the companies were concerned, but there were two roots for this belief. One was the memory of Firth's Redbourn project, and those later, hazy ideas about a second mill, perhaps on Humberside, to which Burn refers.[13] The other source of the idea was the planning at British Iron and Steel Federation level, especially when it was under the guidance of Sir Allan Macdiarmid, chairman of Stewarts and Lloyds, and the driving force behind their radical new departure in building at Corby. The problems came out in the Welsh debate on 17th October, 1944, when the M.P. for Aberavon, Mr. W. G. Cove, referred to rumours of the removal to England, and Mr. D. L. Mort of Swansea East asked for a report on the progress of negotiations, pleading that the mills 'should be established in the areas where the men have worked for years at this hard toil in individual mills', and adding 'we have a right to make that claim'.[14] In reply Mr. Hugh Dalton, as President of the Board of Trade, revealed that as yet he had got little satisfaction from Colonel Bevan, chairman of the Tinplate Conference, or Sir Allan Macdiarmid. 'I have been endeavouring for months to get a simple statement from the tinplate manufacturers, or failing this, from the Iron and Steel Federation as to where they propose to erect these new plants. I have asked this question many times. I have asked it orally and I have asked it in writing'. Mr. Lewis Jones of Swansea West, a member closely associated with the West Wales steel and tinplate interests, assured the House that every effort was being made to find a suitable site and that it was already decided that the plant should be in South Wales, but Mr. Dalton confirmed that he would not approve the tinplate redundancy scheme until 'I am satisfied that the new plants are going to be on sites which are in accord with the public interest', and referred to recent press reports of a plan for development on Humberside.[15] In May, 1946, he outlined the conditions on which he had been willing to approve the redundancy schemes. The basic one was that the industry

should have complete plans for modernisation in South Wales—
'there was an enquiry set up by the Iron and Steel Federation
which thought it much better to move the plants out of South
Wales altogether, leaving South Wales derelict, and setting
them up in some green fields in Lincolnshire or Northampton
. . . . The first reform we had to get was that the new plants
were to be put in the *proper* place for tinplate plants, that is in
South Wales'.[16]   On the location of the hot mill much of this
seems to have been tilting at windmills, but within South Wales,
and in relation to the cold reduction mills, government action
was a much more important locational influence.

Throughout 1945 and 1946 the size of the scheme grew, but
questions of government policy and of company control delayed
construction.   Consequently, with post-war inflation, the
capital investment involved spiralled distressingly.   One
participant in the discussions recalls that at each meeting the
estimated cost of development increased by a few hundred
thousand or perhaps million pounds.[17]   Growth in capacity
was up to a point logical and very desirable.   In March, 1945,
a report to E. H. Lever from the United Engineering and
Foundry Company of Pittsburgh confirmed the Iron and Steel
Control's 1943 conclusions in favour of an 80″ mill.   Cost
structures differed somewhat for sheet/strip and tinplate, and
the Port Talbot mill was intended to supply more of the latter,
but costs of strip increased about $12\frac{1}{2}$ per cent. as width went up
from 54″ to 72″ so that in a 600,000-ton mill, with interest and
depreciation each at 6 per cent., there would be an extra overall
processing cost for the wider material in the hot mill of about 5s.
a ton.   In return for an extra capital outlay of about £0·6
million and such small extra running costs it was argued that a
yet untapped British market for wide strip would be opened.[18]
In April W. F. Cartwright of Guest Keen Baldwins and S. E.
Graeff, an acknowledged American strip mill expert who had
been at Ebbw Vale since 1936, reported on a visit to sixteen
North American strip mills.   Although they were reported as
confirming the need for an 80″ mill it seems that in fact they
believed that they had proved conclusively that it could not
pay, and recommended a 60″ or 66″ mill.[19]   The advice of
Sir Charles Wright concerning the national prestige value of an
80″ mill nevertheless prevailed, and the capacity of such a unit

was naturally bigger than earlier projected installations. By August, 1945, when he approached the Finance Corporation for Industry concerning possible assistance, E. H. Lever was speaking of a Port Talbot hot mill capacity of 900,000 to 950,000 tons a year, an increase of one quarter over the Tinplate Processes report of just over a year earlier and over twice as big as the mill proposed by Latham and James. In December the F.C.I. asked for another technical survey by their own nominee, G. H. Latham, and two months later his report suggested that by fuller utilisation, including concentration on rolling the widest possible coils, the hot mill capacity could be increased by another 300,000 tons a year.[20]

Meanwhile the process of re-organisation and of construction languished. On 6th May, 1945, the Board of Guest Keen Baldwins decided to order an 80″ fully continuous hot strip mill and a four-stand 80″ cold reduction mill from United Engineering and Foundry, after which representatives of that company visited Port Talbot and made a preliminary quotation.[21] However, by 21st May the Labour party had announced its withdrawal from the Coalition Government and on 26th July was successful in the General Election, and G.K.B. decided to wait to see how fully committed the new government was to nationalisation. Eventually progress was resumed, but the attitude of G.K.N. to full participation in the new project produced a longer term delay.

Overcoming their doubts about obsolescent tinplate capacity, by the early spring of 1945, G.K.N. were willing to bring John Lysaght fully into the new organisation. They would retain their predominance in G.K.B. and have the largest role in the Port Talbot developments. This policy was not particularly welcome to the board of Richard Thomas and Baldwins but G.K.N. maintained it for more than a year. On April 17th, 1946, however, the Government's intention of nationalising the steel industry was announced to the House of Commons, and this eased the situation, for the active support that J. H. Jolly in particular had maintained for full G.K.N. participation was weakened. In mid-September, without the full knowledge of their Lysaght subsidiary, G.K.N. agreed with R.T.B. to withdraw from the Port Talbot project. This implied also that the Lysaght Newport works would depend for hot rolled strip on an

Q

independent company.   The logical alternative, not accepted for a further two months, was to separate the Orb mills from the rest of the G.K.N. and Lysaght organisation and transfer them to the new group.   When the decision to build the hot mill at Port Talbot was taken the position of Lysaght was weakened but the defection of G.K.N. made it wholly untenable.   The consequences were far reaching for the location of the cold reduction mills, but before examining them we must consider another matter scarcely touched on above, but soon to engage a good deal of attention and later recalled by a leading participant as 'the Achilles heel of the Port Talbot project'[22]— the problem of Port Talbot docks.

THE DEFICIENCY OF PORT TALBOT DOCK

The case for development at Port Talbot rested on a plant in being, a location favourable for supplying strip mill coil to existing tinplate centres, and near enough to them for the reconstruction to take place with the minimum social disturbance.   The Port Talbot dock itself was recognised as inferior.   Like all others in South Wales it was a 'made' port, reconstructed at the end of the nineteenth century.   There were proposals to improve it in 1914 when Baldwins were contemplating their Margam plant, but by 1946 it was still small, served by a small entrance lock and capable of handling vessels of only 6,000 to 7,000 tons.   In January, 1946, G.K.B. negotiated with the Great Western Railway concerning the handling of the greatly increased inflow of ore, although this was concerned mainly with forwarding rather than with docking.   In January, 1947, the railway company agreed to provide half the necessary investment of £0·9 million.   Searching questions about the suitability of the dock were now asked by the Iron and Steel Board.   They involved the economics of handling small ore carriers.

Even in the 1920s the trend to large vessels had been recognised.   United Steel Companies had realised this in the reconstruction of Workington docks, and this was followed by the elaborate discussions of 1928–1929 on a new deep water based iron and steel plant for the Clyde.[23]   More directly relevant to South Wales experience, Sir William Firth had indicated the significance of efficient deep water ore docks to the Newport Chamber of Commerce in December, 1936. At Rotterdam and other continental ports a 20,000 ton ore carrier could be unloaded in one fifth of the time and at one quarter of the per ton cost of discharging a 5,000 ton ore carrier at Newport docks.[24] Building the key post-war project of British steel modernisation at a similar port naturally aroused doubts in the newly appointed Iron and Steel Board, and from February to September, 1947, it repeatedly returned to this theme in discussion with the representatives of the South Wales companies.

Early in February the Board requested details of Port Talbot's ability to handle large shipments of iron ore, and pointed out that independent shipping interests were already suggesting that new ore boats would carry 12,000 tons ore, double the tonnage which could be discharged there. A 6,000 to 7,000 ton ceiling on tonnage was admitted but it was argued that most of the foreign ore would come over only a medium-length haul from North Africa and that almost all other ports handling this ore were also small. The plan was that the extended works at Port Talbot would use 15,000 tons Oxfordshire ironstone and limestone a week and 28,000 tons foreign ore, and, on Iron and Steel Board queries about delivery if Port Talbot dock was closed, it was reckoned that with more sidings, another ore tippler and more conveyor belts the imported tonnage could, if necessary, be brought in through Swansea. The G.W.R. also suggested use of King's Dock as a possible aid. The Iron and Steel Board suggested using Swansea docks regularly for all imported ore, claiming that, although that port could handle ships of no more than 10,000 tons capacity, landing costs there would be 6s. a ton less whereas rail haulage costs Swansea to Port Talbot would be only 2s. 4d. a ton. Company experts retorted that this exaggerated the saving in unloading at Swansea and that, including the servicing of the extra investment there, the delivered cost of ore was 2s. 1½d. a ton less through Port Talbot. In May a three-party enquiry involving the Board, the company and an independent carrier interest, examined the whole range of possibilities, including the use of Barry, which was able to take 20,000 ton vessels, and had the additional advantage of two entrances. After further Iron and

Steel Board queries in September the company was left free to develop Port Talbot as the ore terminal.

Early in the 1950s, rather than continue to use hire tonnage, the British Iron and Steel Federation arranged for the construction of a number of ore carriers. Eventually 24 were acquired of which it was considered that 11 could use Port Talbot. Of 8,500 tons capacity, they were described as 'especially designed for the shallow ports', including not only Barrow and Workington, relics of the mid-nineteenth century iron and steel industry, but Port Talbot, the location of the biggest plant ever built in Britain.[25]   Eventually, though Port Talbot became a very large user of Swedish ore, brought over a medium-length haul over which small vessels were less disadvantageous, it was to prove desirable to use bigger ore carriers both to make possible delivery of an adequate tonnage and also to widen the range of competition between orefields so as to lower the price at the shipping port as well as the cost of carriage.   These conditions could not be anticipated in 1947, and although choice of Part Talbot was unfortunate it was a matter of making the best of a bad situation, into which a host of perhaps unavoidable prior considerations had forced the development planners.   As E. H. Lever summarised the situation for Sir Archibald Forbes, chairman of the Iron and Steel Board, while vessels of over 6,500 tons could not use Port Talbot the alternative would have been an inland site where, besides the absence of direct unloading, the benefit of the existing plant at Port Talbot would also be sacrificed.

REFERENCES

1   I am grateful for the opportunity to consult a full, unpublished survey of the reorganisation proposals and developments to the end of 1947, entitled 'The History of the Steel Company of Wales Limited' prepared in March 1948 at the direction of Sir Ernest Lever.   In conversation or correspondence I have discussed the developments with Sir Ernest Lever and Messrs. W. F. Cartwright and E. C. Lysaght.   None of the three persons is responsible for my interpretation of the events of those years.
2   J. Malborn in correspondence.
3   G. H. Latham in correspondence.
4   *Iron and Steel* November 1944, p. 698.   D. L. Burn, *The Steel Industry* 1939–1959, p. 80.

5   D. L. Burn, *op. cit.*, p. 106.
6   D. L. Burn, *op. cit.*, p. 121 footnote 3.
7   Annotations by Llanelly Associated Tinplate Companies staff of a copy of the Latham-James memorandum.
8   Annual Statement, Sir Charles Wright, *The Times* 23 March 1945.
9   D. L. Burn, *op. cit.*, p. 81.
10 E. C. Lysaght in conversation.
11 E. C. Lysaght and *The History of the Steel Company of Wales Limited.*
12 T. P. Colclough and S. L. Bengston, *Report on the Modernisation of the British Iron and Steel Industry,* January 1945, unpublished.
13 D. L. Burn, *op. cit.*, p. 103.
14 *Hansard* Fifth Series, 1943–1944 Vol. 403, 17 October 1944. c. 2269, 2270, 2237.
15 *Hansard ibid,* c. 2323.
16 Iron and Steel Debate 27 May 1946. *Hansard* Fifth Series Vol. 423, c. 1009. My italics.
17 *The History of the Steel Company of Wales Limited* and E. C. Lysaght.
18 J. Malborn in correspondence.
19 *The History of the Steel Company of Wales Limited* and W. F. Cartwright in correspondence.
20 *The History of the Steel Company of Wales Limited.*
21 J. Malborn in correspondence.
22 W. F. Cartwright in correspondence.
23 *Iron and Coal Trades Review* 10 September 1920, p. 350. Report by Brasserts on the Scottish Steel Industry 1929.
24 *South Wales Times* 5 December 1936, p. 14. *Engineer* 18 December 1936, p. 657.
25 *The History of the Steel Company of Wales Limited.* Iron and Steel Board, *Development in the Iron and Steel Industry* 1953–1958, 1955, p. 30. W. F. Cartwright 'Big Ships at Port Talbot', *British Steel* August 1968, pp. 10–13 and W. F. Cartwright in correspondence.

CHAPTER 13

The Sheet Trade in the Second World War and under the first post-war Development Plan

II. The Controversy over the Location of cold reduction Mills and Projects outside South Wales

The South Wales re-organisation scheme involved a large investment in cold reduction capacity, and, after the choice of the hot mill site early in 1945, this became the centre of disputes which dragged on for almost another three years. Full concentration of cold reduction at the hot strip mill plant, as at Ebbw Vale and Hawarden Bridge, was considered impracticable, given the wide distribution of old-type plant and the breadth of participating interests. Concentration would have made close quality control easier, economised in administration and management and reduced transport costs. On this last point an R.T.B. technical committee in 1945 showed that for tinplate made at Llanelly and Morriston rather than at Port Talbot, the extra costs of production and delivery in Swansea docks would be 7s. 4d. and 2s. 9d. a ton respectively.[1] Yet there were many arguments in favour of dispersal.

Avoiding the writing off of all the existing tinning plant, at least until electrolytic tinning seemed justified in British conditions, would minimise the effect of labour displacement in the main tinplate areas. In 1942 Lewis, Gilbertson and Padbury had envisaged three cold reduction mills, in 1943 Latham and James had spoken of five, and the technical committee of Tinplate Processes had recommended only two in mid-1944. By 1945 E. C. Lysaght and Sir Charles Bruce-Gardner were advocating the improvement and extension of the existing cold reduction mill for sheet at Newport, the construction of a five-stand cold mill for tinplate at Llanelly and a four-stand cold mill at Port Talbot equipped to roll and finish either sheet or

tinplate.   The last would give the reconstructed industry flexibility to meet whatever balance of sheet and tinplate demand
emerged.[2]   As with the hot strip mill, however, the government
set guide lines limiting the range of choices.   Early in 1945,
announcing the general re-organisation plans, Hugh Dalton,
President of the Board of Trade, outlined this context for planning—'One of the new cold reduction plants will, *unless some
insuperable technical or economic difficulty is encountered*, be located in
the Llanelly area.'[3]   In the spring, pressing the companies for
further decisions on modernisation before approving the Tinplate Redundancy Scheme, Dalton stressed the necessity of
making an early announcement of tinplate cold reduction mills
to be built near Llanelly, Port Talbot or Swansea, and in
Monmouthshire.   The first two were to be controlled by a new
subsidiary of Richard Thomas and Baldwins, the third to be
independently operated, presumably by Monmouthshire Tinplates Ltd., though supplied with hot rolled coil from either
Ebbw Vale or Port Talbot.   At this time it was believed that
Lysaght's, cold reduction sheet mil lwould be independently
modernised by G.K.N.   In September, at the Richard Thomas
and Baldwins' ordinary General Meeting, E. H. Lever summarised the re-organisation scheme.[4]   The Port Talbot strip
mill would be built under the aegis of G.K.B. and was reckoned
likely to produce 18,000 tons hot rolled coil a week.   A new
company with capital subscribed 'roughly proportionate to
their present interests in the old-type mills' would be set up by
Richard Thomas and Baldwins, Llanelly Associated Tinplate
Companies and Briton Ferry Steel Company to build two new
cold reduction mills 'mainly for tinplate' in the Llanelly and
Swansea areas.   'It is possible that a smaller cold reduction
plant will be erected in the Monmouthshire area, but no
responsibility for this will rest upon your company'.   Two
months later, to the outsider a very late date, T. O. Lewis and
H. Leighton Davies began detailed site surveys for a suitable
location for the two West Wales cold mills.

In December, 1945, the British Iron and Steel Federation
delivered its development report for the period to 1953 to the
Minister of Supply.   It confirmed the plans for two West
Wales cold mills, but suggested that initially production equal
to about 110,000 tons out of their rated capacity of some

400,000 tons should be devoted to sheet, not tinplate.[5]   The short-term future of the Orb Works seemed assured because of its key role in supplying the motor trade.   Output there would be increased by installing more powerful mill drives, and coils from Ebbw Vale or Port Talbot would replace the hot mill breakdowns with which it had worked so far.   In fact, in a final fling of their old skill in improvisation, Lysaghts formed another affiliation, one which again sprawled across the map. The old sheet bar mill at Normanby Park, installed in 1911, was reconstructed to roll 32″ slabs.   These went to the Hawarden Bridge hot strip mill for rolling down into coil, which was cold reduced at Newport.   In November, 1946, John Lysaght and All British Carriers formed a new joint company, Monmouthshire Transport, to convey up to 1,000 tons coil a week from Deeside, returning northwards with sheet, some of it for the Trafford Park works of Metropolitan Vickers, an important outlet for their silicon sheet since before the First World War.[6]

Two events of 1946 changed the context of thinking about the cold reduction mills and particularly affected the future of the Orb Works.   In February the technical assessor for the Finance Corporation for Industry, G. H. Latham, delivered his report. Its recommendations broke completely with those of the Latham and James memorandum of three years before.   It argued that it was desirable to minimise the dispersal of cold reduction, and the arrangements Latham suggested to this end seemed a noticeably R.T.B. solution rather than one to benefit all the partners in modernisation.   In his recommendations for tin-plate a Swansea area mill was omitted in favour of removing the existing Ebbw Vale cold mill to Llanelly.   This would be replaced by a new, faster unit at Ebbw Vale, where it would be supplemented by extensions to the hot mill.   A 48″ cold reduction mill for sheet was recommended for Port Talbot and, apparently for the first time, Latham argued that the modernised Orb cold reduction mill should also be moved there.   These proposals were characterised by E. H. Lever as a plan for the virtual extinction of the steel and tinplate industry west of Port Talbot, and the more extreme recommendations were never adopted.   Lysaght and G.K.N. protested about the proposal concerning Orb Works, but G. H. Latham was obdurate. In the spring he became President elect of the British Iron and Steel Federation so that this opinion gained power as almost a semi-official view.[7]

Another event of spring 1946 affected the development planning generally and in particular weakened the forces defending the Orb Works. On 17th April Mr. J. Wilmot, Minister of Supply, announced government plans for nationalising steel and informed the House that in the meantime reconstruction and development would be supervised by an Iron and Steel Board. The Board was headed by Sir Archibald Forbes, an industrialist from the corn-milling trade, who had been at the Ministry of Aircraft Production, and was a director of Spillers. Re-organisation planning slowed down, and when it was actively pushed ahead again in South Wales in mid-September, G.K.N. had decided to withdraw from the project and it was now planned that in place of G.K.B. and new composite concerns for the cold mills, Port Talbot, the old-type tinplate works of Briton Ferry, Llanelly Associated and R.T.B. and the Orb Works should all be operated under Richard Thomas and Baldwins. G.K.N. still objected to loss of control over the Orb Works but in mid-December, 1946, accepted it. Before the implications of G.K.N. withdrawal are examined further it is worthwhile considering separately the decision-taking process with regard to the tinplate cold reduction mills, for apart from its own intrinsic interest within the wider project it provides a contrast with what happened in sheet. The case is better known and may be summarised briefly.

Long before the sites for the tinplate cold reduction mills were bought or indeed before it was decided that one should be at Llanelly and another near Swansea, general planning for these two areas had begun. For overseas markets tinplate had to be delivered at Swansea docks, the biggest home markets were in the east of Britain near the concentrations of population and the chief agricultural districts producing foods for canning. Dispersal of the two mills, however, reduced labour displacement and placed cold reduced coil near two of the main agglomerations of old-type tinplate plant.

It was early agreed that the Llanelly area mill should be at Trostre, near the G.W.R. main line and the Swansea by-pass line, but other sites, including Landore, were considered before

Llangyfelach north of the Morriston-Gorseinon road was chosen for the second mill. Two independent assessments rated these sites on technical and general grounds superior to a site for cold reduction beside the Port Talbot hot mills. An outside commentator must hesitate to write this off as wishful thinking, but the conclusion remains puzzling. On grounds of transport costs dispersal was clearly undesirable. In July, 1945, when the planned capacity of the cold mills was only a modest 4½ million basis boxes each year, negotiations with the G.W.R. on the Llanelly area project had shown the logistical problem—a weekly movement of 7,000 tons hot rolled coil inward and 5,600 tons tinplate and 1,400 tons scrap outward, although some of the scrap might be used at the neighbouring South Wales Works, Llanelly.[8] The Llangyfelach site was ten rail miles, Llanelly 21½, from Port Talbot. Overall, dispersal produced an average of 5s. a ton extra transport costs for export tinplate, small compared with the home price of £52 a ton at the end of 1952 when Trostre was completed, but much more substantial as a reduction of profits. Even on such a moderate assumption of extra freight charges for both foreign and home markets, Trostre's 1953 output of 250,000 tons involved an excess cost of £60,000. For the same amount its 1,600 or so employees could have each been paid an annual subsidy of about £37 10s. 0d. on their journey to work or more than 2s. 6d. for every working day. Although transport costs were lower from the Llangyfelach site this choice seems even less justifiable on grounds of social necessity, for Swansea was quite accessible. For operating efficiency and administrative convenience dispersal is considered by competitors with centralised hot and cold mill operations to be highly undesirable. One must conclude that the planners of 1945–1947 were tempted to make a virtue of necessity.

Not all, however, were persuaded that Trostre and Llangyfelach were suitable, G. H. Latham and Sir Archibald Forbes of the Iron and Steel Board being notably sceptical. The former questioned the need to build two tinplate cold reduction mills immediately, and his opinion was reinforced by a technical enquiry by T. P. Colclough for the Ministry of Supply. Colclough argued that the progress of electrolytic tinning, new opinions about the most suitable widths for coil and a changing

balance of demand between sheet and tinplate might alter the
situation, while at the same time the Port Talbot hot strip mill
might perhaps not be able at first to supply enough coil for two
cold mills. He concluded that the Llangyfelach mill must go
ahead and provision be made for building the second mill at
the same location. The Iron and Steel Board came to the
same conclusion, but again rational locational planning ran
foul of political pressure. In April, 1947, announcing further
stages of planning for the hot mill, Mr. Wilmot informed the
House that the precise location of the cold mills was still being
considered. A day or so later the Iron and Steel Board had
information that site preparation costs could be $£\frac{1}{4}$ million
more at Trostre than at Llangyfelach and that, with this and
the freight charges on hot strip, the cost per basis box would
be about 2d. higher, or almost 3s. a ton more, at Trostre. Site
work had begun at Llangyfelach, but on 19th June, 1947, the
Minister at last announced that, after weighing all the social
and technical factors, the government considered Trostre a
better location. This conclusion in large part probably
reflected the relative influence in government decisions of the
Swansea group of M.P.s led by D. R. Grenfell of Gower on the
one hand and James Griffiths, Minister of National Insurance
and M.P. for Llanelly, on the other. £100,000 had already
been spent on site work at Llangyfelach, but with levelling completed work stopped and development began at Trostre after
negotiations to purchase the site were completed. With tinplate in short supply, both for home and for export demand,
E. H. Lever made clear that R.T.B. regarded this decision as
most unfortunate interference. Disappointed, the Metal Box
Company considered co-operation with others or even a
venture on its own to build a cold reduction mill, but this would
clearly not have been permitted even if the idea had been more
widely accepted.

Although Llanelly might indeed become a problem area,
half the tinplate mills within ten miles of the Llangyfelach site
—a radius which included Morriston and such relatively near
groups of tinplate mills as those of Gorseinon, Pontardulais,
Pontardawe and also Neath, Briton Ferry and the Llanelly area
mills as well—had closed since the war. The government
softened the blow by promising help for light industries for the

Swansea area, but for the wider South Wales strip mill development it could make valuable concessions and, therefore, exercise very strong pressure for any desired locational decision.   Such concessions, already asked for from the Treasury, included compensation for extra capital and servicing costs for locations chosen on social rather than on economic grounds, specially reduced charges for water and power, shipping and railway carriage and concessions on local rates.   By these means the balance of factors could be altered to produce satisfactory overall costs in a naturally less suitable location, one which was, therefore, directly subsidised at the taxpayers' expense.[9] Trostre began work in 1951, Velindre, the new plant on the Llangyfelach site, in 1956, so that, although there was a lag of over four years in production from the location the company itself regarded as the more attractive, the issue between the two was at length settled—except for the possibility, foreseen early in 1947, that both mills would be at Llangyfelach.   The same reasonably happy outcome evaded the controversy over the location of the cold reduction mill for sheet steel.

THE CONTROVERSY
OVER THE COLD REDUCTION MILL FOR SHEET

In 1945 the John Lysaght board had suggested an extension and improvement of the existing Newport cold reduction mill. In August, when he outlined the modernisation scheme to the Finance Corporation for Industry, E. H. Lever accepted this proposal and it was confirmed by the development plan of the British Iron and Steel Federation.   To the beginning of 1947 only G. H. Latham's F.C.I. memorandum of February, 1946, had spoken of possible removal to Port Talbot, but E. H. Lever now asked S. E. Graeff to examine further the relative merits of the F.C.I. and Lysaght's cases (Table 33).

The Graeff report suggested lower transport and operating costs for a mill at Port Talbot.   The existing mill buildings at the Orb Works were described as too lightly constructed to support heavy cranes and too narrow for the material handling trucks that might have been used instead.   Additionally storage space was inadequate both before and at the run-out end of the mill for it to operate at full rated capacity.   Overall,

TABLE 33

Existing and projected sheet steel capacity at Newport Works
according to John Lysaght, January, 1947 (tons per week)

	Existing	Projected
Hand and mechanised hot mills	3,000	2,000
3-stand cold reduction mill	1,000	5,000
Hot finished sheet	—	1,000
TOTAL	4,000	8,000

Source: *The History of the Steel Company of Wales Ltd.*

Graeff put the extra production cost at Newport over Port
Talbot at 32s. a ton, before providing for depreciation and
capital charges. On his estimates of effective annual capacity
and capital cost, allowing 12 per cent. for interest and depreciation, every ton of cold mill product from Newport would carry
overheads of about 40s. as compared with 36s. at Margam.
These figures were challenged by Lysaghts who argued a
lower investment for improvement of the Newport mill and a
higher potential capacity. There was also sharp disagreement
about the mill's quality, which soon extended to acknowledged
engineering experts. The Iron and Steel Board was keenly
interested in securing an unbiased opinion, although some non-
technical members harboured a variety of misconceptions.
One of these was the belief, apparently inculcated by technical
experts, that one reason for keeping hot and cold mills together
was to enable the full test rolling of a sample from each open-
hearth furnace before the charge was poured, in the nature of
things a wildly impracticable idea. Less dispassionately,
throughout the spring and summer of 1947 the local branch
of the Iron and Steel Trades Confederation, the Newport
Chamber of Commerce and Newport Council fought openly
to retain the mill.[10] As memoir was succeeded by counter-
memoir within the industry, it became clear that arbitration
by an outside disinterested assessor was necessary. Although
they had never employed outside consultant engineers, in
March, 1947, Lysaght agreed to an analysis of their proposals
by the International Construction Company. International's
report regarded the Lysaght forecasts of capacity as too

optimistic, and to that firm's consternation added £½ million to their estimates of capital investment for 'imponderables'. In April K. C. Gardner, President of the United Engineering and Foundry Company, was invited to visit Newport and advise, although again Lysaghts were diffident, fearing that the prospect that removal to Port Talbot would provide more construction work than modernisation at Newport might colour United's assessment at points of genuine doubt. After a very brief visit, but complete freedom in the works, the United Engineering and Foundry delegation reported emphatically that Newport should keep the mill, which it believed could be extended to a maximum of 6,000 tons a week—50 per cent. more than S. E. Graeff's estimate. Seeing the conflict of opinion within the associated concerns in South Wales, however, and apparently responding to R.T.B. pressure for Margam, within a week United Engineering and Foundry had made a complete *volte-face* and recommended an entirely new sheet mill at Margam. A Margam mill would cost more and there would have to be expenditure at Newport to find another use for Orb Works, but running-cost savings would counterbalance this and the greater scope for increased output at Margam—its final capacity could be well over 50 per cent. more than at Newport—gave it a further long-term advantage. On 19th April the press announced that construction at Margam had been recommended to the Iron and Steel Board. Work under way at Newport was stopped but the question was not yet resolved.

In June, on a request from the Iron and Steel Board, E. J. Pode furnished information which suggested that a Margam cold mill of initial capacity 7,000 tons a week would have operating costs of 8s. 3d. a ton less than the improved mill at Newport even when the latter was extended to its maximum output of 6,000 tons weekly. Its advantage in transport of hot rolled coil was put at 6s. 9d. a ton, but Pode's figures also suggested a standing charge advantage at Newport of the order of 17s. 2d. a ton. Moreover, as E. C. Lysaght argued, a low rail tariff could be obtained for the regular bulk traffic from Port Talbot to Newport and, for delivering finished sheet to the Midlands or South-eastern England, Newport had a 30 mile advantage over Port Talbot, or, for a heavy lorry, a round-trip advantage of over two hours.   British Railways were unable or unwilling to produce the figures to confirm their part of this assessment.   Newport was well located for exporting sheet and indeed later some Port Talbot strip was exported through Newport docks.   Lysaghts also argued that shortage of sheet was an additional reason for continued production of wide sheet at Newport, even if a new, narrow sheet mill was built at Port Talbot.   Later they made a case for a new mill identical with that planned for Margam.   The Iron and Steel Board appears to have commissioned a report on this project from the International Construction Company and in mid-September the Board visited the Orb Works.   But, as E. H. Lever put it, the decision of the chairmen of R.T.B., G.K.B. and John Lysaght taken in April in the light of the Gardner report, transcended most of the detailed considerations, which had caused controversy among the experts.   He summed up in August 'There comes a time when memoranda and letters on the subject must cease, and I think this point has arrived'. Eventually the locational decision had to cut through apparently interminable arguments among the experts, and on 16th December, eight months after the company decision, Mr. Strauss, Minister of Supply, announced that after consideration of all social and economic factors the government had decided on Margam for the cold reduction mill.[11]

In retrospect it seems clear that the transport cost savings claimed for Margam always ignored the cost of delivery of sheet steel to English markets, in which Newport had an advantage. Bulk movement of hot rolled coil and a shorter haul on the smaller individual loads of more easily damaged cold reduced sheet was attractive.   In France the new steel group, Usinor, was adopting an extreme form of this plan.   Its hot strip mill was at Denain, in the Nord coalfield, but the cold reduction mills were over 100 miles away at Montataire in the Oise valley, from which the great sheet-consuming industries of the Paris area were less than 40 miles away.   It was as if the cold mill had been built at one of the old Baldwin works in the Kidderminster area on the edge of the great Midland sheet market (Figure 17).   Perhaps understandably, this radical solution was never considered, but even development at Newport would have incorporated the idea.   Apart from this,

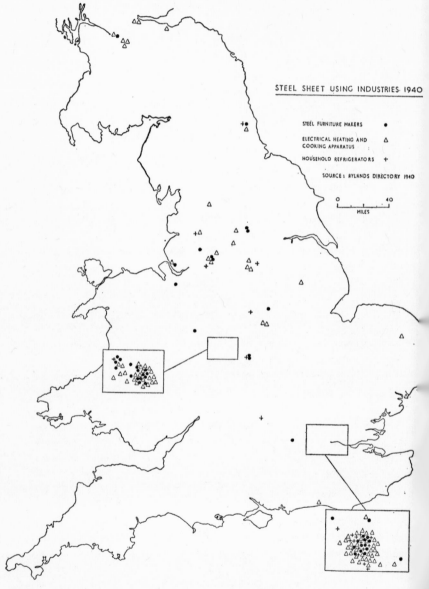

STEEL SHEET USING INDUSTRIES. 1940

STEEL FURNITURE MAKERS •

ELECTRICAL HEATING AND △
COOKING APPARATUS

HOUSEHOLD REFRIGERATORS +

SOURCE: RYLANDS DIRECTORY 1940

Figure 17.   The Mersey–Thames estuary focus of consuming plants was
marked contrast with their absence from Wales.

as E. H. Lever summarised the position, it seemed reasonable that, on an equal output, the service of the additional capital expenditure at Margam would just about be balanced by savings in running costs, so that the prospect of output beyond what was possible at Orb Works turned the scale in favour of Margam. In short, on costs of the cold reduction of sheet the decision was correct, though it was a condemnation of the Trostre and Velindre mills. On balance Lysaght's case for the cold mill was indefensible once Port Talbot had been selected for the hot strip mill. With no inheritance of past plant, taking into account minimum assembly, processing and marketing costs, Newport would have been better for an integrated iron and steel works and hot strip mill than Port Talbot and the cold mill unit would never have been at risk. Ten years later, in their centenary history, Lysaghts provided their own short if rather caustic commentary on the centralisation of sheet manufacture at Margam—'. . . such a transfer had not, of course, been foreseen when the Newport unit was installed in 1935. It was then envisaged that hot strip would ultimately come to the mill—not that Mahomet would, in the end, have to go to a mountain not yet on the map'.[12] In fact it was their scepticism in the early and mid-thirties, hesitancy thereafter and tantalising ill fortune in 1938–1939 which caused John Lysaght to lose their place in the sheet trade. Less than ten years later Richard Thomas and Baldwins' had chosen the coastal flats just to the east of Orb Works as the site for a new integrated steel works and hot strip mill and now spoke of it as the best in Britain for such a plant. The ironies of locational choice could scarcely be more neatly expressed.

Hot rolled sheet production continued in the old-type mills at the Orb Works, narrow strip and stainless steel were considered, but ruled out, and eventually it was decided to specialise further on electrical sheet, in which Baldwins and Lysaghts together already controlled 85 per cent. of national output. At the end of 1948 a new cold mill was announced for Newport, a unit able to make 900 tons silicon steel strip, or, alternatively, 1,250 tons mild steel strip a week. Subsequently the electrical sheet business expanded but more slowly than mild sheet (Table 34).

In January, 1947, the Briton Ferry Steel Company withdrew

R

TABLE 34

Production of Hot and Cold Rolled Sheet and of Electrical Qualities
1950, 1962, 1965 (thousand tons)

	1950	*1962*	*1965*
Hot and cold rolled sheet	1,525	2,868	4,121
Electrical grades	136	187	218

Source: British Iron and Steel Federation, *Annual Statistics*

from the re-organisation scheme.   The sheet cold reduction mill controversy dragged on for another eleven months, but already the various elements of redevelopment in South Wales were being welded together.   Speaking at Port Talbot, early in February, E. H. Lever noted that the companies had met to hammer out a solution, generously sacrificing their personal interests.   Commenting on this speech, and adopting the same benign interpretation, Sheet Metal Industries wrote that 'The firms involved in the scheme have co-operated fully, and individual interests have been subordinated in an effort to ensure the maximum overall efficiency of the South Wales sheet and tinplate industry'.[13]   On 1st May, 1947, the Steel Company of Wales was incorporated to undertake the re-organisation, and by August 2,100 workers were busy on the site of the new Margam works.   By December 9,000 piles had been driven with 16,000 more to drive.[14]   The delay had one very important result—inflation of capital cost.   In each year, 1946, 1947 and 1948, cost of plant in the steel industry advanced by about 12 per cent., and by early 1949 equipment costs were reckoned 140 per cent. over those of 1938.[15]   Early in 1947 Steel Company of Wales development schemes were estimated to cost at least £50 million, but when the first development scheme was completed in 1952 £73 million had been spent, for an output which in 1953 totalled only 1·3 million tons of steel, 400,000 tons tinplate and under 800,000 tons sheet and plate. The older, slower, less sturdy mills at Ebbw Vale and Hawarden Bridge had undoubtedly higher operating costs than Port Talbot but this increase in capital cost burdened the Steel Company of Wales with very high overhead charges.   Other early troubles were eventually overcome.   Men from the old

Port Talbot and Margam works needed training to recognise that small imperfections, acceptable in the heavy plate they had previously rolled, could not be tolerated in deep drawing sheet, and the necessity for attention to detail rather than merely concern with output. Some problems, such as lack of a settled labour force and good labour relations, overmanning and those inherent in a policy of paying tonnage rates before the plant was fully run in with a consequent rocketing of wages as output increased, did not become evident until the perspectives of endlessly growing demand dimmed in the late fifties.

In March, 1951, the new Abbey melting shop at Port Talbot tapped its first steel, and in June the hot strip mill came into production. The Trostre cold reduction mill began work in 1951, the Velindre mill on the Llangyfelach site in 1956. Output now rose rapidly (Table 35), and by 1956 the new chairman

TABLE 35

Production by the Steel Company of Wales, 1948, 1950, 1955
Approximate output (thousand tons)

	1948	1950	1955
Steel ingots	415	460	1,750
Tinplate	225	255	500
Sheet and plate	260	250	1,000

Source: Steel Company of Wales Annual Reports

could legitimately be proud. 'The panorama of Port Talbot, Margam and Abbey Works, covering four and a half miles, is an inspiring sight which has to be seen to be fully appreciated. It forms for all time a memorial to the far-sightedness of those men and of those founder companies who brought it into being and who have laid the most sound foundations for the future prosperity of South Wales'.[16] The autumn before, partly in order to ease the return of the South Wales steel industry to private ownership, the Board of the Steel Company of Wales had been reconstituted separately from that of Richard Thomas and Baldwins. Already by early 1956 the latter was looking to the South Wales coast as the location for yet another hot strip mill.

FURTHER DEVELOPMENT AT HAWARDEN BRIDGE

In both site and location the John Summers strip mill had appeared a more rational development than Ebbw Vale. In 1939 the Iron and Coal Trades Review had even suggested that possibly '. . . no more economic or suitable site could have been found in the whole country'.[17] This judgement was indefensible: the location was far from ideal. The site was ample, requiring infilling and pile driving, but incomparably superior to the wreck-strewn Ebbw valley, and easily extendable to any foreseeable limit. The situation, however, had long been a tidewater one only in a cartographic sense. In 1947 the Rivers Dee and Clwyd Catchment Board submitted a scheme to the Minister of Transport which might have made the Dee navigable for vessels of 1,500 tons up to Connah's Quay, but even had this plan been implemented the steelworks would have still been landlocked for all practical purposes.[18] At the end of the war this mattered little for operations still depended on cold metal. This situation, however, could not be tolerated for long, for supplies were inadequate in both quality and quantity. With ironmaking, the lack of a coastal location would become a pronounced disadvantage. Here, as in South Wales, it was impossible to act in ways untramelled by past commitment in plant.

Late in 1946 the new cold reduction mill came into operation reducing finishing costs in sheet production, but experience with this and with the hot strip mill showed that both could roll larger tonnages than the two steelworks, built in 1902 and in 1917, could supply. Consequently the operating rate and return on the modern mills suffered. The two old melting shops operated on scrap, abundant in the immediate post-war years, and on pig iron, largely from Shelton; for extra deep drawing sheet neither was a satisfactory material. By 1946 a new melting shop was being designed to replace both existing ones, to increase the annual steel output by some 150,000 tons and improve its quality while reducing costs of production.[19] Then scrap supplies tightened, and in 1949, when the company delivered 432,000 tons of sheet and plate, representing approximately 570,000 tons ingots, the Hawarden Bridge melting shops managed only 491,000 tons, and steel had to be bought. The position was worse in 1950, when the hot mill turned out 564,000 tons but Hawarden Bridge and Shelton together made only 760,000 tons steel, and Shelton had its own range of finished products.[20]   Conditions eased in 1951 when the steelworks were completed.   Work was then far advanced on the construction of coke ovens and ironmaking plant.   With an output of 7,000 to 8,000 tons a week, each of the blast furnaces required about 14,000 tons of high-grade iron ore.   The aim was to use as nearly as possible 100 per cent. foreign ore, but for a time supply difficulties necessitated using about 30 per cent. Northampton Sand ore.[21]   With steelworks supply problems solved, John Summers was faced with the problem of a location very indifferently suited for the assembly of iron-making raw materials.

The ore supply problem was tackled energetically.   By agreement with British Railways a shuttle service of trains was run from the docks in Birkenhead 12 miles across the Wirral, using specially built hopper wagons of 50 tons nominal capacity, double the normal size.   The ore dock, though deeper than most in Britain, was poor by international standards, and being at the head of the Birkenhead system difficult to improve to take the bigger ore carriers which could already be foreseen.   Assembly costs on the 3,000 tons coal used daily were also high, the blend consisting largely of coal from West Riding and South Wales pits.[22]   Here, however, the trend of carbonisation technology proved favourable to the plant and a switch to a high percentage of North Wales coal steadily reduced the freight bill, and, incidentally, prolonged survival of the mines in that area.

In the early or mid-1950s the cost of assembling iron-making minerals at Hawarden Bridge was well above that at Port Talbot, where, despite the limitations of the ore dock, nearer coking coal and limestone were a benefit.   Despite its considerable programme of scrapping and rebuilding, however, John Summers obtained its plant at much lower capital cost. In February, 1945, before the full extent of post-war capital cost inflation was foreseen, R. F. Summers observed '. . . if we had put it (the hot strip mill) in after the war it would have cost about twice as much again'.   Hawarden Bridge therefore enjoyed an overall cost advantage over Port Talbot.   In this way, after the Second World War, the apparent logic of a low-cost location was repeatedly confounded.[23]   In marketing, the location of the Summers mills was at least as favourable as that of either of its South Wales rivals.   A motor transport section had been organised in 1928, the new three-mile access road to the works was built in 1936, and, as the Mersey tunnel provided a new motor route to Liverpool, the old fleet of coasting vessels was sold off.   A plant poised so well for an export trade, which once took up to 90 per cent. of its output, was by the late thirties selling about 70 per cent. of its production at home.   While the raw materials, techniques, products and markets of John Summers had changed almost completely, the operations were still conducted in the same location.

THE HAND AND MECHANISED MILLS AFTER 1946: a Case of unexpected Longevity

In 1946 the British Iron and Steel Federation Development Plan anticipated that 75 per cent. of the output of tinplate and sheet would come from the strip mills by 1950–1951.   In fact, delay in the construction of Port Talbot and its cold reduction mills and an apparently insatiable demand gave a new lease of life to older type mills, and in 1953 they still produced one-third of the total output (Table 36).   In a sellers' market it was still

TABLE 36

Sheet & Tinplate deliveries, 1953 (thousand tons)

	Sheet	Tinplate	Total	Percentage of Overall Production
Continuous mills	1,217	475	1,692	66·1
Mechanised mills	189⎫	300	869	33·9
Hand mills	380⎭			
TOTALS	1,786	775	2,561	100·0

Source: Iron and Steel Board, Development in the Iron and Steel Industry 1953–1958, 1955, p. 17

profitable to improve them, by mechanisation, modernisation of bar and pack furnaces and generally continuing the practices pioneered in the twenties in the first American reactions to the automobile makers' demands and to strip mill competition. Special grades, awkward sizes and small lots still remained with them, while the strip mills were fully engaged on standardised orders. In these circumstances some old-type plants even cut and rerolled hot strip mill coils to meet the needs of the market.

By late 1946 the Society of Motor Manufacturers and Traders complained that their allocation of sheet steel, made by the Ministry of Supply, was only 15 per cent. of output as compared with about 40 per cent. of total sheet consumption before the war, and suggested this might cut 1947 motor production to 50 per cent. of their target.[24] Sheet works, closed during wartime concentration of capacity, were reopened to try to fill the gap. In 1946 the Melin sheet mills at Neath and the Whitford works at Briton Ferry were started again. Later, oil-fired bar and pack heating furnaces were installed at the Pontnewynydd 2-high hand mills of Partridge Jones and John Paton, and Llanelly Steel (1907) Ltd., an important sheet maker itself, and supplier of bar to tinplate works, installed a continuous slab, billet and bar mill in 1950 to double its output of bars and improve their quality.[25] Scotland, with no nearby strip mill but with new light industries, provided favourable growth prospects for old-type mills. Smith and McLean's Gartcosh mills retained their reputation for especially wide sheets, and Braby's at their Nethan works, which had been idle for six years, adopted a policy similar to that of sixty years before when in 1948 they replaced the old rod and bar mills with sheet mills. At their Eclipse works, Glasgow, they installed a new 3-high mechanised sheet mill in 1954, expecting improved quality and a 25 per cent. increase in tonnage.[26]

Even in their post-war heyday the old-type mills were burdened with adversities. Semi-finished steel was frequently in short supply, reducing their output and their profit margins. In the early years Midland rerollers were occasionally idle for want of steel, and Scottish mills complained that deliveries were only a quarter of their need. Inconsistencies in national policy increased the confusion. Scottish sheet-using industries languished for want of material while the government delayed its decisions on the future size of Scottish steelmaking, and the newly formed National Coal Board failed to give the necessary assurances about coking coal supplies for which Colvilles were

waiting before making major steel extensions.   When demand
could not be satisfied, Scottish steel companies gave preference
to their traditional heavy industry customers, so that Glen-
garnock, one of the main Scottish sources of sheet bar, re-
designed to take care of that trade in 1936–1937, was now too
busy rolling for the shipyards to turn out its full tonnage of
semi-finished steel.[27]   Sheet bar from cold metal steelworks
was too inconsistent in quality for high-grade sheet, and
when home strip/sheet or foreign coil became available or
demand slackened there was an inevitable shift from the hand
to the mechanised mills and from them to the strip mills.
After December, 1954, a price differential was introduced, the
superior continuous mill coil now selling below the price of
hand or mechanised sheet whose production costs had always
been much higher.   At this time strip coil was 68s. 6d. a ton
cheaper, or 8·5 per cent. of the coil price; by March, 1958, the
differential was 108s. 6d. or 10·6 per cent.   In these circumstances strong discrimination against the old-style mills was
inevitable, and they entered their last decline phase, though
with periodic quickenings of activity.

In the spring of 1951 a special committee of the Iron and
Steel Federation examined plant redundancy in the industry,
and the same year closures occurred in the sheet and allied
trades.   Richard Thomas and Baldwins closed much of the
Whitford works, excepting the galvanised sheet department,
and their Landore and Bryngwyn melting shops.   At Ellesmere
Port John Summers shut down their Wolverhampton Corrugated mills.   Not all these closures were final and by the mid-
fifties, at the time of denationalisation, the bigger companies
were being persuaded to purchase old-style plant and nurse it
towards its final abandonment.   R.T.B. acquired old Siemens
works in South Wales, and in 1956 Summers paid £350,000 to
the Iron and Steel Holding and Rehabilitation Agency for the
Liverpool, Widnes and Ellesmere Port works of Burnell and
Company, their old masters of seventy years earlier.   For a
few years Burnell's mills were kept in full work.   At the end of
the fifties, however, steel demand weakened, and although sheet
was affected less than other lines the low-grade producers were
severely hit.   The position worsened as R.T.B. and the Steel
Company of Wales now joined John Summers in continuous

galvanising, dislodging the old-type mills from another of their refuges.

Some works made headway against the tide until a surprisingly late date—sheet mills of the Neath Sheet and Galvanising Company were mechanised in 1957, and at John Williams Wishaw works in 1959, but generally the decline of the old-type mills now continued more quickly than had been forecast. The Iron and Steel Board in its development report, published in 1957, looked to a 1962 output from non-continuous mills of 600,000 tons, evenly divided between hand and mechanised plant, and in 1961 they predicted a 1965 output of 150,000 tons. The reality was much harsher (Table 37).

TABLE 37

Sheet steel output by type of mill, 1953 to 1963–1964 (thousand tons)

	1953	1956	1960	1962	1963–1964
Continuous mills	1217	1657	2497	2815	3569
Mechanised mills	189	205	175 ⎫	94	94
Hand mills	380	354	156 ⎭		

Source: Iron and Steel Board, Annual Reports and Development Plans

Eleven sheet and tinplate works closed in 1958, seven of them in South Wales, where the Pontardawe sheet and bar mills and the Whitford mills, closing for the second time, were among the victims.   In 1959 R.T.B. West Wales works ceased to roll black plate and their output of galvanised sheet fell sharply, while that at Ebbw Vale went up.   In 1955 the West Wales works had made 12·1 per cent. of the company's plate, coils and sheet but in 1959 only 4·4 per cent. of the group total.[28]   By 1962 R.T.B. had abandoned the old Partridge Jones and John Paton works at Pontnewynydd, which had once been eminent in the Bristol and Welsh sheet trade, the Pontymister works and the Pontardawe and Dyffryn steelworks.   At Bryngwyn complete abandonment was avoided by constructing a new galvanising line and later installing the first continuous line in Britain for manufacturing colour-coated wide sheet.   Other companies also pruned their interests in old plant.   The Iron and Steel

Board approved the mechanisation of the mills at the Gorse Galvanising Works, Llanelly, in 1956 but subsequently the controlling company, Bynea Holdings, had second thoughts, and in 1960 the mills were closed, and shortly the Bynea Steel-works followed.   The last old-style sheet works in the Llanelly area, those of the Llanelly Steel Company, had closed by 1962. The hot mills of Neath Sheet and Galvanising were abandoned in 1964, its galvanising operations thereafter being supplied with purchased coil and control passing to the Steel Company of Wales.   In September, 1966, the hot mills at the Orb Works, Newport, which had been rolling electrical sheet, turned out their last orders.   Elsewhere the decimation of the old mills, although on a smaller scale, was equally thorough.

John Summer's two Merseyside subsidiaries, Burnells and the Birmingham Corrugated Iron Company, went out of produc-tion, the latter on the 50th anniversary of its removal from Birmingham to Widnes.[29]   On Tees-side, two South Durham hand mills were abandoned in 1967, Dorman Long's Bowesfield works at Stockton in 1958, the same company's Ayrton Sheet-works in 1968.   Braby's, buying much of their sheet bar from Colville's, faced considerable difficult'es in the late fifties and eventually sold the mechanised mills they had completed only in 1954.   It was later suggested that losses in the Glasgow works had offset profits in other sections of the group.[30]   Smith and McLean's Gartcosh mills were closed in 1958 and although reopened were abandoned in 1962, when the first cold reduced coils rolled in Scotland became available.   Nothing could more vividly illustrate the contrasts between the old and the new in the sheet business than a journey out from Buchanan Street station, Glasgow, in the spring of 1962.   Passing the derelict Eclipse Works of Braby's one saw, a few miles further on, the black, squat and idle mills of Smith and McLean, but beyond them the long, low, light-coloured buildings of the new cold reduction mill (Table 38).

The final change of the sixties has involved the demise of that long declining sheet-producing district, the West Midlands. Quality and a local market for small lots and special grades had bolstered the surviving Midland mills—in 1957, for instance, when only 9·2 thousand tons of Dorman Long home sheet deliveries went to the North-East coast, 30·7 thousand tons of

R.T.B.'s Midland works deliveries of 65.6 thousand tons went to Midland customers.   After the mid-fifties, however, the area declined sharply, although, with stronger emphasis on electrical sheet, R.T.B. still managed to increase their Midland Works output.   These works functioned as finishing units for Ebbw Vale, which supplied 16·8 thousand tons cold reduced sheet to the Stourvale Works, Kidderminster, and 47·1 thousand tons coil to the Cookley alphasil works at Brierley Hill in 1959.   The hand blackplate mills at Wilden Works closed in 1959, the coated sheet works at Stourvale in 1962.[32]   By the mid-sixties the only surviving corrugated galvanised sheetworks in the Black Country were controlled by James Summerhill and located in the old Beaver Works in Horseley Fields, Wolverhampton.[33]

TABLE 38

Production of coated and uncoated Sheet by Region, 1946–1965
(thousand tons)

	1946	1951	1955	1959	1961	1965
South Wales and Monmouth	595	854	1380	1504	1528	2618
Lancashire, Cheshire, Flint and Denbigh	342	496	632	808	864	1096
Scotland	65	72	75	28	30	402
North East	73	76	67	35⎫	62	48
West Riding	25	19	29	34⎭		
West Midlands	85	80	84	67	41	7
BRITAIN TOTAL	1186	1598	2248	2477	2524	4171

Source: British Iron and Steel Federation, *Annual Statistics*

In the early sixties two Midland plants still rolled electrical sheet on old-style hot mills, the Swindon Works of R.T.B. near Dudley and the Manor Works at Bilston, whose reputation Stephen Thompson had established in the late nineteenth century and which, since then, had been operated by Joseph Sankey.   A new technical development now swept them away. In the United States important advances in rolling and annealing enabled cold reduced 3 per cent. silicon steel strip to replace the old standard 4 per cent. silicon steel sheet.   The new material had improved electrical quality and, still more attractive, more uniform flatness and gauge. The hot rolling stages were now concentrated at the strip mills, where close quality control could be linked with high productivity—a latter-day example of what had happened a quarter of a century earlier with mild steel sheet. Agreements were negotiated with America for the production of cold reduced electrical strip in Britain, and in 1963 Sankey's closed the hot mills at Manor Works and in 1966 R.T.B. abandoned the last hand mills at their Swindon Works.[34] The finishing work on strip mill coil involves cold rolling and heat treatment and is not strongly localised so that in 1966–1967 Richard Thomas and Baldwins announced plans to spend £2 million on Midland processing for electrical and special transformer steels.[35] Although such tenuous links may still be made out by the discerning observer, little else now remains of the once world-dominating Black Country sheet iron trade.

REFERENCES

1 *The History of the Steel Company of Wales Ltd.*
2 E. C. Lysaght in conversation.
3 *The Times* 29 January 1945. My italics.
4 *Sheet Metal Industries* October 1945, p. 1752.
5 British Iron and Steel Federation, *Report to the Ministry of Supply on the Iron and Steel Industry* 1945, pp. 8–9.
6 E. C. Lysaght in conversation and *The History of the Steel Company of Wales Ltd.*
7 E. C. Lysaght in conversation.
8 Discussions with Great Western Railway 3 July 1945.
9 *The History of the Steel Company of Wales Ltd., Iron and Steel* July 1947, p. 368. *Times Review of Industry* July and August 1947.
10 *Times Review of Industry* July and October 1947. May and June 1948.
11 In dealing with the whole controversy over the sheet mill I am indebted to *The History of the Steel Company of Wales Ltd.* and conversation with E. C. Lysaght.
12 *The Lysaght Century* 1857–1957, p. 42.
13 *Sheet Metal Industries* March 1947, p. 517.
14 *Times Review of Industry* August 1947, p. 48, and *The History of the Steel Company of Wales Ltd.*
15 British Iron and Steel Federation, *Progress of the Steel Development Plan* 1949, p. 2.

16 H. Peake, 15 February 1956. The Steel Company of Wales Ltd., *Report and Accounts for* 1955, p. 17.
17 *Iron and Coal Trades Review* 20 January 1939, p. 112.
18 *Times Review of Industry* August 1947, p. 33.
19 John Summers, Extraordinary General Meeting, *Sheet Metal Industries* March 1947, p. 558.
20 *Times Review of Industry* February 1950, p. 50. John Summers Annual Report 1951. *Economist* 2 June 1951.
21 *Journal of the Iron and Steel Institute* 175, p. 313, 178, p. 62.
22 *Coke and Gas* April 1953, p. 118.
23 R. F. Summers *The Birth and Growth of the Firm of John Summers and Sons*, p. 14. *The Economist* 2 August 1952, p. 300 in 'Integrating backwards in steel' provides a concise comparison of Port Talbot and Hawarden Bridge.
24 *Iron and Steel* November 1946, p. 616.
25 *Times Review of Industry* February 1947. *Sheet Metal Industries* June 1950.
26 *Times Review of Industry* June 1948 and *Annual Survey of Industry and Employment in Scotland*.
27 *Times Review of Industry* April 1947, p. 43, July 1947, pp. 43 and 47, January 1948, February 1948.
28 Richard Thomas and Baldwin statistics.
29 *Steel and Coal* 9 February 1962, p. 290, 27 April 1962, p. 826.
30 *Financial Times* 1 February 1962.
32 Richard Thomas and Baldwin statistics, *Times Review of Industry* February 1959, p. 97. *Steel and Coal* 2 February 1962.
33 *Rylands Directory* 1966–1967.
34 I am indebted to Joseph Sankey Ltd. for information on the new developments in electrical sheet and their implications.
35 *R.T.B. Annual Report* 1966.

CHAPTER 14

The Fourth Strip Mill:
the Evaluation of various Locations

In October, 1952, eighteen months after the Abbey Works at Port Talbot made its first steel, the loosening of the close links binding the Steel Company of Wales and Richard Thomas and Baldwins was begun. Cross holdings were removed, co-operative sales agencies were given up and in October, 1955, the virtually identical boards were replaced by separate directorates. Differences of opinion and interest and a desire to ease the process of denationalisation were the two main reasons for this disentangling. Now, though under an independent chairman, the chief executive positions of the Steel Company were occupied by men from Guest Keen Baldwins, both the managing director and assistant managing director having originated with Ebbw Vale's former near neighbour, the old G.K.N. Dowlais works. In short, in carrying out Sir William Firth's vision of a new Bristol Channel strip mill, R.T.B. had played a key role in establishing the Port Talbot complex and now had to face the fact that after creating a coastal rival they were still landlocked themselves. This was a basic consideration in the planning for a fourth strip mill; another stemmed from the market situation.

FINDING A LOAD FOR THE NEW MILL

Shortages of high-quality sheet steel had brought complaints from the consumer durable trades for many years. In the spring of 1953 conditions eased temporarily and home mills delivered 1·78 million tons sheet, of which 68 per cent. was from the three strip mills. The Steel Company of Wales supplied almost one-third of all deliveries. By 1955 the situation was again tight, and although sheet output was 430,000 tons, or

24 per cent. more than in 1953, the number of private cars produced for the home market had advanced by 80 per cent. 462,000 tons of sheet valued at £26 million, or perhaps £6 million more than home supplies would have cost. were imported. Imports of tinplate that year were valued at another £7 million.[1] A long-term threat to Ebbw Vale was indicated by the bulk of the increased home output coming from Port Talbot and Hawarden Bridge. Production of coated and uncoated sheet went up by 456,000 tons in 1953-1955. Steel Company of Wales output was up by 212,000 tons, and Summer's strip mill products, including light plate, by 164,000 tons. Ebbw Vale in 1955 made total deliveries of plate, coil and sheet of only 433,000 tons.[2] These national shortages of sheet and tinplate and their expected persistence seemed to guarantee a market for a well-placed new R.T.B. strip mill. It is difficult to pinpoint the time when the firm began active work on the new project, but in 1954 or 1955 H. F. Spencer, as managing director, pointed out the Severn-side floodlands east of Newport to an apparently rather surprised senior colleague as the site for Britain's next strip mill. After some months of planning the first public announcement of intention to build a new works—but not its location—was made in March, 1956.

To the beginning of 1956, apart from its investment in the Steel Company of Wales, R.T.B.'s post-war outlays had been small—about £12 million at Ebbw Vale, £4 million at Redbourn and smaller amounts at other Welsh and Midland works.[3] The other firms were now actively planning expansion of strip mill capacity; a John Summers scheme for extended steel, rolling and finishing capacity was approved by the Iron and Steel Board in June, 1955, and in February, 1956, plans were announced for all-round expansion at Port Talbot to provide 435,000 tons more sheet and tinplate at a cost of £50 million. At the beginning of 1956 R.T.B. were planning a new South Wales works to make sheet and light plate and also to deliver up to 500,000 tons a year of slabs or coil for finishing at Ebbw Vale. By the spring modified plans were for an increase in the output of steel at Ebbw Vale, and improvement in its quality by converting the Bessemer plant to steam/oxygen blowing, a project the Board approved in November. For a time the company's thinking about the new works seems not to have adjusted to the plans of its competitors or to the reduction in supplies of semi-finished steel destined for Ebbw Vale. Further, an extraordinarily optimistic view of future demand was adopted.

By May, 1956, it was said that, even allowing for Steel Company of Wales expansion plans, and assuming 'middle' rate national trends in supply and demand, there would be a shortfall of $2\frac{1}{4}$ million tons of steel and tinplate by 1962.[4] There were several imponderables, including the future of imports, the amount of strip mill capacity preoccupied with plate and the future of the old-style mills. Moreover, some leading R.T.B. planners doubted the validity of government predictions of national economic growth, on which all demand forecasts depended, so that the new plant was designed with a first-stage finishing capacity of only half the suggested 1962 deficiency. It was expected that ultimately the works would be similar in size to Port Talbot in the mid-fifties. A plant of 1·3 to 1·5 million ingot tons annual capacity was reckoned the balanced minimum on which a start should be made, and to take up some of the slack left by exclusion of supply to Ebbw Vale, tinplate production was added to sheet and light plate. Provision for two cold reduction mills, each capable of up to 500,000 tons production a year, and, in addition, up to 250,000 tons hot finished material, was considered reasonable (Table 39).

TABLE 39

Planned Annual Capacity of the new Richard Thomas and Baldwins Plant, 1956 (thousand tons)

	Stage 1	Ultimate Capacity
Blast Furnaces	3	5
Capacity	1200–1350	2000–2200
Steel ingots	1300–1500	2500–2600
Strip mill products	975–1125	1900–2000

Source: *Richard Thomas and Baldwin records*, May, 1956

Trade developments in 1956 depressed prospects for the new works. The Velindre mill of the Steel Company of Wales started work in July and was expected to increase that company's output of cold reduced tinplate to 900,000 tons within two years.[5]   Meanwhile home consumption was declining—by 22,000 tons 1955–1956. Motor car production fell sharply, sheet production was 150,000 tons down on 1955 and home demand fell by 18 per cent (Table 40).   Some of the impact was absorbed by reduced imports, by closure of old-style mills and by increased production of light plate to meet buoyant demand in that sector, but the decline was mainly passed on to the strip mills. As the margin for short-term expansion narrowed, so R.T.B. reacted violently against their over-optimistic project of only a few months earlier. Development

TABLE 40

Demand and Supply of Sheet, Tinplate and Plate for home use, 1955–1958 (thousand tons)

Sheet	1955	1956	1957	1958
Home consumption by manufacturing industry	2124	1858	1960	2030
Deliveries from strip mills	—	1551	1767	1844
Deliveries from hand and mechanised mills	—	546	453	359
Tinplate				
Total available to home users*	652	630	597	581
Deliveries from continuous mills	—	642	871	972
Deliveries from hand mills	—	252	158	42
Plate				
Home consumption by manufacturing industry	2248	2463	2678	2472
Deliveries from plate mills	—	2171	2313	2091
Deliveries from strip mills	—	493	574	429

* Including exports and imports but not changes in home stocks

Source: *Annual Reports*, Iron and Steel Board

studies were completed in 1956, and early in 1957 a more modest plan was submitted to the British Iron and Steel Federation. In February, 1957, the Federation approved a scheme for two blast furnaces and two steel plants, one with open-hearth furnaces, the other a steam/oxygen blown Bessemer plant, combined ingot capacity only 900,000 tons. The strip mill was deferred until market prospects looked brighter, and meanwhile slabs would be supplied to Ebbw Vale to eliminate both the long, uneconomic haul from Redbourn, then about 200,000 tons a year, and also the smaller supplies of steel of rather uncertain quality from the West Wales works. The residue of over 400,000 tons semi-finished material would presumably go to other rerollers, of which one of the largest in the country, Whiteheads, was in Newport. A strip mill was envisaged in the future and the site would be laid out for an ultimate capacity half as big again as R.T.B. had planned less than a year before. This remarkable change of plan is as difficult to explain as the previous expansive scale of thinking. Now the plans of the company became a shuttlecock among conflicting parties. An early controversy involved the Iron and Steel Board and the Iron and Steel Federation.

In accepting the R.T.B. plan early in 1957, the Federation confirmed its view that another strip mill would not be needed until the mid-sixties. The Board acknowledged the industry's doubts about consumption trends but maintained that without a new mill there would be a shortage of sheet and tinplate by 1962. Their Development Report, submitted in July, 1957, suggested that, after allowing for expansion at existing works, this shortfall would amount to 280,000 tons sheet and 135,000 tons tinplate. If obsolete capacity was retired the gap would widen by 300,000 tons and 200,000 tons respectively, giving a total of 915,000 tons.[6] Early in 1958 evidence about future demand was still inconclusive but the Board considered that in any case such uncertainties were 'no more than academic', for new capacity could hardly be completed until after 1962. They had, however, already rejected the project for a plant producing only semi-finished steel, and in March, 1958, R.T.B. again submitted a scheme for an integrated works with a strip mill as well as semi-finished steel production. This project suggests reversion to the thinking of almost two years before, for the planned ingot capacity was again 1·3 million tons and all strip mill products were to be made.[7] Home consumption of sheet and tinplate went up in 1958, but very little, and during the year the Iron and Steel Board revised its forecasts downward and extended the time span of its projection. It now concluded that a gap of 'at least' three-quarters of a million tons strip mill capacity was likely by 1965.[8] There were to be further oscillations of demand and adjusted forecasts, but by 1962 consumption had already grown very much in accordance with this forceast for 1965—steel sheet home deliveries went up by 619,000 tons over 1957, tinplate used at home by 113,000 tons and exports of tinplate by 49,000 tons. As with the third mill project a dozen years before, the delays in construction had various consequences, some bad, some good.

First, use of new steelmaking techniques was aided by the delay. Introduced in Austria in the early fifties, the new oxygen steel processes had not entirely convinced R.T.B. by mid-1956, and an open-hearth melting shop was planned. For the revised scheme in early 1957 a compromise was contemplated, though it would probably have proved unsatisfactory—a smallish open-hearth shop and an oxygen-blown Bessemer plant. Before their proposals were finally approved by the Iron and Steel Board in March, 1959, the company had decided to install only an oxygen steel plant. There were serious teething troubles with this plant but on balance the delay was fortunate technologically. Cost inflation was serious, estimated investment spiralling from £160 million to £180 million between 1956 and 1958. Yet R.T.B. still wished to go ahead, their eagerness providing some indication of the inadequacies of Ebbw Vale. It was indeed seriously suggested that Ebbw Vale itself should be reconstructed to meet the growing demand. By improving the slab heating furnaces, installing continuous annealing lines and, most important, remotoring the hot mill it could provide a greatly increased strip output. By 1958 the hot mill capacity had been raised from 12,000 tons a week to 16,000 tons, and those familiar with it reckoned that it could be increased to 30,000 tons, which would have met most of the expected growth in demand.[9] The mill, however, was twenty years old, the location and site were both grossly deficient and in the long run overwhelming advantages would lie with a new, tidewater works having scope for expansion to at least four million tons.

The delay permitted the emergence of, and was in turn lengthened by, pressures designed to affect the location of the

new works.   In the end R.T.B. was able to build where it had
planned but in the final stages of the controversy a wholly new
project was born and in 1962 two hot strip mills were completed.   The economics of an expansion programme already
pressing hard on the capacity of the market to absorb its
products became still more questionable.   The locational
controversies which significantly contributed to this outcome
are conveniently considered under two headings—South Wales
versus the rest of Britain, and the dispute within South Wales.

THE PROCESS OF CONFIRMING A COMPANY'S LOCATIONAL CHOICE: *locations outside Wales*

Richard Thomas and Baldwins had no doubt that their new
mill should be in South Wales, and by May, 1956, the International Construction Company's representatives were already
working on the layout of a site stretching east of Newport.   The
Board of Trade, however, had instructed its regional officers to
investigate all possible sites in Wales, England, Scotland and
even Northern Ireland, and the company recognised their
obligation to consider any other possible locations, if only to be
able to elaborate why they were unsuitable.   If the company's
choice was turned down, then, as an R.T.B. director put it, the
responsibility would have passed to others.   There was a
specific doubt about South Wales, for the N.C.B. were extremely
doubtful that their pits there could supply all the coking coal
the new plant would need, but, that apart, much of the trial
boring seems to have been carried out in the spirit of merely
satisfying outside pressure groups that each site had been
examined.   Looked at nationally, however, rather than merely
as a company matter, other locations seemed at first sight
reasonable propositions.   Possibilities were examined both by
the company and by the Iron and Steel Board.   A complete
list has never been published but seems to have involved the
following, including at the end two wild suggestions allegedly
by the Board of Trade, which, if true, indicate little of its
quality except perhaps in faith, in imagination or in sense of
humour—Newport, Swansea and Kidwelly in Wales, Redbourn and Immingham in Lincolnshire, Banbury on the
Oxfordshire orefield, sites on Southampton Water and
Thames-side, and, in Scotland, Grangemouth on the Firth

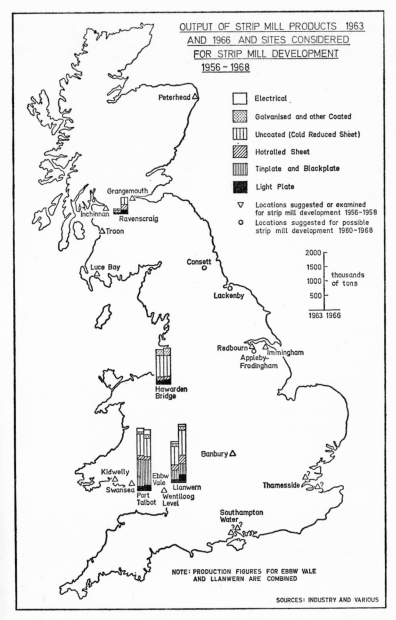

Figure 18.   The mills had very different product ranges.   Queries on Thames-side and Southampton Water indicate that it is not clear which sites were investigated.

of Forth, Inchinnan on the Clyde, Troon on the Firth of Clyde and, beyond the industrial belt, a site on Luce Bay, Wigtownshire or near Peterhead, Aberdeenshire[10] (Figure 18). Avonmouth was mentioned in the company's own discussions but was ruled out immediately on grounds of inadequate water supply.

The Banbury area had obvious market advantages. It lies almost halfway between the sheet markets of the London basin and of the West Midlands, well placed to supply the Cowley press shops or the new Pressed Steel plant decided on for Swindon in 1956. It was very near the Oxfordshire ore quarries, a significant consideration, for, as one Federation technical expert put it, the 'really strong' argument for Newport was its proximity to this ore.[11]   Yet, although the ore was limey and therefore suitable for mixing with silicous foreign ore, its iron content was very low, only 24 per cent. for the ore raised in 1955, and, even with the new techniques of steelmaking, the production of quality sheet would require very large tonnages of imported ore, railed in from Severnside ports. Moreover, in 1956 the whole orefield raised only 1·93 million tons ore, none of it produced by R.T.B. Having such a low-grade burden, the coke rate would be high, and the nearest Welsh coking coal collieries were 95 miles away by rail. Finally, there was a totally inadequate water supply for a major steelworks. In short there is no likelihood that Banbury would have proved a suitable location, and the company seems never to have been interested in the suggestion.

North Lincolnshire was on almost all counts more attractive and, in contrast with the chimeras conjured up by journalists and politicians in 1945–1946, was now seriously considered. R.T.B. had reserves in the Frodingham orefield, there were nearby ports to handle imported material and the lowest cost coking coalfield in Britain was in the hinterland. The immediate market for strip mill products was small but Lincolnshire was as accessible to the biggest national markets as South Wales. Two centres were considered—R.T.B.'s Redbourn works, Scunthorpe and a new site at Immingham. Specific problems involved the suitability of Lincolnshire iron ore for high-grade flat rolled steel and the question of the size of the reserves of this ore.

For the most difficult motor body pressings American strip mills in the late thirties were rolling steel with phosphorus levels below 0·010 per cent. but at Normanby Park Lysaghts had not managed standards consistently below 0·030 per cent. The Sérémange strip mill built by Sollac in the minette orefield of Lorraine in the early fifties employed oxygen and steam in the Bessemer and open-hearth steelmaking operations and produced steel of fair quality. L.D. steelmaking permitted the use of lower-grade ore, but, even so, steel made from Frodingham ore would still have too much phosphorus and sulphur to meet the increasingly stringent requirements for severe deep drawing operations. This difficulty could be overcome by double slagging, which improved quality but reduced output and raised unit costs. Moreover, the low cost of production of iron from Lincolnshire ore depended on minimising coke consumption, and this involved running the blast furnace on what was described as a 'knife edge' practice, slight deviations producing either high silicon or high sulphur iron, each unsuitable for the production of high-quality sheet steel.[12] In the early 1960s the addition of lime in the L.D. process, the modification known as L.D.A.C., made quality sheet from Jurassic belt ore practicable, but by then the locational decisions had been taken. Even if this problem had been overcome earlier there were other obstacles.

Frodingham ore was extremely variable in chemical composition. As James Henderson of Appleby-Frodingham had described it in 1942, a vertical cut might expose layers of stone varying from 14 to 26 per cent. in iron content, 4 to 25 per cent. in silica and 4 to 35 per cent. in lime. Sulphur, inimical to deep drawing quality, increased away from the outcrop.[13] Although ore preparation plants could surmount this difficulty, this would naturally raise iron and steelmaking costs. There were doubts, too, about the size of the workable ore body in Lincolnshire. With very little bought scrap available, a one million ton strip mill would require iron-making capacity of at least 700,000 tons or an annual consumption of almost 2·0 million tons of Frodingham ore and 1·0 million tons of Northampton Sand ore, its essential siliceous mix.

Redbourn in 1956 made only 299,000 tons of iron, insufficient to justify large working faces and economic layout in the R.T.B.

quarries at Crosby and Conesby. The ore burden at Red-bourn, therefore, probably cost 4s. to 5s. more per ton at the furnaces than at the nearby, much bigger United Steel works. Expansion would remedy this, and indeed within a year or so R.T.B. were developing such big, low-cost quarrying operations at their Winterton properties towards the northern end of the outcrop. In the mid-fifties their two quarries produced half their ore needs, but siliceous stone was bought from Stewarts and Lloyds north of the Welland, a cheaper source than their own Irthlingborough mine further south. Search for nearer sources of Northampton Sand ore, near to the old mid-Lincolnshire ore workings at Greetwell and Leadenham was unsuccessful.[14] In summary, the short-term prospect for large additional supplies of Frodingham ore seemed good, of Northampton Sand ore much less so.

Further ahead, supply of both ores seemed likely to be difficult. Given plant life of at least forty years, and even assuming no expansion from an iron-making capacity of as little as 700,000 tons, the new works would require an additional reserve of 80 million tons of north Lincolnshire ore and 40 million tons of Northampton Sand ore. The disappointments of R.T.B. prospecting suggested that the latter would have to be bought and hauled 65 miles over the tortuous Lincolnshire rail network. Even Frodingham ore in the long-term prospect looked most unpromising, as late as 1961 a well-informed local estimate putting workable reserves west of the River Ancholme, and therefore at shallow depths, as only fifteen to twenty years' supply at current iron producing rates for Normanby Park, 100 years for the much bigger United Steel's plant and 35 to 40 years for Redbourn. In these circumstances alone a large new extension at Redbourn seemed a very doubtful proposition.

Beyond the Ancholme the ore bed has now been proved to the outskirts of Grimsby so that the reserves of the three companies are much larger than was estimated only twelve years ago. However, extraction and transport costs will be higher. As of 1961 they were estimated at perhaps 15s. and 3s. 6d. a ton respectively as opposed to 8s. a ton for extraction and 1s. for carriage from one of the smaller existing quarries. At these rates, mining well to the east of the present orefield would increase iron-making costs by over £1 per ton.[15] Finally, the Redbourn site was too small to accommodate a strip mill, all its ancillaries and the necessary expansion of iron and steelmaking plant. The eastward trend in development of the Frodingham orefield was merely one factor pointing to Immingham as an attractive alternative as a strip mill location.

Immingham had already been considered more than once, and in combined access to home and foreign orefields had unrivalled advantages. It had deeper water than almost any other port in Britain, could handle vessels of 25 to 30,000 tons, and already had an iron ore traffic amounting to 310,000 tons in 1954. Low-cost coking coal collieries were 50 miles west and linked to the port by well-equipped mineral lines. N.C.B. pricing policies cancelled out much of this advantage, and tonnages of higher-grade coal, partly from South Wales though mainly from Durham, would be needed for a suitable coke oven mixture, but trends in carbonisation practice suggested greater use of South Yorkshire coal. Site conditions for a major new steelworks were ideal. Immingham lacked a big local market for flat rolled products, but so did all the existing strip mills, and it had good rail connections with the rest of the country. It had, however, no large local metal-working labour force, and in the tight labour markets of 1956 this was a grave disadvantage. Secondly, no development here could contribute to improve operating efficiency at Ebbw Vale, and finally, almost as decisively, there were water supply difficulties. R.T.B. engineers described water quality as unsuitable for cold reduced sheet and tinplate, and the Iron and Steel Federation's technical adviser, T. Colclough, bluntly categorised Immingham as 'one of the worst sites in the country from the point of view of water supply' to which he added, not so convincingly, 'and that is why concentration was on the River Trent'.[16]

Choice of Southampton Water would have involved an intriguing breaking of new ground. Big vessels were already handled there, and for African orefields or the new developments in Venezuela Southampton was probably the most accessible big port in Britain. Supply of coking coal meant a long rail haul from South Wales or coastal movement either from there or from North-East coast ports, although at this time of fuel shortage there was still no Board of Trade ban on the import of coal, and mid-Appalachian mines were already feeding new coastal works on the continent. Hauls on finished steel to London and south-eastern markets would average only about 75 miles, although the area was further from the West Midlands than was Port Talbot. A Southampton area mill, however, might have permitted R.T.B. to divide their markets, the needs of London, Swindon, Cowley, Luton and the scattered smaller consumers in the south-eastern quadrant of England being supplied by the new mill, while Ebbw Vale met the Midland demand. It is noteworthy that in 1959 London and the Home Counties and the very big area south and west of a line from Gloucester, through Oxford, Reading and Portsmouth took 34·6 per cent. and the Midlands 36·3 per cent. of Ebbw Vale deliveries of hot and cold rolled sheet. The South-East, though not the immediate vicinity of Southampton Water, produced large tonnages of high-grade scrap, which despite much smoothing out of inter-regional differences by the British Iron and Steel Federation could still be delivered there at prices lower than in South Wales.

If Southampton Water was a promising location, the marshland belt of the lower Thames estuary seemed even better. Fords had demonstrated for 25 years that pig iron could be smelted cheaply from imported ore and Durham coal carried coastwise, and further down the estuary, near Canvey island or even to the east of Shoeburyness, there were excellent sites for a big integrated works. From Canvey island eastwards, however, wide spreads of sand separated these sites from deep water, making development of a terminal a difficult engineering problem. A north-shore works would have easy access to the Dagenham body shops which consumed some 200,000 tons sheet a year, and a 70-mile road haul to Luton. Given the motor firm policy of splitting orders among the sheet makers, however, R.T.B. could not secure the full custom of either centre, and under the current uniform delivered pricing arrangement there was no incentive to modify this practice to benefit a nearby mill. R.T.B. engineers recognised that the water supply situation on Thames-side made it impossible to locate the whole of the projected plant there. Further, the estuary shared with Southampton Water two other grave disadvantages, not of intrinsic locational values but of the practical

politics of locational choice—neither was a primary metal area
and neither had a large unemployment problem nor any prospect
of one emerging.

R.T.B. had little interest in development prospects in
Scotland. In 1959, for instance, only 1·7 per cent. of Ebbw
Vale hot and cold rolled sheet went north of the border
(Figure 19). Even considered from some supposed superior

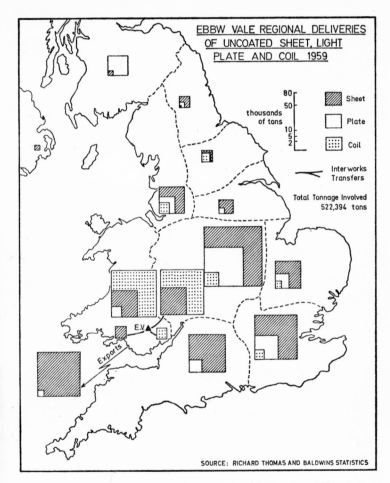

Figure 19.   In sheet the dominance of the Midland and South East
contrasted sharply with the very small deliveries north of the
Humber and Ribble.

national interest, any site in the central lowlands was too
eccentric from the centres of sheet consumption to justify
further examination.   Further, Scotland could offer few possible sites, all of them inferior to Immingham.   Sectional
interests were able to ensure nevertheless that the Scottish case
should be fully examined.   Grangemouth was a port of
moderate quality flanked by suitably large sites for heavy
industry.   The coking coal of east Stirlingshire lay immediately
adjacent but was both inferior and more expensive to produce
than that from South Yorkshire.   The differential price
changes the N.C.B. had introduced in 1954 were estimated to
increase Scottish iron-making costs by about 11s. a ton while
those of Lincolnshire went up by only about 2s. 6d. a ton.[18]
Inchinnan was nearer the centre of Scottish sheet demand
although this outlet was very small by English standards.   It
offered good sites and could be provided with reasonably deepwater access for ore carriers so that it had been regarded for
over 30 years as the ideal situation for the relocation of the
Scottish steel industry.[19]   As with Grangemouth, the haul on
coking coal would be shorter than that to Immingham
although, with the Lanarkshire field dying, substantial tonnages
from Stirlingshire would be required and for a time at least
some high grades from Durham as well.

There were already three Welsh strip mills whereas demand
and growth in consumption were in the Midlands and south-
east, so that, although the company had no doubt that Newport
was the ideal location, from a 'national point of view' there was
something to be said for Immingham, Southampton or Thames-
side in production and marketing costs.   On regional economic
planning grounds, and regarding the strip mill's contribution to
employment, and perhaps even to 'leader' development, promoting the growth of sheet fabricating industries, a case could
possibly be made out for the Clyde, the Forth or even the Tees.
In practice rational consideration of the best location for the
new plant from the company point of view or from that of
society was submerged in a flood of partisanship which scarcely
ebbed through the $2\frac{1}{2}$ years after R.T.B. first revealed their
intentions.   The strength of the advocacy seemed in almost
inverse proportion to the suitability of the location.   Thus
nothing was heard on behalf of the Thames or Southampton

Water, the arguments for Immingham were restrained, Teesside was too busy planning heavy plate or beam mills to raise a voice, while Grangemouth or Kidwelly became emotive names which gave high colour if little substance to speeches and sent the delegations hurrying off to London. Much of this controversy is irrelevant, but certain key points indicate the range of factors which now affected locational decisions and their changing relative values.

REFERENCES

1 J. S. Crawford in *Financial Times*. Steel Supplement 28 February 1955. Steel Supplement 19 August 1957. *The Times* 2 May 1956.

2 Steel Company of Wales and John Summers *Annual Reports*. Richard Thomas and Baldwin unpublished statistics.

3 *South Wales Evening Post*, Industrial Supplement 16 January 1956.

4 The projections are contained in an unpublished Richard Thomas and Baldwins document of May 1956.

5 Steel Company of Wales, *Annual Report* 1956, p. 18.

6 Iron and Steel Board, *Development in the Iron and Steel Industry. Special Report*, 1957, pp. 7, 59, 60. *Steel Review* 6. April 1957, p. 7, 13. January 1959, p. 7.

7 Iron and Steel Board, *Annual Report for* 1957, July 1958, pp. 20, 22.

8 Iron and Steel Board *Annual Report for* 1958 June, 1959, p. 19.

9 C. T. Thomas in conversation.

10 Iron and Steel Board *Annual Report for* 1958, p. 20. T. M. Thomas, 'Geographical and Economic Factors in the siting of a major integrated steelworks', *Tidschrift Vor Econ en Soc Geografie* August/September 1963.

11 T. Colclough.

12 H. H. Stanley and A. Jackson in correspondence.

13 J. Henderson presidential address, *Journal of the Iron and Steel Institute* 1942, 1, p. 45.

14 I am indebted to the ore mining branch at Redbourn for enlightening discussion of the problems of ore supply.

15 Based on discussions at Redbourn 1961.

16 T. Colclough May 1956.

17 R.T.B. statistics.

18 *Iron and Steel* July 1954, p. 383.

19 See K. Warren, 'Locational Problems of the Scottish Iron and Steel industry since 1760', *Scottish Geographical Magazine* April and September 1965.

CHAPTER 15

Politics before Economics*: the Choice and Consequence of strip mill Location, 1956-63

The case for some of the possible strip mill sites was not made effectively because they were not backed by national pressure groups and frequently had little local support either. This was so, for instance, with the most reasonable English contender, Immingham, although local M.P.s and notably the member for Grimsby, Kenneth Younger, did something to advance its claims. The virtues of this location had to be argued on its economic merits and the decision was taken on other grounds. The Scottish case was mostly conducted from this wider perspective.

The idea for a Scottish strip mill had appeared and was then apparently extinguished in 1945. In the summer of that year Colvilles chairman, Sir John Craig, had admitted that, good as the Gartcosh sheet mill's product was, that from the strip mill was better. Colvilles had considered such a plant, but had preferred to use the resources at their disposal to perfect current methods of production. The correspondent of the journal *Iron and Steel* reckoned that Scotland would never be secure in the new consumption goods trades without a strip mill, which should be established 'regardless of cost', and by a combination of firms or a wholly new concern if Colvilles would not do it. 'It is in fact only lack of enterprise that prevents the continuous mill being planned right away . . .' was his parting shot.[1] In fact at that time Colvilles undoubtedly had a big enough job completing the rationalisation and modernisation programme they had begun only ten years earlier, and demand for plate seemed quite as insatiable as that for strip sheet. Moreover it

* The title of *The Times* editorial, 19th November, 1958.

was incorrect to claim, as did the same correspondent in 1947, that there was a sufficient market for a full strip mill, at any rate north of the border.[2]   Similar arguments were advanced once or twice in the early fifties but the issue was never actively canvassed until R.T.B. announced their project.[3]

Fulfilling their obligation to look at suggested sites, and believing they could justify an elimination they had already decided on in principle, R.T.B. examined a site near the River Carron, just north of Grangemouth, in 1956.   Their proposal for Newport was submitted to the British Iron and Steel Federation a few months later.   Having been pressed twenty years earlier to shoulder their social responsibilities in West Wales, where they had plant, they were now harried to consider Scotland, where they had none.   Local authorities, the nation's M.P.s, the Scottish Trades Union Council and the Scottish Council (Development and Industry) were all prominent in the agitation.

There were persistent fears that inadequate coking coal reserves, which had delayed both immediate post-war developments and the decision to build the new blast furnaces and melting shop at Ravenscraig, would make another integrated works in Scotland impossible.   The N.C.B. ten-year development plan was expected to produce 2·35 million tons coking coal a year by the early sixties, but Scottish works already carbonised 1·5 million tons, and the new R.T.B. works would require up to another 1·5 million tons.   For a time it was argued that developments in the Kinneil and Airth areas near the proposed steelworks site could provide this, but the case was not convincing, and geological difficulties soon made it necessary to scale down the Coal Board's targets.[4]   Grangemouth was perhaps suitable for vessels carrying ore on the short haul from Sweden, and it could be deepened to take the bigger carriers necessary on longer hauls.   On balance, because of the doubtful coal prospect, the raw material supply situation was unfavourable for a Scottish mill.   Then the argument was switched, so that by the middle of 1957 the Scottish T.U.C. was saying, 'The General Council considers that assertions of insufficient coking coal and deposits of iron ore, *if not entirely irrelevant*, detract from the main issue',[5] and a few months later the Scottish Council claimed as the result of a two months' cost analysis that, as compared with South Wales, '. . . on the economic factor it is believed that any difference would be marginal and probably favour the Scottish location'.[6]

In fact the Scottish claim focused from the start on the stimulus a strip mill might give steel fabrication, helping to make good jobs lost through the closure of Royal Ordnance factories, Admiralty depots and private industry. Early in 1958 the Scottish T.U.C. summed this up . . . 'To site a fourth strip mill in Wales would be tantamount to a flagrant disregard of the relationship of steel production to industrial development', and the government seemed to endorse this opinion, even though it ignored the fact that the locational link between sheet production and consumption is weak and failed to recognise that Wales used little of the sheet it made.[7]   In the late fifties Scottish sheet and strip consumption was only about 250,000 tons a year; if the R.T.B. mill had been located there almost three-quarters of its output would have to be sold in England, largely in the Midlands or south   Yet, even if the whole project could not be in Scotland, there remained an alternative, to graft the plant on to an existing works. By the early autumn of 1958 Scottish interests were pointing out suitable 'host' plants.[8]

Stewarts and Lloyds had only one steel plant in Scotland and this was small, unintegrated and confined to the tube trade, so that a host could only mean Colvilles, whose attitude was therefore decisive. Colvilles believed that there was no proof that coking coal supplies were adequate for their own long-term plans for extension of iron capacity, never mind those of R.T.B.[9] They probably also feared a loss of workers. Logically enough, therefore, they opposed the idea of a Scottish strip mill and in the summer of 1957 refused an invitation to open a fighting fund for the new mill, stating that they considered the project was not necessary. After the fight was over, John Long, the Scottish Secretary of the British Iron and Steel and Kindred Trades Association, revealed that he and George Middleton of the Scottish T.U.C. had seen the Colville directors about the strip mill. 'Sir Andrew McCance (Colvilles chairman) made it very clear to that deputation that under no circumstances whatever would they consider having the strip mill in Scotland and that it should go to Newport.'[10]   During 1958 conditions developed which made Colvilles willing to modify their attitude.

Demand for sheet grew in 1958 but the strip mills were now biting deeply into the business of the old-type sheet mills, deliveries from which fell away by 20·3 per cent. from the 1957 level. Output in Scotland fell by 27·6 per cent. More decisive were the changes in the plate trade situation. There had been a persistent shortage into the mid-fifties, but by 1957 six new plate mills had been approved by the Iron and Steel Board. In July, 1956, Colvilles had received permission to replace the plate mill at their Clydebridge works by 1962 and that at the Dalzell works over a longer period.[11] In 1958 plate demand slipped sharply while political pressure for the strip mill continued unabated. In addition to the threat that, if R.T.B. were persuaded to build at Grangemouth, Colvilles would face serious competition for labour, fuel, and other steelworks supplies and services, and that a Grangemouth strip mill would also make lighter plates more cheaply than a conventional plate mill, there was the prospect of long-term underemployment of the Ravenscraig iron and steel works. By the end of September, 1957, when this works made its first steel, it had cost £22·3 million. In the financial year 1956–1957 Ravenscraig made almost no contribution to the Colville steel output of 2·095 million tons. After that some old furnaces at the nearby Dalzell works were closed, but even so, in the next financial year, with the new works active, steel production was down by 31·2 per cent. to 1·442 million tons.

These changes suggested that, if Colvilles were host to a Scottish strip mill, they might avoid a major new competitor and find another outlet for their Ravenscraig steel and the second blast furnace and new slabbing mill already approved. This meant that a new site, on tidewater, was impracticable. On 18th November, 1968, the Prime Minister told the House of Commons that two strip mills were to be built, one of them by R.T.B. at Newport and '. . . the Board of Colvilles Limited have agreed in principle to undertake the other project'. The tone of the sentence suggested that the initiative had come from others, an impression confirmed by suggestions elsewhere that Colvilles had been persuaded 'to their great act of faith', partly by the Ministry of Power and partly by the Scottish Office. There is supporting evidence too; for instance, not

T

until two months after the decision to build was announced did Colvilles make a survey of home and overseas markets. In May, 1959, in discussions with the Scottish T.U.C., Mr. Macmillan noted that if technical reasons had been dominant, or if a single large unit had been considered essential, Scotland would have had no share in the development.[12]

EAST & WEST WALES

In the seven years before R.T.B.'s announcement of a plan for a new strip mill there had been rumour or report of surveys for steelworks development at Burry Port, Llanelly, Barry and on the Pengam Moors airfield, Cardiff.[13] Now the prospects of intraregional rivalries were increased by the coincidence of darkening economic prospects for West Wales with news of the R.T.B. plans. Although the new mill was never intended primarily for tinplate and was finally not equipped to make any, it fell victim to the same pressures from the tinplate area that were already appearing in 1934-1936 and had dominated discussions ten years later.

In 1947 the Steel Company of Wales had taken over eighteen old tinplate works, fourteen of them from Richard Thomas and Baldwins. Under the management of H. Leighton Davies they had done excellent work. When the Trostre cold reduction mill and tinning plant started work in 1951, they went through a sharp crisis in the early stages, but things then improved, and early in 1956, when R.T.B. were actively planning their new mill, the Steel Company still had twelve old-type works. In South Wales there were 28 such plants, employing 13,970 workers in January, 1957, and still concentrated mostly in the Llanelly and Swansea areas. With Velindre coming into full production, and able to turn out 1,500 tons tinplate a day, the equivalent of a week's work on four old-type mills, the closure rate accelerated. By midsummer, 1957, 2,100 men were unemployed at the Kings Dock Works, Swansea, one of the newest old-style mills, and at the Old Castle Works, Llanelly, the oldest and biggest plant in the country, and by November of the 28 works active ten months before twelve were either idle or scheduled to close.[14] By early 1958 no old-type mill which had operated under the red dragon of the Steel Company of Wales

was still in production.   The sheet mills were also disappearing.
Seven more South Wales sheet and tinplate mills closed during
1958.   Most displaced workers soon found new jobs, so that
of 3,500 displaced in 1957 fewer than 750 were wholly
unemployed at the end of the year, but there was ground for
genuine subregional concern, and this helped to power a strong
West Wales pressure group.   In February, 1958, the government appointed a team to study the industrial problems of that
area.[15]   Long before this R.T.B. were already examining the
possibility of development in the west and drawing up a balance
sheet comparing it with Monmouthshire.

By the summer of 1956 R.T.B. had made site surveys both
east and west of the Usk, on a site near Swansea and on the flats
between Pembrey and Kidwelly six miles west of Llanelly.[16]
Whereas Newport could already take 20,000-ton vessels and the
British Transport Commission was soon committed to spend
£1 million on extensions of the ore-handling plant, Kidwelly
had no harbour facilities at all nor the prospect of their low-cost
development.   Newport was soon proved a very inadequate
iron-ore terminal by West European standards but it was better
than any other in South Wales.   Proximity to Oxfordshire
ironstone quarries was regarded as an important asset of
Newport, avoidance of the need to carry this ore through the
bottleneck of the town even being urged in favour of the site to
the east as opposed to the one on the Wentlloog levels.   The
main Welsh coking coal collieries were well to the east of
Swansea Bay, a large group in the immediate hinterland of
Newport, although the sites surveyed both east and west of the
town lay outside the coalfield.   At Kidwelly good coal of non-
coking quality lay under the site and would have been sterilised
if the plant had been built there.[17]   Site conditions at Newport
were by no means ideal.   The one west of the river was not
acceptable and any plant there would have had its ore stockyard 1¼ miles from the docks.   To the east there were difficulties with clay and peat and the need for deeper piling than
at Port Talbot.   Water supply conditions, however, were
favourable.   Some 20 million gallons a day were needed and
providing this at either Kidwelly or near Llanelly would prove
difficult, while developments near Pontypool were expected to
insure ample water for the Newport area.[18]

Newport had a great advantage for marketing.   The 'logical development' of the growth of a motor or motor component industry in South Wales had not happened on any substantial scale and by the early 1950s only about 4 per cent. of national sheet consumption was in the Principality.   By 1959 7·5 per cent. of Ebbw Vale's total home deliveries of sheet were made in Wales and Monmouthshire, as opposed to 19·1 per cent. in London and the Home Counties and 36·3 per cent. to the Midlands.[19]   Via the A.48 Kidwelly was 70 miles farther from these English markets, an especially serious disadvantage if the works concentrated on sheet.   There was, however, something to be said for West Wales in terms of labour and social provision.   Some opposition to development on the site east of Newport was expressed by the local population, and there was inadequate housing in the area for the large labour force of the mill; West Wales had men trained in steel and millwork and fixed capital in established communities.   Yet on further examination the relative disability of the east shrank even on these points.   The skills learned in the melting shops of West Wales were not directly transferable to the operation of the oxygen converters on which R.T.B. eventually decided to rely, and hand-mill men had to forget and relearn a good deal in moving to a strip mill.   Even before the locational choice was finalised by R.T.B. it was clear that few of those displaced from West Wales hand mills would be out of work long enough to work in a new mill which might take five years to complete. In Development Scheme 'M' the Steel Company of Wales was planning to add another 3,000 to its work force in the western half of industrial South Wales, and by early 1957 it already had 1,600 more workers than a year before.   Finally, it was obvious that no West Wales mill could contribute as effectively as a plant at Newport to improving operating efficiency at Ebbw Vale.

R.T.B.'s conviction grew that Newport was the only practicable proposition.   As Sir Ernest Lever remarked to the Swansea and District Metallurgical Society early in 1957, his company had become convinced that British sites suitable for strip-mill development could be counted on the fingers of one hand, and the closest analysis of many factors and all other possible alternatives had convinced them that their original intuition about Newport had been correct.[20]   A few weeks later Mr. Julian Pode, managing director of the Steel Company of Wales, supported R.T.B.'s decision in a speech in Cardiff. 'Prosperity,' he observed, 'cannot be forced into unnatural channels by Act of Parliament, and the construction of immense new units at immense costs must surely be undertaken at the site which is economically sound.'[21]   The conclusion in the first part of this sentence was again soon to prove incorrect, and his advice that the rest of South Wales should accept R.T.B.'s Newport choice and co-operate in tackling any resulting problems failed to temper the feuds within South Wales.

In March, 1957, the West Wales Federation of Trade Councils opened a 'fighting fund' to win the strip mill for Pembrey-Kidwelly.   Social arguments were again advanced. As a trade union leader put it '. . . a new strip mill should come to the area where dozens of old-type tinplate works will have to be inevitably closed and provide employment for the men who will become redundant'.   Early in 1958 a working committee reported to a meeting of twelve local authorities that the strip mill for the Kidwelly Flats was the only solution to the major long-term problems in West Wales, and in April Lady Megan Lloyd George, M.P. for Caernarvon, reaffirmed this, pointed out that here at any rate there was social capital in schools and homes to serve the new works, and argued that, on sociological grounds, the case for putting the mill in the area was overwhelming.[22]   Towards the end, however, the West Wales advocacy weakened and Grangemouth seemed to become the most dangerous rival to Llanwern, although certainly not through any R.T.B. interest.

NEWPORT AND RAVENSCRAIG, 1958-1963

On 18th November, announcing the two strip mills, his cabinet's 'judgement of Solomon', as he rather unfortunately called it, the Prime Minister revealed that the Scottish developments would cost about £50 million.   It was soon agreed that up to £50 million would be loaned to Colvilles, and R.T.B. would receive a government loan of £60 million for a project which early in 1959 was estimated as likely to cost £100 million.

Both the Ravenscraig expansion and the new Spencer Works,

as R.T.B. called the Llanwern plant, in honour of their managing director, involved two blast furnaces. For Colvilles this would treble the annual tonnage over the seventeen mile route from the new ore unloading plant at General Terminus Quay in Glasgow and thereby throw more doubt on the long-term justification for the 1954 choice of Ravenscraig as the focus for new developments in Scottish steel-making. For Llanwern iron ore had to be carried across the Usk, through Newport and out to the blast furnaces, even though these were erected within sight of the Severn estuary. In spite of the intention to use considerable tonnages of Oxfordshire ore, the amount smelted has been much smaller and, as costs moved more strongly in favour of foreign ore, R.T.B. showed little concern when its application to open new quarries south of Banbury was refused.[23] Oxygen steelmaking plant was installed in each works, although at Ravenscraig another open-hearth furnace was also added. The choice of mill by Colvilles proved very revealing, indicating the diffidence of a new entrant to the quality sheet trade in a very uncertain market.

Each strip mill was announced in November, 1958, as a semi-continuous unit capable of 500,000 tons flat rolled products a year. At Llanwern this was to be mostly sheet, partly light plate, but tinplate was no longer mentioned; at Ravenscraig half the output would be light plate. Only 150,000 tons of Colville's sheet output would be a net addition, the rest replacing the tonnage of the Gartcosh hand mills, although the quality was far higher. Both the Iron and Steel Board and Sir Andrew McCance argued that a semi-continuous mill was on balance by no means an inferior plant to a fully continuous unit.[24] Given the relatively small outputs planned, this con-clusion was difficult to gainsay, and it might have seemed churlish to remark that one unit would have been in a much better position. For a time, uncertain of market prospects, Colvilles even considered installing a Steckel mill, which would have a lower capital cost and an even smaller output but which could later be converted into a semi-continuous mill. They believed that the Steckel mill could produce not only good sheet but also tube strip, another new line for the company, but by the early weeks of 1959 they had decided, like certain

Welsh interests in 1946, that Steckel sheet would be inferior in quality to that from a strip mill.   In the spring they were contemplating a plate/strip mill combination, a 120″-plate mill which would also act as the rougher unit for four 4-high 62″ wide finishing stands rolling strip.   Later in the year greater emphasis was given to sheet, and the choice of a semi-continuous strip mill was confirmed.   There was hesitation about the width of this unit but eventually it was decided that the six-stand hot mill would be 68″ wide, enabling it to meet the great majority of orders, the wider range of sheets used in the motor industry being the main omission.   For cold reduction, a reversing mill was again considered but was shown to have insufficient capacity and to be likely to require conversion to continuous operation at an early date.

Whereas R.T.B. had abundant experience in thin flat-rolled steel and could immediately call on Ebbw Vale expertise, Colvilles had much greater difficulty.   They selected three men from senior posts in their existing works to form a committee to develop the scheme and this committee visited existing strip mills; Port Talbot in January, 1959, and shortly afterwards Ijmuiden, Bremen and Italian and Austrian works.   By early April R.T.B. engineers were in Pittsburgh for consultations with the United Engineering and Foundry Company but, although already in correspondence with the same firm, Colvilles had not yet reached this stage.   They now made heroic efforts to make up the leeway, the result of their extremely rudimentary thinking on strip mill development before the Prime Minister's announcement.   They were belated converts to the idea.

Newport was to be completely integrated from the start, with no question on this occasion that the cold reduction mills should be in the same plant as the hot mills.   Colvilles planned to sell half the initial 500,000 tons from the Ravenscraig mill either as hot rolled sheet or as light plate and to transport the rest eight miles as coil for cold reduction on a site at Gartcosh.   It was suggested that there was ample space there for new factories to work up the steel strip.

By early summer, 1959, an increase of 500,000 tons hot rolled coil at Port Talbot and 300,000 tons sheet at Hawarden Bridge was expected within the year from development schemes under way. It was believed that the supply position would ease within eighteen months, but by autumn, 1959, the Society of Motor Manufacturers and Traders had submitted increased assessments of the industry's requirements over the next six years, and the Iron and Steel Board requested the submission of schemes for further expansion. Surprisingly, when these were quickly submitted, it approved schemes for both Llanwern and Ravenscraig and totalling 500,000 tons more sheet a year. Yet the opportunity to permit expansion at Llanwern while checking further growth at Ravenscraig had been available, for the R.T.B. expansion proposals came some weeks before those from Colvilles. Extensions approved for Llanwern involved increase of ingot capacity from 1·0 to 1·4 million tons, the installation of a fully continuous strip mill and an increase in cold reduced sheet output by 235,000 tons. With no assurance that Scotland could absorb any significant share of the increase, Colvilles was allowed to change its development from 250,000 tons plate and 250,000 tons sheet to 175,000 tons and 500,000 tons respectively. A semi-continuous mill was still retained. A third expansion scheme, submitted by the Steel Company of Wales, proposed a second hot strip mill for Port Talbot. This would be a 48″ mill, concentrating on tinplate strip, so freeing the 80″ mill for longer runs on motor body stock, which might have improved the efficiency of the Steel Company of Wales very greatly. Although a provisional contract for the mill was placed, the Iron and Steel Board, committed to expansion at Llanwern and Ravenscraig, had to turn the proposal down. A compromise was arranged under which the Llanwern works would hire-roll slabs from Port Talbot, returning them to the Steel Company for cold rolling.[25] This repeated the mistakes in dispersion that had been forced upon the Steel Company in the location of Velindre and Trostre and again denied the logic that the first Iron and Steel Board had used to justify the removal of Lysaght's cold reduction mill to Port Talbot. On the other hand it seemed to permit the expansion of steel and cold rolling capacity at Port Talbot while providing a very desirable improvement in the load factor at the new R.T.B. hot mill. The planned interchange was up to 400,000 tons a year, but in fact never became very important. In August, 1962, well ahead of schedule, the hot mill at Llanwern was commissioned, and early in December the first coils were rolled in the Ravenscraig strip mill.   By then the rate of growth in demand had slipped below the forecast.   In other respects, too, the sheet and strip situation was changing rapidly.

REFERENCES

1   *Iron and Steel* July 1945.
2   *Iron and Steel* March 1947, p. 115.
3   See K. Warren, *Scottish Geographical Magazine* April and September 1965.
4   *Times Review of Industry* June 1957, p. 68.   *Iron and Coal Trades Review* 4 October, 1957, p. 767.   *Iron and Coal Trades Review* 21 February 1958, p. 424.
5   *Iron and Coal Trades Review* 23 August, 1957 p. 417, my italics.
6   *Times Review of Industry* January 1958, p. 63.   *Iron and Coal Trades Review* 25 October 1957, p. 990.
7   *Iron and Coal Trades Review* 21 February 1958, p. 424.   See also *Iron and Coal Trades Review* 13 April 1956, p. 344.   *Manchester Guardian* 10 April 1958.   *The Times* 5 June 1957 and 19 November 1958.
8   *Manchester Guardian* 17 October 1958.
9   Colvilles Limited, *Chairman's Statement* 7 February 1958, 'Development'.
10   *Times Review of Industry* June 1957, p. 45.   *Iron and Coal Trades Review* 27 September 1957, p. 711.   *Manchester Guardian* 9 February 1959.
11   Iron and Steel Board, *Development in the Iron and Steel Industry, Special Report* 1957, p. 88.
12   *The Times* 19 November 1958.   *Times Review of Industry* July 1959, p. 50.   G. D. N. Worswick and P. H. Ady, *The British Economy in the 1950s* 1962, pp. 349-350.   For full discussion see D. L. Burn, 'The Steel Industry 1939-1959', pp. 639-657.   K. Warren, *Scottish Geographical Magazine* September 1965, especially pp. 94-97.
13   *Times Review of Industry* May 1949, July 1949 and August 1955.
14   *Times Review of Industry* May 1957, p. 46.   *Iron and Coal Trades Review* November 1957, p. 1004.   Iron and Steel Board, *Annual Report for 1956*, p. 29.   *Annual Report for 1957*, p. 33.
15   *Manchester Guardian* 20 January 1958.
16   *Times Review of Industry* June 1956, pp. 55, 77.   Iron and Steel Board, *Annual Report for 1958*, p. 20.
17   H. Brooke Minister for Welsh Affairs, *The Times* 19 November 1958.
18   R.T.B. spring 1958.

19   The idea of 'logical development' was referred to in *Iron and Steel* November 1944, p. 698.   British Iron and Steel Federation *The South Wales Steel Industry* November 1956, p. 9.   R.T.B. statistics for 1959.

20   *Iron and Coal Trades Review* 29 March 1957.

21   J. Pode, 'Steel in 1957 with particular reference to South Wales'.   Annual Conference of Chartered Institute of Secretaries, *Iron and Coal Trades Review* 17 May 1957, p. 1117.

22   *Iron and Coal Trades Review* 22 March 1957, p. 699.   *Times* 14 March 1957.   *Manchester Guardian* 12 November 1957, 25 January 1958.

23   See K. Warren, *Scottish Geographical Magazine* September 1965, pp. 91–97 and Chapter IV 'The Steel Industry' in G. Manners (Ed) *South Wales in the Sixties*, 1964, p. 112.

24   Iron and Steel Board, *Report for 1958*, p. 20.   Colvilles Limited, *Chairman's Statement for 1958*, pp. 10–11.

25   Iron and Steel Board, *Annual Report for 1958*, p. 23, *for 1959*, pp. 21–24.

CHAPTER 16

Sheet Developments 1963-68, and the Widening Horizons beyond

THE EXPERIENCE OF STRIP MILLS AND SHEET CONSUMING
DISTRICTS, 1963–68

In the early sixties sheet consumption grew more slowly than the Iron and Steel Board's forecast, and much less than had been assumed by R.T.B. in 1956. By 1963 both Llanwern and Ravenscraig were getting into their stride, with a combined hot and cold rolled output rather greater than R.T.B. had then planned for a single new works. The older strip mills were increasing their output, the buffer of old-type mills had almost gone, and after 1961 imports of sheet rose again. Between 1960 and 1963 production of light plate declined by almost 100,000 tons or nearly one-fifth at the strip mills while tinplate production scarcely changed, so that sharpening competition between the mills was concentrated on sheet.

Exports of sheet and coil increased but much of this business proved unremunerative. For instance, in order to operate Llanwern as near as possible to capacity, R.T.B. sold large tonnages abroad, but, although the early foreign business was done at prices only a few pounds below the home level, by 1965 they made sales for as little as £35 a ton, little over two-thirds the home price level. Although there was some loosening, growth in British sheet consumption broadly reflected the existing pattern. (Table 41.) The South East and Midlands consume almost half the sheet fabricated by British industry. The high figure for the Eastern Region largely reflects the concentration of the automobile industry in the Luton—Dunstable-Bedford area. Motor manufacturers are the chief consumers of sheet, in 1962, for instance, taking 708,000 tons of cold reduced sheet, 36 per cent. of all home deliveries. Collectively the next eight ranking consuming trades, according to the British Iron and Steel Federation's classification, consumed

TABLE 41

Recorded Sheet Steel Consumption by Ministry of Labour Regions, 1965 (thousand tons)

Wales and Monmouth	95
Scotland	105
North Western	335
South Western and Southern	355
London and South Eastern	354
Eastern	259
West Midlands	550
East and West Riding	63
East Midlands	48
Northern	37
Northern Ireland	3
TOTAL	2,204

Note: figures refer only to firms making returns in the Consumer's Census

Source: Iron and Steel Board and British Iron and Steel Federation, *Statistical Departments*

114,000 tons less. Many members of this group, notably the makers of electrical equipment, metal furniture, domestic appliances, are also strongly localised in the same areas as the motor industry.[1]

Pricing policy has hardly strengthened the agglomerative force linking sheet production and consumption. Until 1957 sheet steel was quoted at a uniform delivered price throughout England and Wales. Then a concession of £1 a ton below the basis price was introduced for a few months for the area within 25 miles of Hawarden Bridge and for seven years in South Wales. When new price increases were announced in 1966, John Summers and then the Steel Company of Wales introduced selective increases zoned outwards from their works, but after the British Steel Corporation took control in the summer of 1967 uniform delivered pricing was restored.[2] Government development area policy had secured some dispersal of consumption towards the steel districts. For example, new domestic appliance factories were built at such otherwise unlikely locations as Merthyr Tydfil, Llandudno Junction or

Bromborough.   Yet, until the government interfered with its ambitious expansion programme, the motor industry remained firmly entrenched in its old locations.   When the companies were induced to build in the development areas they gave strong preference to those nearest their existing plants. Merseyside, therefore, was the chief beneficiary and Hawarden Bridge consequently the favoured strip mill.   At the same time, the motor firms were able to obtain permission from the Board of Trade for major extensions at the existing works in return for building elsewhere.   In the mid-sixties the Midlands retained its lead in sheet consumption although its relative share has declined. (Table 42.)

TABLE 42

Recorded Sheet Steel Consumption by Ministry of Labour Regions, 1963 & 1965 (thousand tons)

	1963	*1965*
East and West Midlands	580	597
London and South Eastern	398	354
North west	226	335
Scotland	88	105
Wales and Monmouth	76	95
All others	663	718

Source: British Iron and Steel Federation, *Statistical Department*

Carefully avoiding further dispersal of its widely spread private car production, the British Motor Corporation centralised the domestic appliance business of its Fisher and Ludlow subsidiary on the Kirkby Industrial Estate, Liverpool. Standard Triumph was said to contemplate big new body-making developments at Speke, but the site had only storage facilities until after 1966.   Vauxhalls announced that it would move its commercial vehicle plant from Dunstable to Hooton Park near Ellesmere Port, had second thoughts and developed component manufacture there instead.   Its early products— gearboxes, axles, engines and other mechanical parts—provided virtually no outlet for Hawarden Bridge sheet.   By 1964 it had been decided to make up to 90,000 Vauxhall Viva cars at Ellesmere Port annually, but the bodies were to come from

Luton.   While about a third of the sheet used by Vauxhalls in
Bedfordshire came from the Steel Company of Wales, 190 miles
away, John Summers, only ten miles from the Viva assembly
line, delivered 120 tons of sheet a day in their own lorries alone
to the press shops at the other end of the axial belt.   They
returned with scrap on roads they shared with vehicles carrying
bodies made from that sheet.   The economics of concentration
in quick-action pressing had given rise to apparently irrational
patterns of movement.

The Ford Motor Company's new assembly plant at Halewood
on the south-eastern edge of the Liverpool industrial area represented a more hopeful development.   Completed in 1963 at a
cost of £30 million, it was equipped not only to assemble cars
but also to produce stampings for Dagenham in exchange for
engines and other mechanical parts.   By mid-1964 the Halewood assembly line was capable of 1,000 vehicles a day, representing yearly sheet consumption of perhaps 160,000 tons.
Compared with this, all other projects in the fringe areas were
insignificant.   Between 1963 and 1968 home deliveries of
coated and uncoated sheet steel increased by 5·4 per cent. but
in the north-west by 48·2 per cent.   Although the motor firms
still refused to tie themselves wholly to one supplier, Summer's
regional concession system, introduced in April, 1966, no doubt
helped them in a bad year for the sheetmakers.

Welsh developments were less important.   Pressed Steel
agreed in 1960 to build a large new refrigerator plant on
Crumlyn Burrows, between Port Talbot and Swansea, one of
the possible strip mill sites examined fifteen years before.
B.M.C. extended the radiator works at Felinfoel, Llanelly, and
constructed a £7½ million body pressings plant nearby.
Rover, with leanings to Scotland or County Durham, eventually came to an agreement with Cardiff Corporation for a new
motor works on Pengam Moors.[3]   Together these seemed to
promise substantial benefits to the South Wales steel firms,
especially the Steel Company of Wales, but results were disappointing.   Rovers continued to bring bodies from the Pressed
Steel works in the South Midlands, the B.M.C. development
was not very big, and, after a promising excursion into washing
machines in liaison with a direct sales organisation, Prestcold
closed down at Crumlyn Burrows in 1964.   In 1965 Ford

acquired this works for engine components, transmission systems and exhaust and axle units for direct daily shipment by liner train to Ford assembly plants. None of these products gives scope for much sheet consumption. In 1965 recorded sheet consumption for the whole of Wales and Monmouth was only 3·6 per cent. the output of coated and uncoated sheet from South Wales mills.

Scotland was estimated to consume 100 to 125,000 tons sheet annually by 1959. Even first-stage levels of planning for Ravenscraig and Gartcosh involved 250,000 tons cold reduced strip and 125,000 tons hot rolled material. The new sheet industry had to be made into a 'leader' trade for new metal fabricating. In February, 1959, the Scottish Council (Development and Industry) resolved to press the Secretary of State for Scotland for advance factories to take advantage of the quality sheet now available, and soon was suggesting with especial vigour that Continental and American firms should consider branch factories in Scotland. Success was considerable.

Pressed Steel had already decided to make motor bodies at its Linwood works for Volvo in Sweden, and in 1960 bigger steps were taken to develop a new Scottish motor industry. The British Motor Corporation agreed with the Board of Trade to build a commercial vehicle and tractor plant at Bathgate, and Rootes a private car works near the expanding Linwood body shops. Business for the strip mills still grew only slowly, so that Colvilles began an active canvass for Continental business, and at home were forced into long-distance marketing. Their lorries soon became a familiar sight, speeding down the A1 or negotiating the streets of West Midland towns where they mingled with the familiar fleets from Hawarden Bridge, Port Talbot and Ebbw Vale. By early 1964 annual Scottish consumption of sheet and light plate together was running at 175,000 to 200,000 tons, no more than quarter to one-third that country's capacity. That year the Ravenscraig mill made a 'substantial' contribution to its own depreciation charges but none to the interest payable on the government loan. More sheet outlets were essential, and at Rothesay in 1965 the Scottish T.U.C. pleaded for a tinplate mill at Ravenscraig. As the Scottish Secretary of the Iron and Steel Trades Confederation hopefully put it, this would not only take strip and provide 400 jobs but ensure '. . . the certainty of thousands more developing in food canning and similar industries and in direct export markets'.   Colville's 1965–1970 expansion proposals included a tinplate works and a galvanising line, but, pressed for a decision early in 1967, the Minister of Power observed that this project would have to wait.[4]   Renewed calls for more component manufacturers in Scotland, a brief hope that Rootes/Chrysler might centre its operations there, still leave Scotland producing far more high-grade sheet than it can consume in further manufacturing for many years to come.[5] In 1962 Scotland's proportion of Britain's coated and uncoated sheet output was 3·6 per cent., in 1967 with over eight times the tonnage its share was 12·2 per cent.

TRENDS IN DEMAND & MARKETING

The Benson Report of mid-1966 suggested that within ten years home tinplate consumption would increase by almost half beyond the high levels of 1965 and that motor industry steel consumption would grow by 40 per cent. (Table 43.)   A reliable industry source has suggested a slower rate of growth for tinplate and a much more rapid increase for sheet, especially for cold reduced material. (Table 44.)   Whichever is correct

TABLE 43

Benson Report Forecasts of tinplate and automobile steel demand to 1975 (thousand tons)

	Tinplate	Automobile Steels
1965	826	2378
1975	1200	3330

substantial growth seems certain, and this will have to be satisfied from existing works.   New delivery methods suggest that the more distant mills will be able to share in this trade with less difficulty than at present.

Until the mid-1960s there had been a long period trend to increased road delivery of strip mill products, reflecting the advantage of speed, of the avoidance of damage suffered in rail transhipment and shunting and of the possibility of eliminating

TABLE 44

Home and Export Demand for Strip Mill Products 1966, 1975 & 1980 (million tons)

	1966	1975	1980
Tinplate and blackplate	1·22	1·60	1·74
Cold reduced sheet	3·08	4·88	5·50
Hot rolled sheet	0·67	1·00	1·10
Light plate	0·80	0·80	0·80
TOTAL	5·77	8·28	9·14

Source: Unpublished market analysis 1967

expensive storage facilities at the consumer's works. Except for small loads, rail transport was cheaper even over short distances. (Table 45.) By autumn, 1964, 85 to 90 per cent. of

TABLE 45

Road and Rail delivery Charges for flat-rolled Steel Products c. 1962 (per ton)

	RAIL						ROAD	
Distance	*Wagon load charges per ton*							
miles	*10 tons and over*		*3–10 tons*		*Under 3 tons*			
	s.	*d.*	*s.*	*d.*	*s.*	*d.*	*s.*	*d.*
36	11	11	14	11	29	10	14	0
72	18	3	22	10	45	8	22	6
108	24	7	30	9	61	6	30	0
180	35	3	44	1	88	2	39	0
288	47	6	59	5	118	9	60	6

Source: Unpublished Statistics

the 24,000 to 25,000 tons strip-mill products John Summers dispatched weekly left the works by road.[6] In the mid-sixties came a sharp reaction to rail transport. This was helped on the consumer's side by the growing popularity of coil rather than sheet, and on British Railways' part by new coil cars which solved troublesome problems of condensation of moisture. At the same time the liner, or better still company train principle reduces both delay and damage. Sometimes, notably in the new Pressed Steel body shop, built on old

U

railway property at Swindon, big consumers have laid out their plant for rail delivery, and even for the smaller consumer the establishment of British Railways freightliner depots and rationalisation of steel delivery to main centres of demand has caused the transfer of traffic from the roads.[7] The 1968 Transport Bill should accentuate this drift.   By the beginning of 1967 rail shipment from Hawarden Bridge had edged up to between 20 and 25 per cent. as against only 10 to 15 per cent. two years before.[8]   Economically perhaps, to society at large certainly, the increased emphasis on rail delivery makes the separation of strip mill and sheet consumer more acceptable. It is certain that not all the existing units will expand at the same rate and possible that the sheet steel trade may develop in new areas of Britain.

THE POSSIBILITY OF NEW STRIP MILL PROJECTS

The Iron and Steel Board until its disestablishment in 1967 was convinced there was no early prospect for another strip mill. Existing heavy steel firms were not so sure, and for a time hopes of more imaginative planning by the British Steel Corporation involved huge new complexes which might well include new strip mills.   The Iron and Steel Federation's Benson Report of 1966 rejected the idea of a deepwater plant on the Thames Estuary but spoke of a possible large scrap-using steel plant north of London.   No mention was made of sheet steel but the area within 70 miles of the mouth of the Medway already has over a fifth of Britain's home sheet consumption, and ample sites fringe the mouth of that river, which could be easily developed to take 100,000-ton ore carriers.   British membership of the Common Market and increased growth rates in the whole South East would further increase the attractiveness of such a project.   Development area policy, however, and the danger of regional overheating provide strong counter-arguments.   The Thames Estuary has in fact poorer prospects for handling really big ore carriers than Southampton Water. There, if amenity problems in particular can be overcome, a very large new steel complex may be built, perhaps even by the private sector of the industry.[9]   In the short term new sheet capacity seems likely to be provided in a much less spectacular way.

The 1961 and 1964 Development Reports of the Iron and Steel Board both referred to the fact that more than one producer of heavy plate contemplated entering the market for wide strip.   Increasingly exacting plate specifications and new oxygen converter plants make the old suggestion that these works cannot produce material of sheet quality much less tenable than in the past.   Their existing primary capacity and modern 4-high plate mills will reduce the capital cost of a breakthrough into the new product range.   Market margins will certainly be narrow, but sheet and strip demand has proved more buoyant in time of recession than that for plate, and projections suggest that some heavy steel outlets will grow only slowly in the medium term. (Table 46.)   Of six plate-makers in Britain, the Patent Shaft Steel Company at Wednesbury is too small for such a plant, Colvilles already have a fully-fledged strip mill and the South Durham Steel and Iron Company is preoccupied with tube and pipe manufacture for home and

TABLE 46

Recent and Projected Demand for Steel by selected Home Industries
(thousand tons)

	1960–63 (average)	1965	1975
All home consumption	14,292	16,645	22,450
Shipbuilding	671	671	550
Construction	2,615	3,200	4,520
Motor vehicles	2,025	2,378	3,330
Tinplate	697	826	1,200

Source: Benson Report 1966, p. 10

overseas natural gas distribution systems.   Consett has already supplied very high quality plate for nuclear reactor shells and hull steel for Polaris submarines, and in 1960, when Ford contemplated an assembly plant, body works and other stamping operations at Washington, County Durham, indicated its willingness to build strip mill stands on to the new Hownsgill plate mill.   Even a superficial glance at that plant suggests that the site was prepared and the mill laid out with this in mind.   The British Steel Corporation, however, seems unlikely
U*

to consider any further major development at a location so ill-favoured for low-cost ironmaking.   Dorman Long on Teesside and Appleby-Frodingham in North Lincolnshire are more likely prospects for plate/sheet developments.

Dorman Long commissioned an automated universal plate mill at Lackenby in 1965, and in 1966 began work on a four-stand-80" wide extension to roll light plate to be coiled for delivery.   Much of this will go to the new tube and pipe mills on the north bank of the Tees at Greatham, but two further finishing stands were provided for.   These would permit production of strip down to 18g and further stands and cold reduction mills could produce motor body grades.   The Iron and Steel Board disallowed the additional two stands.[10]   Even though the annual sheet consumption of the whole Northern Region and the East and West Ridings is only about 100,000 tons, such a flexible unit would prove a valuable asset in conditions like those of 1966, when the Dorman Long coke and iron-making plant operated at below 50 per cent. of capacity.[11]

In the spring of 1966 United Steel Companies announced its 'Anchor' project for North Lincolnshire.   At one stage Immingham was considered, but for various reasons, not wholly convincing to an outside judgement, it was decided to focus expansion at the existing Appleby-Frodingham works, Scunthorpe.   Ingot capacity there would be increased by 700,000 tons to 2·5 million tons, two very large L.D. converters would replace the melting shop and a new universal slabbing mill and a semi-continuous mill for coiled light plate was planned.   By 1975 a third oxygen furnace to expand steel capacity to 4 or 5 million tons, a new blooming mill, billet and rerolling mills were further possibilities.[12]   In September, 1967, the company's advisers, W. S. Atkins and Partners, submitted a revised plan which included Redbourn, by then associated in the Midland Group of the British Steel Corporation.   It suggested a target of 5¼ million tons crude steel.   Thick strip was mentioned, and, although never made explicit, strip/sheet is an obvious further development.[13]   Ability to produce this grade would be increased by the new steel-making plant, the high-quality light plate installation and the proposed switch to a mixed home/foreign ore burden.   Immingham dock improvements, shared with the oil companies and the National Coal

Board, were an integral part of the scheme.   Here in the shadowy outlines of possible future developments, one discerns the descendant of past schemes—the vision of Lincolnshire pack mills which excited Frank Thomas, the mechanised sheet mills which Lysaghts once considered for Normanby Park and the Redbourn project with which Sir William Firth introduced strip mill development to Britain.   Whatever their hopes of eventual realisation, initiative in the near future lies with the five existing strip mills.   It is essential to examine their various opportunities and limitations.

DEVELOPMENT PROSPECTS AT THE EXISTING STRIP MILLS

By 1965 3 to 4 million tons was already being suggested as the minimum efficient size of a new, fully continuous strip mill.   In line with this the Benson Committee suggested that within ten years the optimum size of a strip mill plant would involve 5 million tons steel-making capacity.   Home consumption of sheet, tinplate and blackplate was only 3·8 million tons in 1965 and the Benson forecast for 1975 was 5·9 million tons.[14]   Even allowing for the continuance of 0·8 million tons of light plate production at the strip mills and for substantial exports, Britain could accommodate no more than two of these 'ideal' new plants.   Given the trend of ore costs and the economics of bulk delivery, they should be at deepwater ore docks, able to handle vessels of 200,000 tons capacity.   Britain now has five strip mills and only at one, Port Talbot, is the ore unloaded into the furnace stockyard without a land haul.   Planning in the sheet and allied trades must therefore aim at the nearest practicable approach to the ideal pattern from the very different present position.   It proceeds within a framework of constraints, including availability of capital and government policy on plant closure.   Already built, subject to a bewildering range of cost-disturbing factors—for instance the notorious and widely varying incidence of local rates[15]—it is not easy to make a cost comparison between the strip mills.

In regional output of strip mill products South Wales seems likely to maintain or increase its predominance.   Its three mills made 67·2 per cent. of all the tinplate, sheet products and light plate rolled by the five British mills in 1965.   Forecasts—by a Welsh firm—suggest that by 1975 the plants of Richard Thomas and Baldwins and the Steel Company of Wales will increase their share to 73·5 per cent. and by 1980 to 75·8 per cent. Summers remain vitally interested in strip mill products, but Colville's Ravenscraig plant is in rather a special position.

Always part of a multi-product complex, having a small Scottish market but one relatively secure from home producers' competition, the Ravenscraig mill seems a marginal competitor for the other strip mills.   It will continue to make incursions into the English markets, even achieving such sparkling successes as the contract to supply sheet to Fords, but it will not be engaged in the same life and death struggle as the other mills whether under national or private ownership.   Tinplate or galvanised sheet production may change the situation, but informed industry estimates, made in 1967, suggest that, although it will still be much the smallest of the five operations, Ravenscraig/Gartcosh will expand less between 1966 and 1975 than the rest of the strip mill industry.   In the following five years its growth may be very much less.   Strip mill output there in 1975 will probably be only a little over ¾ million tons, about 38 per cent. of the 1966 total of the Steel Company of Wales, and only just over 19 per cent. of the four million tons suggested as desirable for a strip mill unit by the mid-seventies.   Capital charges are lower than at Port Talbot or Newport, but the N.C.B. move to more realistic pricing has already pushed up Colville's fuel bill by £1 million, marketing hauls are long and the whole complex lies inland.   The situation with regard to foreign ore, however, may be changed greatly if the Scottish and North Western group plan for an ore terminal at Ardmore Point, Hunterston or Wemyss Bay is realised.   By 1973 such a terminal could handle 150,000 or even up to 250,000-ton carriers as against the 27,000 tons limit of General Terminus Quay.[16]   By the late 1980s a great new four- to five-million-ton steel complex at the ore terminal might well revolutionise the competitive position of a relocated Scottish strip mill industry, but that is too far ahead for any certainty.

At first consideration Ebbw Vale is likely to be dismissed as hopeless.   Twenty miles inland from its ore dock, some 900 feet above sea level and with a strip mill which, though modernised, is 30 years old, it has assembly and process costs higher than those of more recently built, coastal mills although the outsider cannot gauge by how much. Coal mining has moved away down the valley, the traffic in sintered ore from Northampton-shire was abandoned in 1966, so that over 1·2 million tons foreign ore a year is now landed at Newport for Ebbw Vale. Understandably, as Llanwern neared completion in 1962 and home and international competition increased, it was suggested that Ebbw Vale would soon be swept out of existence. In April, 1962, 1,500 men were declared redundant and one blast furnace was closed in an attempt to improve productivity, and in October, during an inter-union dispute, the management warned that if the works closed it might never re-open.[17] Yet R.T.B. engineers had planned that the Llanwern operation should also reduce costs at Ebbw Vale, the new ore tonnage justifying improvement at Newport docks, the Llanwern sinter plant permitting the closure of one blast furnace and some coking capacity at the older works. Early in 1962 the R.T.B. managing director told trades union representatives 'If R.T.B. had not been vital and persistent enough to undertake the Llanwern project there would be no Ebbw Vale in a year or two', and ten months later, to a local authority conference, he added 'If those works had not come to Llanwern—if for example they had been built on the east coast—then the life of Ebbw Vale would have been exceedingly short. . . .'[18]

Within Richard Thomas and Baldwins, Ebbw Vale remained vitally important as the only tinplate producer. National out-put of tinplate and blackplate failed to increase between 1963 and 1966, output at Velindre and Trostre fell by 7·3 per cent., but at Ebbw Vale went up by 16·2 per cent. In sheet the production of stainless material, of R.T.B.'s alphasil and con-tinuous galvanised material was actively developed. Even for ordinary grades of mild steel sheet, Ebbw Vale could be run on small orders or a wide variety of sizes while Llanwern spread its great overheads over bulk production of a smaller range of specifications. Meanwhile operating efficiency has improved. The labour force has been cut while iron production has been maintained and, with the new L.D. plant, installed in 1960, quality, costs and steel-making self sufficiency have all shown improvement (Table 47). Steel costs are now claimed to be very low, and mill throughput has been increased so that the slabbing mill, installed in 1938 to roll 500,000 tons a year, produced 1 million tons in 1966, while the strip mill of initial nominal capacity 12,000 tons a week was rolling up to 25,000 by 1967. Scope for further improvement remains—the second

TABLE 47

Pig Iron and Steel Ingot production at Ebbw Vale 1956, 1960 & 1965 (thousand tons)

	Pig Iron	Ingot Steel
1956	557	694
1960	592	803
1965	611	1,016

galvanising line, installed in 1966, was anticipated, for instance, to have operating costs £4 a ton below the existing unit, and a new reversing slabbing mill was planned in 1967 to improve primary mill costs. Interest and depreciation charges at Ebbw Vale in 1966 were at least £4 a ton below those at Llanwern, and in 1967, while the latter still made a regular overall loss, Ebbw Vale was performing at an almost exactly similar profit. At this point the planning context changed; it was grouped with the other main plants in the British Steel Corporation South Wales Group. In this wider perspective the prospects seemed to dim again.

In the second half of 1969 the new Port Talbot tidal ore basin will come into operation, enabling vessels of at least 100,000 tons to unload at that plant. For some years at least the new ore dock is likely to supply Llanwern through a shuttle service of large iron-ore wagons in a never-dismantled train, the 'merry-go-round'. Ebbw Vale, at the head of a narrow side valley, and with smaller ore requirements, does not fit well into such a scheme and the relative cost disadvantages of such a land haul increase as the delivered cost of foreign ore on the coast declines. Speaking to the Ebbw Vale Metallurgical Society in the spring of 1968, the managing director of the South Wales Group stressed that Ebbw Vale was secure for some years, but his emphasis on how much even South Wales lagged behind the

United States and Japan in steel output per man year must
have warned his hearers that Ebbw Vale, whose plant had
already been pushed to production levels never anticipated by
those who installed the units, would then fall a victim, in spite
of Steel Corporation approval of modest extensions in 1967 and
1968.[19] This need not involve complete closure and the
creation of a stranded community. The Benson Report had
implied that Ebbw Vale should have cold-metal steelmaking
operations, but a more likely prospect would be the abandonment of steelmaking too, so that the mill would roll down and
finish slabs from the coastal works. Eventually, when it
becomes essential to replace the hot mill, the logical development, on merely economic criteria, will be to transfer those
operations too to Llanwern.

Hawarden Bridge has much better prospects, although below
the surface weaknesses may be discerned. Bidston dock is
certainly inadequate, but fuel supply has been steadily ration-
alised so that by 1967 the 23,000 to 24,000 tons coal needed
weekly was delivered from North Staffordshire and Lancashire
pits. The regional market for sheet has also been growing
faster than in any other strip mill hinterland. By 1966
Summers were even claiming the lowest iron cost of all the
high-quality ironmakers, and, as the plant was cheaply built
and modernised, standing charges per ton of product have
ranged from £3 10s. 0d. to £4 a ton lower than for the Steel
Company of Wales.[20] Yet a possible corollary of low overheads is the purchase of present profitability at the expense of
the continuing modernisation of plant, which is essential to
long-term success. Various disinterested observers suggest that
Summers have fallen into this trap. The evidence is conflicting.

In 1965–1966 John Summers announced a £4 million 'tidying
up' operation to increase weekly steel capacity to 40,000 tons.
The scheme involved reconstruction of the open-hearth furnaces
to increase their heat capacity from 150 to 250 tons. Meanwhile the Steel Company of Wales had decided to replace a
melting shop of similar age and the even more recent Port
Talbot V.L.N. converter plant with L.D. vessels, to increase
weekly capacity from 50,000 to 80,000 tons. A second strip
mill was also proposed. Together these developments were
estimated to cost £60 million. Too heavy capitalisation has

dogged the Steel Company before, but such a unit, run at capacity, might well cause the past successes of Hawarden Bridge to fade in future years. If present intergroup competition is replaced by allocation of orders from a central Steel Corporation sales office, however, the large regional consumption of the North West will stand Summers in good stead. Three other Hawarden Bridge weaknesses or potential weaknesses are the need to bring in slabs from outside, the adherence to steel-producing methods which are generally being discarded and an inadequate ore dock.

Plans to extend the capacity of the Summers' strip mill announced in 1965 involved the transfer of 2,000 to 4,000 tons a week of slabs from Shelton Works.[21] Apart from freight charges and heat loss, this involves dependence on a plant which, although almost wholly rebuilt in the last six years, has rather high iron-making costs. Its Kaldo steelmaking operations and continuous casting went through considerable initial difficulties and continuing losses. External evidence confirms that the Kaldo process is a more costly producer of steel even in the most favourable conditions than the new generation of L.D. converters.[22] The present Hawarden Bridge melting shop is similarly at an operating-cost disadvantage although this could not have been anticipated when it was commissioned in 1951. The extension of steel furnace capacity can be only a patching operation which some independent steel engineers consider undesirable. By the spring of 1967, however, experiments with spray steelmaking were underway at Shelton. If they prove successful, and the teething troubles with continuous casting teach valuable lessons at the price of waiting a little longer, Hawarden Bridge may yet break into the new technologies at a more highly developed stage and so avoid such immense investments as are represented by the Llanwern slabbing mill.

The ore dock problem appears much more intractable. Bidston's limitations were already obvious in the fifties, and in the mid-sixties the announcement of the big new South Wales ore dock scheme promised to render the disability acute. By 1966, however, plans began taking shape for a new Mersey ore dock to service not only Hawarden Bridge but Shelton, Irlam and presumably Bilston as well. During 1968 the idea

of a new ore dock was even transmuted in the minds of some
into a new ore dock and integrated plant on the lines which the
Scottish and North Western group was planning for the Clyde.
On all accounts the conditions for engineering such a project
are less favourable. The five-fathom line lies six miles west of
Formby Point and above that the Mersey channel winds land-
ward between broad banks. By the summer of 1968 it was
suggested that a partial solution might perhaps be found in a
bulk movement which was combined with that of the new
Clydeside terminal—very deep draught ore carriers would
unload part of their cargo in the Clyde and then enter the
Mersey half loaded to tranship at a new ore terminal at Rock
Ferry between Port Sunlight and Tranmere.[23] By sacrificing
the full benefit accruing to the Scottish mill, Hawarden Bridge
would be enabled to reap many of the advantages of very large
carriers, but the haul across the Wirral to the furnaces would
remain.

John Summers's trading profits fell rather more than those of
the Steel Company of Wales between 1963 and 1966. In 1966
the Benson Report anticipated only small short-term growth
there, but felt that after 1975 Deeside might again become a
major national growth point.[24] In 1967 well-informed industry
sources suggested a similar pattern but with any growth spurt
delayed until after 1980 (Table 48). Over the next ten or

TABLE 48

Deliveries of Strip Mill Products by British Producers 1963, 1966,
1975 & 1980 (thousand tons)

	1963	1966	1975 estimate	1980 estimate
John Summers	1,155	1,197	1,340	1,345
Richard Thomas & Baldwins	1,390	1,958 ⎫	6,095	6,925
Steel Company of Wales	2,088	2,010 ⎭		
Colvilles	192	553	770	780

Source: An unpublished industry report 1967

fifteen years the gap will widen further between the tonnage
from Hawarden Bridge and from the two coastal strip mills in

South Wales. For them there seems promise of substantial expansion, although its rate will be conditioned by the competition from over-extended mills throughout the world.

The Steel Company of Wales built up its operations in the fifties at a time when increasing output seemed more important than minimising costs. Since then it has had to rationalise its operations, trim its labour force, and improve raw material supply. In pursuit of the first object the old Port Talbot melting shop was closed in 1961 and in 1963 the forty-six-year-old Margam shop followed, so severing the steelmaking connection which ensured that the hot strip mill should be located at Port Talbot. The 1965 plans for a new strip mill had to be withdrawn like those of 1959 when the Iron and Steel Board decided that increased demand could best be served by increasing output at Llanwern from $1\frac{1}{2}$ to 2 million tons at the very low cost of £$3\frac{1}{2}$ million. This was a rational enough decision but was later counter-balanced by trends in raw material supply favouring Port Talbot.[25] Early in 1966 the Steel Company decided to spend £39 million to replace all its existing steelmaking plant with two large L.D. vessels capable of 3 million tons a year, subsequently extended to 3·25 million tons. These steps to rationalisation have not resulted in any downward overall cost trends.[26] By 1964 American consultants in location analysis and in labour productivity were called in. In number of workers and their average wage levels the Steel Company retains an unenviable record. Early in 1967 it was admitted that the work force at Port Talbot could be cut from 16,000 to 10,000 without imperilling output, and concurrently American manning in a very similar plant was 5,000. As the Steel Company's managing director revealed, steel output per man year in 1967 in South Wales was 110 tons, in the United States 210 tons.[27] Through 1968 vigorous efforts were made to reduce the labour force. In 1969 the Achilles heel of inadequate dock facilities will also at last be covered.

The Steel Company of Wales has reduced the disadvantages of possessing facilities only for shallow draught vessels by concentrating on medium distance ore, so that in 1967, for instance, Port Talbot was the largest single user of Swedish ore in the world. As ore carrier size increased, however, so lack of access to cheaper, distant ores and of flexibility in purchasing became more obviously disadvantageous.   A few years earlier American offers of coking coal which could have given coking coal costs £1 below the delivered price from Welsh pits, would have been barred in any case by the Board of Trade embargo on coal imports.   By 1967 the Steel Company was suggesting that Australian coal could be delivered 45s. a ton cheaper than British coal, which starkly exposed the inadequacy of Port Talbot, for such a cargo would have to be carried in 100,000-ton carriers.   Australian ore, beginning to trickle into South Wales by 1968, must be transhipped into smaller vessels at Rotterdam.[28]   The need to tackle the growing inadequacy of Port Talbot dock was realised by 1957, when a joint scheme with Guest Keen Iron and Steel at Angle Bay, Milford Haven, was projected.   It was believed that 100,000-ton carriers could unload there, that ore could be railed to Port Talbot for 6s. a ton—9s. to Llanwern—or, better, that it could be shipped on by shallow draught vessels.   There were disadvantages to this scheme and by 1960–1961 the Steel Company had turned to the prospect of big developments at Port Talbot dock.   After three or four schemes had been proposed, work began on a tidal harbour in the autumn of 1966 and will be completed in 1969. It will then be possible to dock 100,000-ton carriers, and, with relatively small further expenditure, vessels of up to 200,000 tons.   Estimates of the cost saving have varied widely, but, with the rich ores from Western Australia, which promise immense changes for ironmaking in all seaboard metal districts of the world, the saving may amount to as much as 55s. per ton of pig iron.[29]   A reduction approaching even nearly to this amount will give Port Talbot a great fillip in competition with all other British strip mills.

The Llanwern works was planned with the realisation that a short land haul on imported ore from the North Dock, Newport, was unavoidable.   A 4½-mile overhead conveyor was originally considered, but the ore is carried by British Railways. Annoyed by freight rate increases, and realising the advantages of new, very much bigger, and wholly company controlled ore unloading facilities R.T.B. promoted a Private Bill in 1962 for a new ore jetty running from Goldcliff out over the mudflats to Newport Deeps.[30]   This aroused the anxiety of eighbouring

Severnside and Bristol Channel ports, and in 1963 a new proposal for a jetty into Bristol Deeps did little to allay these fears.
In 1964 the National Ports Council instituted an enquiry and,
in 1965, after reviewing various possibilities, including development at Cardiff and Milford Haven, or, jointly for R.T.B. and
the Steel Company of Wales, a new terminal at either Port
Talbot or Bristol Deeps, declared in favour of independent construction of the last two.[31]   But by now R.T.B. were again
reconsidering the whole issue, and eventually decided on an
impounded terminal at Uskmouth.[32]   Even this would involve
a conveyor link to the furnaces.   Following nationalisation the
question of ore unloading in South Wales was re-opened in 1968
and, as it has prospects of handling giant ore carriers and an
annual throughput of up to 20 million tons, the Port Talbot
terminal will possibly supply Llanwern as well over a rail haul
of 45 miles, in spite of the 1965 White Paper.[33]   Although the
haul will be through the Vale of Glamorgan, its extra length
would make Llanwern's ore supply position very similar to that
of Ebbw Vale in relation to Newport Docks.

Llanwern began operations with a few advantages and
many liabilities.   The work force was kept well below the Port
Talbot levels per unit of capacity, and Richard Thomas and
Baldwins were firm that they would not pay wages on the same
inflated scales as the Steel Company of Wales.   Computer
control was introduced into an increasing proportion of the
operations, and by the end of 1964 it was claimed that the sheet
rejection rate was below that of any competitor.[34]   The plant,
however, came into production against keen competition and
in addition had quite exceptional running-in difficulties,
notably in the oxygen steel plant.   The excessively large
slabbing mill was consequently grossly under-employed.   The
target output of 1·4 million ingot tons was reached in the
operating year 1963–1964, but standing charges were so high
that almost £10 was lost for every ton produced and by 1967
its finished product costs were still, apparently, £2 a ton higher
than those of Hawarden Bridge.   Beyond the years of over-
capacity, if the ore supply situation can be satisfactorily
improved, the prospects are much brighter.   As most of the
plant has a much higher potential output than any which has
been even nearly approached yet, growth in production will

yield lower unit costs. The Llanwern universal slabbing mill was reckoned by some to have a potential throughput of six million tons even though as yet it has dealt with less than 1·5 million tons, and the hot mill could roll twice its present output of coil.[35] Eventually, perhaps, this most rationally located of all the British strip mills may really be allowed to show its paces.

Schemes vaguely suggested in 1968 for wholly new steel-making complexes on Clydeside, perhaps even on Deeside or Southampton Water, are highly attractive theoretically, but, for both economic and social reasons, existing major producing centres are much less easily abandoned and replaced by new ones than in the past. Significantly, speaking at Ebbw Vale, the managing director of the British Steel Corporation's South Wales Group made a plea for greater labour mobility.[36] This may occur, and other factors contributing to change include possible entry to the Common Market, or, even without it, sharply accentuated competition in the British market from foreign mills. Giant ore terminals, new concepts in bulk rail transport, the slowly expanding motorway network, rapid changes in the technology of iron and steel making, government preference for Development Area economic growth are a very varied bunch of factors which will influence the future pattern of strip mill location in Britain. Whatever happens, it is impossible in the foreseeable future to cancel out the past, to plan as if sheet making in Britain had no economic history or its former activities no longer shaped its geography.

From the time of the first iron sheet mills in Pontypool early in the eighteenth century, or the galvanising shops and mills along the Birmingham Canal in the early Victorian age, through the large new coastal works at Newport, Ellesmere Port and elsewhere at the turn of the century, the splendid new mills sprouting in the wastelands of Ebbw Vale after 1936, to Llanwern's establishment in Severnside meadowlands twenty-years later the sheet trade has never been free from the trammels of the past. Its changing locations have reflected the influence of technical change, of new demands added to or replacing old ones and increasingly the policies of governments both at home and overseas. Theoretically optimum locations have a beauty all their own and rational development has, alas, all too often been lacking, but the result in industry, as in other aspects of life, is a richness of variety and colour. The future will be conditioned by this inheritance.

REFERENCES

1 British Iron and Steel Federation, *Annual Statistics for 1962*, p. 82. See also Figures 4.5, 4.6 and 4.7 in G. Manners (Ed.), *South Wales in the Sixties* 1964 and *Ministry of Labour Gazette*. Annual analysis of regional employment patterns.

2 K. Warren, 'Steel pricing, regional economic growth and public policy', *Urban Studies* November 1966, pp. 185–199.

3 *Times Review of Industry* May 1960, p. 70, June 1960, p. 66.

4 *Iron and Steel* February 1966, p. 79. February 1967.

5 Report of Meeting of Confederation of Shipbuilding and Engineering Unions, *Guardian* 13 May 1966.

6 John Summers, *Works Statistics* November, 1964.

7 *Steel Times* 10 January 1967.

8 John Summers, *Works Relations Department* January 1967.

9 *Steel Times* July 1968, p. 413.

10 Dorman Long, *Chairman's Statement* 1964–1965, 1965–1966. *Iron and Steel* April 1966, p. 163 and conversations at Lackenby.

11 British Iron and Steel Federation statistics and Dorman Long, *Chairman's Statement* 1965–1966, p. 13.

12 J. D. Joy, Presidential address to Lincolnshire Iron and Steel Institute October 1967 quoted *App-Frod Record* 12 October, 1967, pp. 1–2.

13 A. J. Peech, Managing Director, Midland Group, British Steel Corporation, quoted *Steel Times* May 1968 I am also indebted to a general, earlier correspondence about strip/sheet prospects in Lincolnshire with A. Jackson of Appleby-Frodingham.

14 D. Burn and others, *The Future of Steel* Institute of Economic Affairs 1965, p. 12. British Iron and Steel Federation, *The Steel Industry. The Stage I Report of the Development Co-ordinating Committee (Benson Report)* July 1966, pp. 43, 45, 211.

15 *Iron and Steel* March 1966, p. 122. October, 1966 p. 505.

16 *Steel Times* September 1968, p. 549.

17 See also *Statist* 8 February 1963.

18 *Iron and Steel* March 1962, p. 122. *South Wales Argus* 18 January 1963.

19 *Steel Times* May 1968, p. 340.

20 John Summers and Steel Company of Wales *Annual Reports for 1964 and 1966*.

21 *Guardian* 17 December 1965.

22 John Summers *Chairman's Statement* 2 February 1967, pp. 4–5.

Consett Iron Company, *Chairman's Statement* for the year to April 1966, p. 11. *Benson Report* July 1966, pp. 38–40.

23 *Steel Times* July 1968, p. 413.

24 *Benson Report* p. 79.

25 *Iron and Steel Board Annual Report for* 1965, 1966, pp. 44–45. *R.T.B. Report and Accounts* 1966, p. 7.

26 Steel Company of Wales *Annual Report and Accounts 1966*, p. 6. See also costs of production and other charges per ton of saleable products as listed in Profit and Loss Account.

27 *Economist* 18 January 1964. *Iron and Steel* January 1967. *Steel Times* May 1968, p. 340.

28 W. F. Cartwright 'Big Ships at Port Talbot', *British Steel* August 1968, pp. 10–13 and in correspondence.

29 Based on W. F. Cartwright, *British Steel* August 1968, p. 13.

30 *Times Review of Industry* April 1959, p. 78. *Iron and Coal Trades Review* 11 August 1961, p. 276. *Iron and Steel* January 1963, p. 42.

31 *Guardian* 12 February 1960, 8 March 1963, 13 March 1963. *Times Review of Industry* March 1960. *Western Mail* 3, 4 July 1964. *Times* 11 August 1965 and H.M.S.O. Cmnd. 2706. *Iron Ore Imports into South Wales* July 1965.

32 *Guardian* 2 July 1965. 20 January 1967. *Iron and Steel* January 1967, p. 38.

33 W. F. Cartwright, 'Big Ships at Port Talbot', *British Steel* August 1968, pp. 12–13 and *Iron Ore Imports into South Wales* July 1965, especially pp. 5, 6.

34 *Guardian* 11 December 1964.

35 *Steel and Coal*, Supplement on Spencer Works November 1962, p. 24. *Guardian* 11 December 1964.

36 *Steel Times* May 1968, p. 340.

Index